USENET:
NETNEWS FOR EVERYONE

Jenny A. Fristrup

Hewlett-Packard Laboratories

Prentice Hall PTR
Englewood Cliffs, New Jersey 07632

Library of Congress Cataloging-in-Publication Data

Fristrup, Jenny A.

USENET: netnews for everyone / Jenny A. Fristrup

p. cm. — (Hewlett-Packard professional books)

Includes index.

ISBN 0-13-123167-7

1. USENET.   I. Title   II. Series

QA76.76.063F79   1994

384.3'3—dc20

94-15379

CIP

Editorial/Production Supervision: Lisa Iarkowski
Interior Design: Gail Cocker-Bogusz and Lisa Iarkowski
Acquisitions Editor: Karen Gettman
Manufacturing Manager: Alexis R. Heydt
Cover Photo: The Image Bank, Jane Sterret
Cover Design: Doug DeLuca

© 1994 Prentice Hall PTR
Prentice-Hall, Inc.
A Paramount Communications Comp
Englewood Cliffs, NJ 07632

The publisher offers discounts on this book when o
For more information, contact:

Corporate Sales Department
Prentice Hall PTR
113 Sylvan Avenue
Englewood Cliffs, NJ 07632
Phone: 201-592-2863
FAX: 201-592-2249.

Printed in the United States of America

10 9 8 7 6 5 4 3 2

ISBN 0-13-123167-7

Prentice-Hall International (UK) Limited, London
Prentice-Hall of Australia Pty. Limited, Sydney
Prentice-Hall of Canada, Inc., Toronto
Prentice-Hall Hispanoamericana S.A., Mexico
Prentice-Hall of India Private Limited, New Delhi
Prentice-Hall of Japan, Inc., Tokyo
Simon & Schuster Asia Pte. Ltd., Singapore
Editora Prentice-Hall do Brasil, Ltda., Rio de Janeiro

Date Due

BRODART, INC.   Cat. No. 23 233   Printed in U.S.A.

To Stephen Benelisha,
my best friend,
my beloved partner in life.
Thank you.

Hewlett-Packard Professional Books

Costa	Planning and Designing High Speed Networks Using 100VG-AnyLAN
Fristrup	USENET: Netnews for Everyone
Grady	Practical Software Metrics for Project Management and Process Improvement
Grosvenor, Ichiro, O'Brien	Mainframe Downsizing to Upsize Your Business: IT-Preneuring
Gunn	A Guide to NetWare® for UNIX®
Helsel	Cutting Your Test Development Time with HP VEE: An Iconic Programming Language
Madell, Parsons, Abegg	Developing and Localizing International Software
McMinds/Whitty	Writing Your Own OSF/Motif Widgets
Poniatowski	The HP-UX System Administrator's "How To" Book
Thomas	Cable Television Proof-of-Performance: A Practical Guide to Cable TV Compliance Measurements Using a Spectrum Analyzer.
Witte	Electronic Test Instruments
Witte	Spectrum & Network Measurements

Contents

Preface   XV

PART ONE Introduction to USENET   1

1 Meet the USENET Community   3

Welcome… People are Talking, 4
People Exchanging Information, 4
How They are Doing This, 5
Many People, Much Talk, 6
What this Means to You, 6

2 People Using USENET   9

USENET in the Past, 10
USENET in the Present, 10
USENET in the Future, 15
Putting USENET to Work for You, 15

3 An Overview of USENET   17

USENET Newsgroup Organization, 18
The Structure Behind USENET, 19
How it Looks to You and Me, 20
USENET Growth and Maintenance, 21

4 Basic Terms and Conventions   23

Basic USENET Terminology, 24
Evolution of USENET Etiquette, 26
Recommended New User Conduct, 27
Summary, 29

5   Close Examination of a Newsgroup   31

About This Newsgroup, 32
The Charter, 32
The Index, 32
The Articles, 34
Getting the FAQs, 37
Interesting Events, 38

PART TWO   The Newsgroups of USENET   41

6   About this Part of the Book 43

How Part Two is Organized, 44
What Each Chapter in Part Two Covers, 44
How to Use Part Two, 44

7   Computers: The "comp" Newsgroups   47

comp.admin, 48
comp.ai, 48
comp.answers, 49
comp.apps, 50
comp.arch, 51
comp.archives, 51
comp.bbs, 51
comp.benchmarks, 52
comp.binaries, 52
comp.bugs, 53
comp.cad, 54
comp.client-server, 54

comp.cog-eng, 54
comp.compilers, 54
comp.compression, 54
comp.databases, 55
comp.dcom, 55
comp.doc, 56
comp.dsp, 57
comp.editors, 57
comp.edu, 57
comp.emacs, 57
comp.fonts, 57
comp.graphics, 58

comp.groupware, 59

comp.human-factors, 59

comp.infosystems, 60

comp.lang, 60

comp.lsi, 65

comp.mail, 65

comp.misc, 71

comp.multimedia, 71

comp.music, 71

comp.newprod, 71

comp.object, 71

comp.org, 72

comp.os, 72

comp.parallel, 78

comp.patents, 78

comp.periphs, 79

comp.programming, 79

comp.protocols, 79

comp.realtime, 80

comp.research, 80

comp.risks, 80

comp.robotics, 80

comp.security, 81

comp.simulation, 81

comp.society, 81

comp.soft-sys, 81

comp.software-eng, 82

comp.software, 82

comp.sources, 82

comp.specification, 84

comp.speech, 84

comp.std, 85

comp.sw, 85

comp.sys, 85

comp.terminals, 97

comp.text, 97

comp.unix, 98

comp.virus, 101

comp.windows, 102

8   Miscellaneous: The "misc" Newsgroups   105

misc.activism, 106

misc.answers, 106

misc.books, 106

misc.consumers, 106

misc.education, 107

misc.emergency-services, 107

misc.entrepreneurs, 107

misc.fitness, 107

misc.forsale, 107

misc.handicap, 108

misc.headlines, 108

misc.health, 108

misc.int-property, 108

misc.invest, 108

misc.jobs, 109

misc.kids, 109

misc.legal, 110

misc.misc, 110

misc.news, 110

misc.rural, 110

misc.taxes, 110

misc.test, 110

misc.wanted, 110

misc.writers, 110

misc.writing, 110

9 Network News: The "news" Newsgroups 113

news.admin, 114

news.announce, 115

news.answers, 116

news.config, 120

news.future, 120

news.groups, 120

news.lists, 121

news.misc, 123

news.newsites, 124

news.newusers, 124

news.software, 124

10 Recreation: The "rec" Newsgroups 127

rec.answers, 128

rec.antiques, 129

rec.aquaria, 129

rec.arts, 129

rec.audio, 138

rec.autos, 138

rec.aviation, 139

rec.backcountry, 139

rec.bicycles, 140

rec.birds, 141

rec.boats, 141

rec.climbing, 141

rec.collecting, 141

rec.crafts, 141

rec.equestrian, 142

rec.folk-dancing, 142

rec.food, 142

rec.gambling, 143

rec.games, 143

rec.gardens, 148

rec.guns, 148

rec.heraldry, 148

rec.humor, 148

rec.hunting, 149

rec.juggling, 149

rec.kites, 149

rec.mag, 149

rec.martial-arts, 149

rec.misc, 149

rec.models, 149

rec.motorcycles, 150

rec.music, 151

rec.nude, 155

rec.org, 156

rec.outdoors, 156

rec.pets, 157

rec.photo, 158

rec.puzzles, 158

rec.pyrotechnics, 159

rec.radio, 159

rec.railroad, 164

rec.roller-coaster, 164

rec.running, 164

rec.scouting, 164

rec.scuba, 165

rec.skate, 165

rec.skiing, 165

rec.skydiving, 165

rec.sport, 165

rec.travel, 168

rec.video, 168

rec.windsurfing, 168

rec.woodworking, 169

11   Science: The "sci" Newsgroups   171

sci.aeronautics, 172

sci.answers, 172

sci.anthropology, 172

sci.aquaria, 172

sci.archaeology, 172

sci.astro, 173

sci.bio, 173

sci.chem, 173

sci.classics, 174

sci.cognitive, 174

sci.comp-aided, 174

sci.cryonics, 174

sci.crypt, 174

sci.data, 175

sci.econ, 175

sci.edu, 175

sci.electronics, 175

sci.energy, 175

sci.engr, 176

sci.environment, 176

sci.fractals, 176

sci.geo, 176

sci.image, 177

sci.lang, 177

sci.logic, 177

sci.materials, 177

sci.math, 177

sci.med, 178

sci.military, 178

sci.misc, 178

sci.nanotech, 178

sci.optics, 179

sci.philosophy, 179

sci.physics, 179

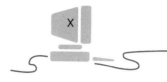

sci.research, 179

sci.skeptic, 179

sci.space, 179

sci.systems, 180

sci.virtual, 180

12   Society: The "soc" Newsgroups   183

soc.answers, 184

soc.bi, 184

soc.college, 184

soc.couples, 184

soc.culture, 185

soc.feminism, 190

soc.history, 191

soc.libraries, 191

soc.men, 191

soc.misc, 191

soc.motss, 191

soc.net-people, 191

soc.penpals, 192

soc.politics, 192

soc.religion, 192

13   Talk: The "talk" Newsgroups   195

talk.abortion, 196

talk.answers, 196

talk.bizarre, 196

talk.environment, 196

talk.origins, 196

talk.philosophy, 196

talk.politics, 196

talk.rape, 197

talk.religion, 197

talk.rumors, 197

14   Worthy Mentions from the Alternative Set   199

Binary Files, 200

Rabid Fandom, 203

The Finer Aspects of Reproduction, 206

Couch Potatoes Unite!, 208

15 Other Available Hierarchies   213

bionet, 214

bit, 216

biz, 224

clari, 226

gnu, 236

HEPnet, 237

ieee, 238

Inet/DDN, 239

info, 242

k12, 244

relcom, 246

VMSnet, 249

PART THREE   Accessing USENET   253

16 Boning Up on the Basics   255

USENET Basics,   256

Computer Basics,   256

Computer File Systems,   257

Editors,   258

Terminals, Terminal Emulators and Communication,   259

News Readers,   260

17 Gaining USENET Access   263

Typical Configurations,   264

Equipment You Will Need,   264

Pursuing Existing Avenues,   265

Encouraging Avenues to Exist,   266

Creating Your Own Avenue,   266

18 Topics for Further Exploration 269

Archie, 270
Electronic Mail, 271
File Transfers and "anonymous ftp", 271
Gopher, 274
Mailing Lists, 274
Remote Access via Telnet, 275
WAIS, 275
World Wide Web, 275

Appendices 277

A Articles from the Source 277

What is USENET?, 278
How to Use USENET (Proper Netiquette), 286
Frequently Asked Questions About USENET, 295
Getting USENET Access, 314

B List of the Alternative Hierarchy 335

C A Word About News Readers 359

News Reader Basic Functions, 360
Types of News Readers Available, 360
Some Available News Readers, 361
Command Summary for rn, 364

Command Summary for trn,   365
Command Summary for tin,   367
Where to Go for More Information,   368

D   **Recommended Reading**   371

Glossary   375

Index   388

Preface

Have you ever felt that you could get more done if you just knew where to go to get answers to the questions you have? I know I have. Between automated answering systems and voice mail, getting the information you need can be a daunting task.

The purpose of this book is to introduce you to a group of people who can, and are willing to, help you get the information you need. They are a group of people worldwide who voluntarily share what they know with those who know enough to ask. From the subject of "business and free trade" to the subject of "convincing your toddler not to bite" people are talking about it. They will share what they know, offer advice and even give moral support. It is done through USENET—a collaborative effort of people sharing information.

This book will show you how you can utilize these folks to get answers to your questions. It will show you how to expand your network of personal and professional contacts using USENET. You will learn how to make USENET work for you.

I have organized this book into three parts:

Part I: Introduction to USENET
Part II: The Newsgroups of USENET
Part III: Accessing USENET

Read Part I if you are totally unfamiliar with the concept of USENET and its newsgroups. It covers how the conversations are organized and distributed. It also takes a close look at an existing newsgroup. Here you will see the dynamics of the discussions and learn the basic terminology. (By the way, if you are unfamiliar with the concept, I applaud your curiosity!) Throughout this book, I will avoid the technical details that can turn learning about USENET into an experience on the same level as learning your multiplication tables.

Part II is a reference section. It contains a list of the core USENET newsgroups available at the time of this writing. It lists the basic newsgroup and any subgroups, gives a description of each and lists the group's available FAQs (a FAQ is a collection of information intended to be passed on to other people). Browse it. Read only the parts that interest you. It is

not meant to be read in its entirety unless 1) you are having trouble going to sleep at night or 2) are just plain masochistic. Part II begins with a long chapter on computers. Certainly don't feel obligated to start there. Chapter 10, the chapter on recreation, is much more enjoyable browsing.

Part III is a guide to getting access to USENET both from the office and from the home. It gives you the basic questions to ask and points you in the right direction for further reading. There are many well written books on the subject of computers and computer communication. Part III does not attempt to duplicate these efforts. Part III is only a guide. In here you will find conspicuous references to other people's works.

I have also included four appendices. Appendix A contains four USENET articles that are full of important and useful information about USENET usage. They are recommended reading for all people new to USENET. Appendix B contains a list of an alternative set of USENET's newsgroups. In here you will find a fascinating view of unstructured humanity. Appendix C contains an overview of some available new readers (programs that allow you to participate in USENET conversations). Appendix D contains a short list of books for further reading on specific topics.

Since my effort in writing this book is directed at reaching those of you who are not computer software and hardware professionals, I have included a glossary of terms that you may not be familiar with. The first time I use a term that is included in the glossary, I italicize it. I hope this helps.

My special thanks goes to the people of the USENET community that invest their time in keeping and maintaining the FAQ files. In chapter 5, Diane C. Lin of the "misc.kids" newsgroup has provided an ideal example of a cooperative, supportive and well organized newsgroup environment. Appendix A is the product of Chip Salzenberg, Jerry Schwarz, Chuq Von Rospach, Jonathan I. Kamens and Gene Spafford. These people are sages of USENET. Their effort has benefited many people. I would also like to thank Stephen Benelisha, Amy Chan, Pat Pekary and the kind folks at Prentice Hall, especially Karen Gettman, Lisa Iarkowski, and Barbara Alfieri,

for their encouragement and support. Thank you to Eleanor Benelisha for taking the time to read and improve the book while in its draft state. Thank you also to the artists at T/Maker for the clip art.

If you are the type of person who wants to make the best use of your time, this book will help put you in touch with resources that will do just that.

Jenny A. Fristrup
fristrup@hpl.hp.com

Introduction
to USENET

1

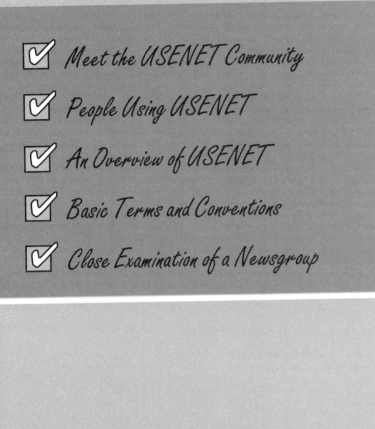

☑ *Meet the USENET Community*

☑ *People Using USENET*

☑ *An Overview of USENET*

☑ *Basic Terms and Conventions*

☑ *Close Examination of a Newsgroup*

The purpose of this chapter is to introduce you to a community of individuals that can serve as a valuable resource in your personal and professional life. In this chapter you will sample who is using USENET and how it can be useful to you.

You have questions? The USENET Community has answers. Come in. Meet the people who are willing to share their life experiences with you.

Meet the USENET Community

1

Welcome... People are Talking

Welcome to the USENET Community. Allow me to introduce you to a group of people who like to talk and have plenty to say. These people are available to answer your questions and give you advice. Some will give you the latest on the leading edge of technology. Others will provide a shoulder for you to cry on.

If you are looking to improve your network of contacts, you have come to the right place. The USENET community is a place to easily network with people who have interests similar to your own. You will meet experts in many fields. You will make friends. Eavesdropping on other peoples' conversation is encouraged. Come learn as much as you care to absorb.

People Exchanging Information

People use USENET in many ways. A Canadian consumer talks with people from a consumer newsgroup about troubles he is having replacing a tool at a Canadian branch of a well-known American store. The consumer experts advise him to visit an American branch of the store.

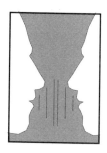

In the travel newsgroup, a traveler wants to learn from other people's experience what it is like to travel alone in Europe for an extended period of time. Many people eagerly share their experiences and encourage him on. The people provide him with a wealth of information, both things to watch out for and things to take advantage of.

A doctor asks for opinions regarding an ethical dilemma he is facing. He is attracted to one of his young patient's single mother. He asks whether or not he should pursue the relationship. The overwhelming advice to him is don't mix business with pleasure. It can only lead to problems when you are dating someone that you are also billing.

A software developer seeks information on spreadsheet development. She consults with the spreadsheet experts from one of the computer *newsgroups*. The experts direct her to the appropriate manuals in her local technical book store.

A group of people from one of the news newsgroups discusses the relevance of USENET to non-technical professions. Some feel that USENET is only for the technological elite. Many people from non-technical professionals voice a different opinion.

How They are Doing This

People use *electronic messages* from their home or from their work to hold conversations. Using a *terminal* (or *terminal emulator* on a *personal computer*) people *log in* to a *computer* that is *networked* to other computers and exchange messages. They read the messages with programs called *news readers*.

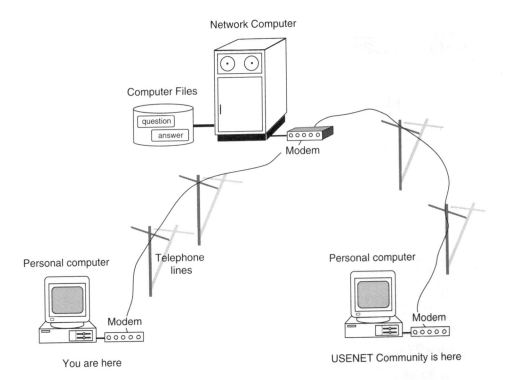

Network Computer

Computer Files

question

answer

Modem

Telephone lines

Personal computer

Modem

You are here

Personal computer

Modem

USENET Community is here

In the same way that you are able to make a long distance telephone call without understanding the inner-workings of the telephone network, you can exchange electronic messages with people around the world without feeling obligated to understand the inner-workings of computers and networks. Just like the telephone, USENET is a very powerful communication tool.

Many People, Much Talk

There are thousands of people using USENET to exchange ideas and share information. Hundreds of thousands of conversations are taking place at this moment. USENET reaches from Canada to the Antarctic, from the Ukraine to New Zealand. Each USENET participant brings a lifetime's experience to the newsgroups he or she visits.

What this Means to You

In your professional life, in your personal life, you have much to gain from these people. If you are struggling with a problem, ask yourself, "Has anyone ever struggled with this problem before or am I the first?" If you are not the first then there is someone out there who has first hand experience that you could benefit from. The beauty of USENET is, you don't even need to know whom to ask. The people with the experience will come to you with answers.

It doesn't matter what your interest is. Be it business or pleasure, there are people here interested in it too and they want to talk to you. They are interested in your experience and want to hear what you have to say.

USENET is a tool. Each person who uses USENET uses it in a different way. Each uses it for a different purpose. This chapter touches on how USENET has been used by different people in the past, present and how it might be used in the future.

2

People Using
USENET

USENET in the Past

USENET grew out of a need for students and researchers to share technical information and observations about their work. In 1979 Tom Truscott and James Elliott of Duke University developed the software that made the sharing of such information possible. The original two *site* users were Duke University and the University of North Carolina.

It was such a successful method of sharing information that the number of organizations subscribing to the USENET newsgroups increased rapidly.

USENET in the Present

Today USENET is not limited to students and researchers. It is available world wide to most anybody interested in participating. USENET has over 99,000 participating sites and over 2,700,000 users. People use USENET for many different reasons. The thing they all have in common is the need for exchanging information. The following samples were taken from different USENET newsgroups.

A Student at School

The following student was looking for information about a particular type of graduate program. He posed the question to the newsgroup devoted to graduate school discussion. Someone answered his question.

 "Would be interested in learning about ANY popular culture graduate programs of any type in the USA and Canada. The only ones I have heard of as yet are the ones at Bowling Green State and Morgan State. I don't need a lot of info at this point, just a short notice that a program exists at a given school. The usual grad school directories don't have much to say about this. Thanks."

 "The New School for Social Research has an M.A. in Media Studies that may address your needs. It has both an 'in-person' version as well as one done completely through computer conferencing, including a thesis.

The number for the New School's Media Studies department is 212-229-8903."

A System Administrator at Work

A *computer system administrator* faces many technical questions that need answering during the course of the day. Here is an example of one such system administrator.

 "I am looking for some news readers to install on a SPARCstation 10 under SUN-OS 4.1.3. I DO NOT want graphical readers. These readers will be used by people from tty terminals and vt100 terminals. In addition, I would like them to be stand alone programs, not some funky emacs extension or anything."

 "I use tin and I like it. The keystrokes clash with elm, & I'm going mad! Otherwise it does everything I need (so far). On an ordinary terminal too. Qume QVT119. C.news is the daemon. It all installed without too much trouble."

Asking a question and getting an answer from someone with experience is valuable. When it can be done without hunting down the correct person to ask, it is even better. The system administrator took less than two minutes to type in the question. In a short period of time, typically a day, the question was answered.

A Writer at Home

Here is an example of a question that an aspiring writer posed to USENET. It received an answer.

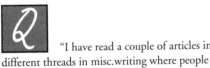 "I have read a couple of articles in different threads in misc.writing where people sound like they expect to impress editors with the query letter or the cover letter. Is that actually possible?"

 "I suspect that most editors see far too much 'impressive' writing and would prefer a professional (and SHORT) letter.

Except for some rare special cases, these letters are in the unpleasant class of situations where you can either lose or not lose. Triumph is not an option. Keep your letter simple, and blow them away with the work itself."

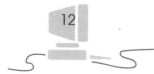

The White House

The Clinton Administration used USENET to keep its constituents informed. Press releases, official comments, and other items for the record were distributed in USENET newsgroups. Here is what President Clinton had to say when the basketball player Michael Jordon retired.

The White House
Office of the Press Secretary

For Immediate Release   October 6, 1993

Statement by the President

As a sports fan who has had the great pleasure of watching Michael Jordan play his incandescent brand of basketball since the early 1980s, I was saddened to hear his announcement today that he was retiring from the game. But, at the same time, I think we can all understand his wish to take his leave and devote himself to more private concerns.

We will miss him -- here and all around America, in every small-town backyard and paved city lot where kids play one-on-one and dream of being like Mike.

His gift to us all has been in giving everything he had game after game, year in and year out. It has been our privilege for the last decade to see him gracing the hardwood, lighting up our tv screens and brightening the lives of the young at heart all around the world.

I want to wish Michael and his family the very best. I know that the past several months have been difficult ones and I hope that he can enjoy the peace of mind that he richly deserves.

-30-

This is of course a trivial example but placing the entire text of the Clinton Health Plan would take up too many pages.

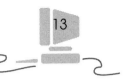

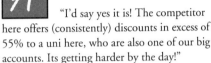

A Marketing Professional at Work

Here is an example of someone using USENET to try to further expand his company's market.

"One of our sales guys just got back from a visit to a local university (a good customer of ours), with a rather glum look on his face...

Our competitor is offering a 75% (that's Seventy-Five percent!) discount on some boxes and peripherals, to universities around here. Jeeeeez!

Is this known to be a general policy of theirs? If so, can we play in this kind of price war in order to stay in the university market?

Our efforts at selling to these sites are gonna take a real kicking, and just when we're beginning to win over the educational crowd."

"I'd say yes it is! The competitor here offers (consistently) discounts in excess of 55% to a uni here, who are also one of our big accounts. Its getting harder by the day!"

It is not surprising that some science fiction fans are able to thoroughly integrate computer conversation into their daily lives. What is surprising is that some members of the Hollywood community are able to do the same.

J. Michael Straczynski created a science fiction show called "Babylon-5." The show's pilot aired for the first time in early 1993. Throughout the year between the pilot's airing and the start of the television series, Mr. Straczynski kept in touch with "Babylon-5" fans. Using newsgroups devoted to the subject, and other electronic means, he and the fans discussed all aspects of the series. He kept the fans informed of the progress of the series and answered questions regarding the series story line.

Yes, Even Hollywood

The following is a question asked between the time of the pilot's airing and the start of the series. The individual is surprised that a newsgroup can exist for a series that doesn't.

 "Do you people know something that I don't know? I would've thought that the logical reaction would have been like mine. Namely, intrigued, but waiting until the series. Where did all of this rabid fandom come from? Do you guys have complete, detailed episode guides? What's sustaining all of the enthusiasm?"

 "What's sustaining the enthusiasm is all the tidbits that JMS keeps dropping about the show, mixed in with the occasional bombshell that pulls our entire concept of the characters out from underneath us and forces us to spend a week or so rewatching the pilot to get our bearings again. :-)"

 "Well, Joe Straczynski, the mover and shaker behind the whole show, is in constant contact with us lowly fans...both here and on GEnie. He's always there to tease with some new tidbit of info, some cast change, let us know that B5 has won an Emmy for Best Visual Effects...

What a fantastic way to build a following for a show that didn't yet exist. As you can see, USENET is indeed a powerful tool.

A Cook at Home

Have you ever had problems trying to poach an egg? This person did.

 "How can I make a decent looking poached egg? I don't have any special equipment. When I try to do it using a pot of boiling water, the egg turns into a stringy mess..."

 "A tip from one of JC's cookbooks is to dip the intended vicitm (the egg, not the guest) in boiling water for ten seconds before opening it and dropping it into the poaching water. This virtually eliminates the stringy spreading egg threads, makes the egg stay appealingly globular, and looks very professional."

USENET in the Future

It is easier to use a computer than it ever has been. Many of the frustrations of years ago have been removed. Personal computers are on their way to becoming as common as toasters in the home. When this happens, USENET will become an even more valuable tool.

Skeptical? Think back to when the telephone first came to be. People of that time period couldn't imagine using such a high technology device in their everyday life either.

Putting USENET to Work for You

Here is just a sample of how USENET can work for you.

✔ Developing your network of professional contacts

✔ Expanding your network of personal contacts

✔ Searching and finding technical information

✔ Expanding your customer base

✔ Enhancing your hobbies and recreational activities

✔ Finding a job

✔ Finding answers to difficult questions

✔ Voicing your opinion to your government

✔ Recruiting for your business

✔ Bargain hunting

✔ Finding a pen-pal

✔ Adding your experience to the collective knowledge in your field

Whether you work for a company, own your own business, manage a household, or are retired, USENET can work for you. Whatever you are interested in, be it Bible Study, Creative Writing or Effective Advertising, there is a group of people interested in your thoughts and willing to share theirs. In your area of expertise, USENET can be used to develop contacts, share ideas and exchange information in that area.

USENET is a powerful tool waiting for you to use it.

Without going into too much detail, this chapter covers how USENET works. It covers how the newsgroup conversations are organized, accessed, managed and distributed. It also talks a little about the physical structure that makes USENET possible.

3

An Overview
of USENET

USENET Newsgroup Organization

USENET conversations are organized in *hierarchical* newsgroup trees. There are seven core newsgroup hierarchies or trees: comp (computers), misc (miscellaneous topics), news (newsgroup information), rec (recreation), sci (science), soc (society), and talk (conversation). Each tree branches into different levels of newsgroup sub-topics. (If you are familiar with a computer *file directory* organization, you are already familiar with the concept of tree hierarchy organization).

Highlighted is a branch from the "rec" newsgroup tree.

A Branch of the USENET Newsgroup Tree

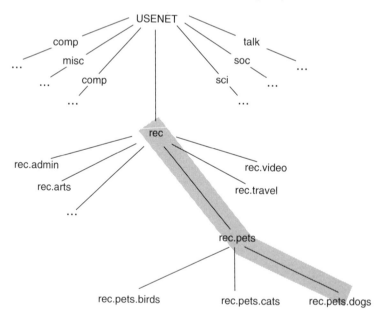

Each newsgroup contains electronic messages called *articles*. An article is any bit of text that someone cares to write. Each article is stored in a computer file and has a number that is used to uniquely identify it. The number is useful in keeping track of which articles refer to which other ones.

The Structure Behind USENET

The structure that supports the distribution and management of USENET articles is made up of several distinct layers. Each layer exists on its own independent of the other layers.

Computers

The bottom most layer is a network of computers. A *networked computer* is a computer that can share information with other computers in the form of computer files.

Networks

The next is the *network protocol* layer. A network protocol can be thought of as the language the computers speak when exchanging information among themselves. (UUCP is an example of a network protocol.) There are many computers in the world. Some computers are limited to a single network protocol to exchange information. Others are able to use any number of different protocols. It is these "multi-lingual" computers that are used to tie all the other computers together.

Physical Connections

Providing the physical link for this computer communication is a jigsaw puzzle of various telephone lines, modems, and cable connectors hooking all of the computers together. These pieces make up the physical connection layer.

Newsgroup Distribution Software

The next layer is the newsgroup distribution software layer. It is a set of programs that allow groups of USENET articles to be sent to one another on a regular basis. Properly set up, these programs can operate pretty much on their own.

Newsgroup Management Software

Newsgroup management software is the next layer. It consists of a set of programs that allow the person in charge of the computer to manage the hundreds of articles that arrive via the network distribution programs. These programs allow the person in charge to select the set of newsgroups best suited for the set of people using the computer.

News Reading Software

The final layer and the one most apparent to the person using USENET is the news reading software. Most everyone who accesses USENET newsgroup articles does so using a program called a *news reader*. There are many different news readers available. Some are easier to use than others. This layer is also known as the *user interface* layer. A news reader is a program that presents the articles in a form that makes sense conversationally. Most present the articles in a *threaded* fashion. Threaded means that each response to an article is linked to the article that it is responding to. The news reader allows you to pick and choose which conversations you want to read and/or participate in.

How it Looks to You and Me

The USENET community is made up of individuals (like you and me) who access newsgroup articles using a *computer terminal* (or *terminal emulator* on a PC) and a *news reader*. Individual articles get propagated from computer to computer. Others read the articles and reply to them. These replies are new articles that get propagated as well from machine to machine.

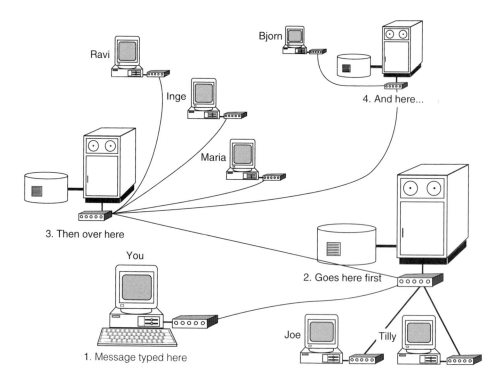

The ever growing number of computers using newsgroup distribution and management software combined with the ever growing number of people using these computers to share information are the elements that make up USENET.

USENET Growth and Maintenance

Everyday more computers are added to the network. Everyday more people are using computers. Everyday new newsgroups are added to USENET. As more people begin sharing information, the range of topics people care to exchange information on grows too.

New newsgroups are created through a voluntary democratic process. Someone will propose a new newsgroup and members of the USENET community vote on it. *Computer system administrators* at individual *sites* are left to add the new newsgroup on the newsgroup distribution list.

The set of newsgroups that make up USENET is constantly changing. New ones are being added. Old ones are being deleted. Any document listing the complete set of USENET newsgroups is bound to be out of date before it reaches the eyes of those who read it (including this one). A complete and frequently updated list is maintained in the "news.announce.newgroups" newsgroup.

J ust as a different geographical re-
gions have their own driving conventions to facilitate traffic flow, different
USENET newsgroups have devel-
oped their own set of conventions
that help facilitate information flow.
Certain conventions appear common to most all newsgroups. This
chapter covers a few of the more
common USENET conventions and
basic terminology.

4

Basic Terms
and Conventions

Basic USENET Terminology

Like most communities, USENET has its own language. Some of the terms used have meaning unique to USENET. Here are definitions for a few of the more basic ones.

Acronyms

USENET is full of acronyms. Acronyms save *bandwidth*. (Taking up a lot of bandwidth is the network equivalent of personally taking up a lot of room on a crowded bus or train. It is discouraged.) Here are some of the more common acronyms. These are ones you may see in any newsgroup.

Common Acronyms	
BTW	by the way
FYI	for your information
IMHO	in my humble opinion
IMNSHO	in my not so humble opinion
RTFM	read the f***ing manual
YMMV	your mileage may vary
Smileys	
:-)	happily
;-)	just kidding
:-(	unfortunately

Appendix A contains a copy of an article that is periodically posting to the "news.announce.newusers" newsgroup titled "Answers to Frequently Asked Questions about USENET." It has many more of these tidbits and a lot of other useful information.

Article

An article is a USENET conversation element. It is a computer file that contains a question or piece of information made available to the USENET community by posting to a newsgroup.

FAQs

A FAQ is a file that contains the answers to a newsgroup's frequently asked questions. It may also contain other information of interest to a newsgroup's audience. FAQs are very important. FAQs reflect the self worth of a newsgroup. If a newsgroup has a well developed and maintained set of FAQs, the newsgroup participants take their subject matter seriously. FAQs (the substantial ones) are effort intensive to develop and time consuming to maintain.

Flames

A flame is a heated, emotionally packed, reply to an article. Flames can get personally insulting and quite nasty. A flame can contain explicit obscenities and A LOT OF SHOUTING!!!. The participants of newsgroups that have been around a while know what topics will result in flames and try to avoid them (not because they want to remain civil, though some do, but because they have seen it all before).

Hierarchy

A hierarchy is a group of things arranged in order of rank. A USENET newsgroup hierarchy refers to the set of all newsgroups contained within a specific broad subject category.

Index

An index is a numbered list of articles and replies. It is what a news reader presents its user with.

Lurker

A lurker is a person who regularly reads the articles associated with a particular newsgroup but seldom participates.

Moderator

A moderator is a person who controls what gets posted to a particular newsgroup. A moderator is used to ensure that a newsgroup's articles stick to the agreed upon subject matter. A newsgroup may or may not have a moderator.

Newsgroup

A USENET newsgroup is a place of people to have conversations about a well-defined topic. Physically it is made of the computer files that contain the conversation elements to the discussions currently in progress about the agreed upon topic.

News Reader

A news reader is a program that organizes the conversation elements in a sensible and presentable manner. The news reader allows the person using it to read and/or participate in those conversations.

Posting

Posting is the act of making an article or reply available to a newsgroup for distribution. It is done through a news reader.

Reply

A reply is also a USENET conversation element. It differs from an article in that it refers to a previously posted article.

Spoiler

When the word "spoiler" appears in an article's subject line it indicates that the body of the article may contain more information about a movie, book, television show, etc. than some people want to know before actually experiencing the event. A spoiler warning is usually attached to the review of such an event.

Evolution of USENET Etiquette

USENET is big. USENET gets bigger every day. An article that gets posted to a USENET newsgroup get distributed to 99,000 sites world wide. At those sites, an estimated 2,700,000 people read USENET newsgroups.[1] People all over the world read USENET newsgroup.

As you can imagine, 2.7 million people around the world having conversations results in heavy network traffic. Just as our freeways get congested, so do our computer networks. To minimize the impact USENET has on a site's net-

---

1. These figures were taken from "USENET_READERSHIP_SUMMARY_REPORT_FOR_AUG_93" as archived at rtfm.mit.edu in /pub/usenet-by-hierarchy/news/lists.

work traffic, an efficient code of behavior has evolved. This code of behavior is called USENET Etiquette.

USENET Etiquette, or Netiquette as it is sometimes called, involves following a set of recommended guidelines prior to posting to a newsgroup. The guidelines are periodically posted to individual newsgroups and are always available in the "news.announce.newusers" newsgroup.

Recommended New User Conduct

Before posting to a newsgroup, there are a few things a new USENET user should do. Reviewing the articles in "news.announce.newusers" is one of them. The articles in this newsgroup give an overview of what is considered good Netiquette. Before soliciting advice from a newsgroup, check out the FAQs available for the newsgroup in the appropriate "*.answers" newsgroup. (If you are considering posting to "rec.motorcycles", look for FAQs in "rec.answers".) There is a good chance that someone has asked the question before.

Here are some other guidelines to follow when interacting with a newsgroup.

Respond via E-mail

The urge to post a reply is strong when you know the answer to a question that someone has asked. Rather than posting the answer, it is better Netiquette to *e-mail* a reply directly to the person who asked the question. The answers go to the person who needs them and duplicates are not propagated world-wide to people who don't.

Post a Summary

If you are the person asking a question, you may receive many e-mail replies. Many of the replies you receive may be redundant. It is considered good form to post a summary (redundancies removed) to the newsgroup you posed the question to. This is an efficient way to share the information.

Read All Follow-ups Before Posting

Before posting a reply to someone, read all the replies that have been posted so far. If someone has already covered the material that you were going to post, there is no need to post it again.

Limit the Amount of Material Included from Previous Postings

When replying to an article, it makes it easier for others to read it if you include one or two relevant lines from the article that you are replying to. It may take a day or two for your reply to propagate around the world. By then, the local replies may have gone off on a tangent. It is considered bad form to include the entire original article.

Watch Your Attributions Carefully

People do not like to have their words misquoted or misconstrued. Clarifying such occurrences takes up a lot of *bandwidth* and is generally not of interest to the newsgroup's audience.

Avoid Cross-postings

Sometimes, in the desire to receive an answer to a question, someone will post an article to more than one newsgroup. The redundancy that cross-posting creates is inefficient use of the network and considered bad form. Unless an article truly has interest to multiple newsgroups, do not cross-post.

Check Your Subject Line Carefully

In some newsgroups, there are literally hundreds of articles at any one time. If you are seeking advice or an answer to a question, be specific in the subject line about what it is you are looking for. Knowledgeable USENET people tend to share what they know if they recognize that their knowledge is needed. Subject lines like "Help!" and "I have a question..." aren't specific enough for the knowledgeable people to recognize themselves as such.

Remember USENET has a World-Wide Readership

It isn't effective use of USENET to post articles of local interest to newsgroups that get distributed world-wide. For example, a car for sale in the San Francisco Bay Area is unlikely to receive replies from people in New Zealand. Use your news reader to limit your article's distribution to the appropriate geographical locations.

4 • Basic Terms and Conventions

Spelling and/or Grammatical Errors should not be Pointed Out

Imagine if everyone who recognized a typo in an article posted a reply pointing it out. Or even if they e-mailed their replies to the author. I wouldn't like receiving 200 messages all stating that "miscellaneous" is spelled with two "ls" not one, would you?

Refrain from Name-calling, Tantrums or Other Hysterics

It happens. People irritate one another. Flames do occur. Be considerate of the newsgroup's audience. If someone irritates you take it to e-mail if you must. Watching two people one up each other on "Oooooh YEAH?!!!s" in not interesting reading (at least not after the first couple of times.)

Summary

The best way to get a feel for how to properly interact with a newsgroup is to watch it in action over a couple of weeks. Observe the regular players, the names that appear frequently. See how they behave. Each newsgroup has a slightly different flavor to it. If you are considering posting to a newsgroup, make sure you have a good understanding for how its members  prefer to operate. If you don't, you may get some first hand experience at how flames work ;-).

This chapter armed you with the basics. You now know the basic terms and typical newsgroup conventions. You now have a feel for how a USENET newsgroup works. In the next chapter we will take a close look at a newsgroup in action.

The best way to understand how a newsgroup works is to visit one. The next best way is to read this chapter.

5

Close Examination
of a Newsgroup

About This Newsgroup

The "misc.kids" newsgroup consists of a friendly and helpful bunch of parents and soon-to-be parents. They are orderly and generally conduct themselves in a manner that other newsgroups would do well to emulate. These kind people are an ideal example of how useful and powerful USENET can be.

The Charter

The following is an excerpt from the "Welcome to Misc.kids/FAQ File Index" periodic posting. It was written by Diane C. Lin.

"Welcome to misc.kids, the newsgroup for parents, soon-to-be parents, and other people interested in children. In this group, we discuss issues relevant to pregnancy and child rearing, solicit advice from other netters on a host of parenting concerns, and generally seek and provide support and encouragement with respect to raising kids. This is a group intended for parents of children of *all* ages, though questions about babies and younger children seem to predominate."

As you can see, the "misc.kid"-ers have a well defined charter for their newsgroup.

The Index

Here is a sample of what the "misc.kids" index looks like. This is only a couple of screen fulls. There are a couple of hundred articles in here.

177 +	LOGO for kids
178 + 2	Pregnant- yay! Amnio/CVS decision - boo.
179 +	Daycare update
180 + 1	need advice on biking with baby
181 +	Girl Scouting (long)
182 +	control one's temper (Was: Discipline....)
183 +	To those who requested the baby stuff faq
184 +	Children Architecture-Ethnographical Studio
185 +	Lullabies
186 + 1	Length of Time to Get Pregnant & the pill

187 +   JDB Committee: child rights issue

188 +   Earlobes, Was Re: circumcision as mutilation

189 + 1   Kids & Guns

190 +   Seasonal births (was Length of Time to Get Pregnant

191 + 4   2 Year Old Not Talking

192 + 2   How to stop young child undoing seat belt

193 +   Birth Announcement/Story

194 +   On the Blubbering Verge....

195 +   "One Step Ahead 'Nature's Nest'" Infant Hamm

196 +   Sloane was Re: trendy names

197 +   my *baby* turns 5 today

198 + 3   Color Chart was Communicating with a 5 year old

199 +   Washington D.C./Baltimore area picnic

200 +   Reasons for Adopting an Infant

201 +   Getting your Ph.D and having children

202 + 3   My mother's in denial over baby's name!

203 + 2   Emily (was Re: trendy names)

204 + 2   Tubal Pregnancies

205 +   Fetal Arythmia

206 +   biking with baby (summary)

207 + 1   Color Chart WAS Communicating with 5 yo

208 +   are those $30 Kolcraft matress ok?

209 +   Potshots at religion (was Re: circumcision as mutilation)

210 +   Southern California Picnic Location

211 +   Smelly sneakers

212 +   Cylert & ADHD

213 +   HELP ME! 6yr old urinary prob

214 +   New Year

215 +   Going out of parenting sale - Mtn. View CA, books/games/etc

216 +   Does Comfy Carrier still exist?

217 +   Halloween Costume Ideas?

218 +   home birth questions

219 +   Seeking a private adoption

220 +   Nanny needed

221 +   THANKYOU

222 +	Kids and prostletyzin
223 +	Looking for info on how to test for Lead paint in a house
224 +	Young computerists: unite!
225 +	Children's ....
226 +	New England picnic is tomorrow (9/18)!!
227 + 6	Real Food for 5 mo?

The number at the front of each line is the *article number*. It is how you tell your news reader which article you want to read. The "+" indicates (in this particular news reader) that an article has not been read yet. The next number, if any, shows how many replies an article has received (this is a threaded news reader—more on that later.) The remainder of the line is the article title (also called the *subject line*) which may appear truncated. Some news readers can handle longer titles than others.

Scanning the index you will see: people seeking advice (#180, #192, #213, ...), people looking for answers to specific questions (#208, #216, #217, ...), on-going discussions (#182, #188, #190, #203, ...), announcements of regional events (#199, #210, #226), and many instances of people giving and receiving support (#178, #186, #191, #202, ...).

The Articles

Let's take a look at a couple of articles. This is a generic representation of an article and its replies. How the article and its replies appear to you will depend on the type news reader program you use.

Article #192

 "Has anyone any good ideas on how to stop a 20 mo child from undoing the seatbelt holding his car seat in place?"

 "Get a different car seat. We have a Century 2000E, I think. There's no way for the child to reach either the car's seat belt or the car seat's strap release."

 "Can you twist the buckle so the button is underneath, and therefore harder to undo?"

Here is another article and its many replies.

Article #227

 "In the last week, my 5 month old baby has gotten a strong desire to hold/suck on the food my husband and I are eating. This is mainly a problem when we go out to dinner. Is there any safe "finger food" that we can give her to suck on - she doesn't have any teeth yet. I thought baby biscuits were made for this purpose, but my husband says they are for babies with teeth."

 "Well, it isn't exactly food, but it kept our 5.5 month old occupied at a restaurant last week. We took one of those cellophane-wrapped melba toasts that came with the bread basket. Worked for a while, and after that, we crushed up the melba toasts in the package for a whole new texture sensation. (For the confused, we gave her the melba toasts still wrapped so she couldn't get to the crumbly insides.)"

 "For the last 18 months, I've carried 1-2 bagels in my backpack (never could stand purses) ...perfect for pre-teethers, toddlers, etc. My son (2) loves them..."

Article #227 (Continued)

 "You need foods that dissolve quickly in the mouth. Teeth actually make the situation worse, since the front teeth come in well before the molars, so the baby can take bites but not chew them…"

 "We are just entering this stage. Tonight Alec got cooked peas with the jackets sliced through and removed. He also got some cucumbers sliced up into little slimy squares. They both worked fine. The problem is that we are avoiding wheat at this stage, and Cheerios and most crackers and teething bisquits contain wheat. I found some non-wheat teething bisquits, and I have heard rumors of "oat-ee-o's" at health food stores, but I haven't found any."

 "This isn't a problem. This is a neat new phase. Your baby is probably telling you that she's ready for real food. So give it to her. You've probably got your own list of things you don't want her to have until some magic age. But otherwise, just make sure you keep the pieces small (maybe tiny in the case of things like steak or okra), or too large to swallow for things too solid to bite a piece off of.

Taking good things along never hurts either. Rice cakes, oatios, and peas always work for Corey. He's a big fan of the round food group… "

Article #227 (Continued)

"I used to give my daughter a strip of steak to suck on when she was 5, 6 months old. She often worked on the steak until it turned white (all the juices were gone). Just be careful not to put too much salt on the steak."

Getting the FAQs

As was explained in Chapter 4, a FAQ is a file containing answers to a newsgroup's frequently asked questions. A FAQ provides a means to easily bring new members up to date. The "misc.kids" folks have worked out an orderly method for making FAQs available to people. Rather than post each FAQ on a periodic basis, they maintain an index to the FAQs and post the index.

There are dozens of FAQs associated with "misc.kids". Instead of burdening one individual with maintaining all of the FAQs, they recruit a volunteer for each. If a person desires a particular FAQ, the person contacts the FAQ maintainer to request a copy of it. (Article #183 is an example of the system in action.) The FAQ maintainers change from time to time. The changes are reflected in the "Welcome to Misc.kids/FAQ File Index" periodic posting.

Here is an excerpt from "Welcome to Misc.kids/FAQ File Index". It describes the system they have worked out.

*** Index to FAQ Files ***

If you are interested in any of the following topics, please e-mail the contact person directly, who will then send you a copy of the file. Please be specific when requesting files, as some folks maintain more than one FAQ file. If you would like to add something to the files listed, please also do so via e-mail, and indicate that you would like your comments added to the FAQ file.

If you ask for an FAQ file and don't get it within a week, it may have bounced. When you ask again, please be sure to include your e-mail address in the body of your request, in case 'reply' doesn't work. ("Rec." = "Recommendations")

The index itself is quite large and contains names and addresses of people to contact. The "misc.kids" section of Chapter 8 contains a list of the FAQs that are available.

Interesting Events

A newsgroup can have many notable events in its lifetime. The newsgroup "misc.kids" is no exception. Regional get togethers are common for "misc.kid"-ers. Articles #199, #210 and #226 are examples of such events in progress.

One of the side effects of becoming a regular visitor to a newsgroup is that you begin to recognize the other regulars. Each regular develops into a complete and familiar personality. The only thing missing is the face to go with it. The "misc.kids" community undertook a project of great magnitude to remedy this. They compiled a yearbook of the regulars. Participation was voluntary and distribution was limited to those who participated. It was a success.

The "misc.kids" yearbook illustrates what a powerful tool for getting things done USENET can be. Here a group of people define a project plan and implement it using a newsgroup. Recruiting, problem solving, everything, was done within the electronic newsgroup. Considering the different geographical locations involved, that was an incredible accomplishment.

The Newsgroups
of USENET

2

☑ About this Part of the Book

☑ Computers: The "comp" Newsgroup

☑ Miscellaneous: The "misc" Newsgroups

☑ Network News: The "news" Newsgroups

☑ Recreation: The "rec" Newsgroups

☑ Science: The "sci" Newsgroups

☑ Society: The "soc" Newsgroups

☑ Talk: The "talk" Newsgroups

☑ Worthy Mentions from the Alternative Set

☑ Other Available Heirarchies

U SENET is constantly changing. Newsgroups are being added and removed daily. Part Two of this book can be thought of as a snapshot of USENET. It contains a list of existing USENET newsgroups at the time of this writing.

6

About this Part
of the Book

How Part Two is Organized

The organization of this part of the book reflects the organization of USENET itself. A chapter is devoted to each major branch of the core newsgroups in the USENET hierarchy. The chapters are arranged alphabetically. This part of the book also contains two other chapters. One chapter is devoted to four high volume subgroups of the "alt" hierarchy. The other final chapter describes other (non-USENET) newsgroup hierarchies that are available.

What Each Chapter in Part Two Covers

Within each chapter you will find a listing of all of the newgroups belonging to that particular tree along with any available FAQs they may have. The main newsgroup will be in **bold type**. The subgroups and their descriptions will be in regular type. Any available FAQs will be listed in *italic type*.

---

rec.travel.*:

rec.travel	Traveling around the world.
rec.travel.air	Airline travel around the world. Tickets and accommodations
rec.travel.market place	wanted and for sale.

Directory of tourist information offices worldwide
Directory of travel information available via internet
Index to rec.travel ftp archive
Simple suggestions for travel (net reminders really)

rec.travel.air:

FAQ: How to Get Cheap Airtickets 1 2 [Monthly Posting]
FAQ: How to Get Cheap Airtickets 2 2 [Monthly Posting]

How to Use Part Two

Part Two of this book is not meant to be read from start to finished. It is meant to be either browsed or used as a reference. If you have a passion for a particular topic, determine which chapter it might be in and scan the list of subgroups. Whatever it is that you love, you are likely to find others, like yourself, who love it too.

All things related to computers are discussed in this branch of the USENET newsgroup tree. There is a considerable amount of traffic in these newsgroups. If you have a computer-related interest, this is the list for you.

7

Computers: The "comp" Newsgroups

comp.admin.*:

comp.admin	Discussions of computer system administration.
comp.admin.policy	Discussions of site administration policies.

comp.ai.*:

comp.ai.edu	Applications of Artificial Intelligence.
comp.ai.fuzzy	Fuzzy set theory, aka fuzzy logic.
comp.ai.genetic	Genetic algorithms in computing.
comp.ai.jair.announce	Journal of Artificial Intelligence announcements.
comp.ai.jair.papers	Journal of Artificial Intelligence papers.
comp.ai.nat-lang	Artificial Intelligence and Natural Language.
comp.ai.neural-nets	All aspects of neural networks.
comp.ai.nlang-know-rep	Natural Language and Knowledge Representation.
comp.ai.philosophy	Philosophical aspects of Artificial Intelligence.
comp.ai.shells	Artificial intelligence applied to shells.
comp.ai.vision	Artificial Intelligence Vision Research.

FAQ: AI Newsgroups and Mailing Lists 2 6 [Monthly posting]
FAQ: Artificial Intelligence Bibliography 3 6 [Monthly posting]
FAQ: Artificial Intelligence FTP Resources 4 6 [Monthly posting]
FAQ: Artificial Intelligence FTP Resources 5 6 [Monthly posting]
FAQ: Artificial Intelligence Questions & Answers 1 6 [Monthly posting]
FAQ: Commercial Expert System Shells 6 6 [Monthly posting]
FAQ: Expert System Shells 6 6 [Monthly posting]

comp.ai.fuzzy:

FAQ: Fuzzy Logic and Fuzzy Expert Systems 1 1 [Monthly posting]

comp.ai.genetic:

FAQ: comp.ai.genetic part 1 3 (A Guide to Frequently Asked Questions)
FAQ: comp.ai.genetic part 2 3 (A Guide to Frequently Asked Questions)
FAQ: comp.ai.genetic part 3 3 (A Guide to Frequently Asked Questions)

FAQ: genetic-faq part1 (A Guide to Frequently Asked Questions)
FAQ: genetic-faq part2 (A Guide to Frequently Asked Questions)
FAQ: genetic-faq part3 (A Guide to Frequently Asked Questions)

comp.ai.neural-nets:

FAQ in comp.ai.neural-nets—monthly posting
Periodic neural network patent posting
changes to FAQ in comp.ai.neural-nets—monthly posting

comp.ai.shells:

FAQ: Commercial Expert System Shells 6 6 [Monthly posting]
FAQ: Expert System Shells 6 6 [Monthly posting]

comp.answers:

comp.answers   Repository for periodic USENET articles.

                                 (Moderated)

3b1-faq	*books*
3b2-faq	*cdrom-faq*
C-faq	*cell-relay-faq*
ForthFaq	*comp-lang-ada*
GNU-Emacs-FAQ	*comp-speech-faq*
Intel-Unix-X-faq	*comp-sys-sun-faq*
Modula-2-faq	*compilers-faq*
Modula-3-faq	*compression-faq*
Oberon-FAQ	*computer-virus-faq*
Objective-C	*csas-faq*
PCsoundcards	*dec-faq*
Solaris2	*dsp-faq*
Xt-FAQ	*editor-faq*
acorn	*eiffel-faq*
ai-faq	*elm*
aix-faq	*fax-faq*
amiga	*finding-addresses*
apollo-faq	*finding-sources*
audio-fmts	*fonts-faq*
aux-faq	*fortran-faq*

comp.answers (continued):

frame	*os2-faq*
free-compilers	*osi-protocols*
fuzzy-logic	*pc-games-FAQ*
g++-FAQ	*pcgeos-faq*
gopher-faq	*perl-faq*
graphics	*pex-faq*
groupware-intro	*postscript*
hp-faq	*ppp-faq*
ibm-rt-faq	*proj-plan-faq*
ibmpc-tcp-ip	*prolog*
idl-faq	*realtime-computing*
index	*ripem*
index-	*scheme-faq*
info-vax	*scsi-faq*
jpeg-faq	*sgi*
linux-faq	*snmp-faq*
lisp-faq	*software-eng*
lsi-cad-faq	*sources-test-faq*
mach-faq	*ssn-privacy*
macintosh	*standards-faq*
mail	*sybase-faq*
meta-lang-faq	*tcl-faq*
mh-faq	*techreport-sites*
minix-faq	*tex-faq-supplement*
minix-info	*text-faq*
modems	*typing-injury-faq*
motif-faq	*unix-faq*
msdos-archives	*uucp-internals*
msdos-programmer-faq	*waffle-faq*
music	*wais-faq*
net-privacy	*windows-misc-faq*
neural-net-faq	*x-faq*
news-answers	*z-faq*

comp.apps:

comp.apps	Discussion of computer applications.
comp.apps.spreadsheets	Spreadsheets on various platforms.

comp.arch:

comp.arch	Computer architecture.
comp.arch.storage	Storage system issues, both hardware and software.

A reminder about posting to comp.arch (last mod 06 14 90)

comp.archives.*:

comp.archives	Descriptions of public access archives.
comp.archives.admin	Issues relating to computer archives.
comp.archives.msdos.announce	Announcements about MSDOS archives.
comp.archives.msdos.d	Discussion of materials available for MSDOS.

comp.archives.admin:

Catalog of compilers, interpreters, and other language tools [p1of4]
Catalog of compilers, interpreters, and other language tools [p2of4]
Catalog of compilers, interpreters, and other language tools [p3of4]
Catalog of compilers, interpreters, and other language tools [p4of4]

comp.archives.msdos.d:

Useful MSDOS Programs at SIMTEL20 and Garbo (Part 1 of 2)
Useful MSDOS Programs at SIMTEL20 and Garbo (Part 2 of 2)

comp.bbs:

comp.bbs	Discussion of computer bulletin board systems.
comp.bbs.misc	All aspects of computer bulletin board systems.
comp.bbs.waffle	The Waffle BBS & USENET system all platforms.

comp.bbs.misc:

Changes to UNIX BBS Software FAQ with Answers (v 0.6)
Nixpub Posting (Long)
Nixpub Posting (Short)

comp.bbs.misc (continued):

UNIX BBS Software FAQ with Answers
UNIX BBS Software FAQ with Answers (v 0.6)

comp.bbs.waffle:

Waffle Frequently Asked Questions (FAQ)

comp.benchmarks:

comp.benchmarks   Discussion of benchmarking techniques.

[l m 10 14 92] SLALOM (13 28) c.be FAQ
[l m 11 2 92] good conceptual benchmarking (2 28) c.be FAQ
[l m 12 1 92] TPC Transaction Processing Council (21 28) c.be FAQ
[l m 1 31 92] benchmark source info-Intro—netiquette (1 28) c.be FAQ
[l m 3 17 92] Measurement environments (12 28) c.be FAQ
[l m 3 17 92] Other misc. benchmarks (26 28) c.be FAQ
[l m 3 17 92] PERFECT CLUB (3 28) c.be FAQ
[l m 3 17 92] RFC 1242—terminology (22 28) c.be FAQ
[l m 3 17 92] Equivalence (20 28) c.be FAQ
[l m 4 14 93] music to benchmark by (7 28) c.be FAQ
[l m 4 28 92] References (28 28) c.be FAQ
[l m 4 6 92] New FAQ scaffold (6 28) c.be FAQ
[l m 5 12 93] NIST source and .orgs (11 28) c.be FAQ
[l m 5 5 93] Performance metrics (5 28) c.be FAQ
[l m 7 15 93] Linpack (9 28) c.be FAQ

comp.binaries.*:

comp.binaries	Discussion of public domain programs.
comp.binaries.acorn	Binary-only postings for Acorn machine.
comp.binaries.amiga	Encoded public domain programs for the Amiga.
comp.binaries.apple2	Binary-only postings for the Apple II.
comp.binaries.atari.st	Binary-only postings for the Atari.
comp.binaries.ibm.pc	Binary-only postings for IBM PC.
comp.binaries.ibm.pc.archives	IBM PC archives.
comp.binaries.ibm.pc.d	Discussions about IBM/PC binaries.
comp.binaries.ibm.pc.wanted	Requests for IBM PC and compatibles.

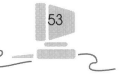

Computers

comp.binaries.mac	Encoded Macintosh programs in binary form.
comp.binaries.ms-windows	Binary programs for Microsoft Windows.
comp.binaries.os2	Binaries for use under the OS/2 operating system.

comp.binaries.ibm.pc:

v22inf10: admin1, IMPORTANT administrative note (part 01 01)
v23inf01: policy, CBIP policy (part 01 01)
v23inf02: starter.kit, CBIP Starter s Kit V1.9.1 (part 01 01)
v23inf03: charter, CBIP newsgroups charter (part 01 01)
v23inf04: bin.man, Beginner s Guide to Binaries V1.4 (part 01 01)
v23inf05: ftp.man, Beginner s Guide to FTP V1.7 (part 01 01)
v23inf06: brik2exe, Executable of brik2 (part 01 01)
v23inf07: briksrc1.shar, brik source (part 01 01)
v23inf08: briksrc2.shar, brik source (part 01 01)
v23inf09: briksrc3.shar, brik source (part 01 01)

comp.binaries.ibm.pc.wanted:

Useful MSDOS Programs at SIMTEL20 and Garbo (Part 1 of 2)
Useful MSDOS Programs at SIMTEL20 and Garbo (Part 2 of 2)

comp.bugs.*:

comp.bugs	Discussion of computer related problems (bugs).
comp.bugs.2bsd	Reports of UNIX* version 2BSD related bugs.
comp.bugs.4bsd	Reports of UNIX version 4BSD related bugs.
comp.bugs.misc	General UNIX bug reports and fixes.
comp.bugs.sys5	Reports of USG (System III, V, etc.).
comp.bugs.4bsd.ucb-fixes	Bug reports/fixes for BSD Unix. (Moderated)

comp.bugs.sys5:

Known Bugs in the USL UNIX distribution

comp.cad.*:

comp.cad	Discussion of computer aided design.
comp.cad.cadence	Users of Cadence Design Systems products.
comp.cad.compass	Users of Compass products.
comp.cad.pro-engineer	Users of Pro-Engineer products.
comp.cad.synthesis	Users of Synthesis products.

comp.client-server:

comp.client-server	Topics relating to client/server technology.

comp.cog-eng:

comp.cog-eng	Cognitive engineering.

comp.compilers:

comp.compilers	Compiler construction, theory, etc. (Moderated)

Catalog of compilers, interpreters, and other language tools [p1of4]
Catalog of compilers, interpreters, and other language tools [p2of4]
Catalog of compilers, interpreters, and other language tools [p3of4]
Catalog of compilers, interpreters, and other language tools [p4of4]
Comp.compilers 1990 Annual
comp.compilers monthly message and Frequently Asked Questions

comp.compression:

comp.compression	Data compression algorithms and theory.
comp.compression.research	Discussions about data compression research.

comp.compression FAQ (reminder)
comp.compression Frequently Asked Questions (part 1 3)
comp.compression Frequently Asked Questions (part 2 3)
comp.compression Frequently Asked Questions (part 3 3)

comp.compression.research:

comp.compression Frequently Asked Questions (part 1 3)
comp.compression Frequently Asked Questions (part 2 3)
comp.compression Frequently Asked Questions (part 3 3)

comp.databases:

comp.databases	Database and data management issues.
comp.databases.informix	Informix database management software.
comp.databases.ingres	Issues relating to INGRES products.
comp.databases.ms-access	MS Access discussion.
comp.databases.object	Object oriented databases.
comp.databases.oracle	The SQL database products of the Oracle.
comp.databases.pick	Discussion of the Pick database.
comp.databases.theory	Discussing advances in database techniques.
comp.databases.sybase	Implementations of the SQL Server.

comp.databases.sybase Frequently Asked Questions (FAQ)

comp.databases.sybase:

comp.databases.sybase Frequently Asked Questions (FAQ)

comp.dcom.*:

comp.dcom.cell-relay	Forum for discussion of Cell Relay.
comp.dcom.fax	Fax hardware, software, and protocols.
comp.dcom.isdn	The Integrated Services Digital Network.
comp.dcom.lans	Discussion of Local Area Networks.
comp.dcom.lans.ethernet	Discussions of the Ethernet/IEEE 8.
comp.dcom.lans.fddi	Discussions of the FDDI protocol.
comp.dcom.lans.hyperchannel	Hyperchannel networks within an IP…
comp.dcom.lans.misc	Local area network hardware and software.
comp.dcom.modems	Data communications hardware and software.
comp.dcom.sys.cisco	Info on Cisco routers and bridges.
comp.dcom.servers	Selecting and operating data communications.
comp.dcom.sys.wellfleet	Wellfleet bridge & router systems.
comp.dcom.telecom	Telecommunications digest. (Moderated)
comp.dcom.telecom.digest	Telecommunication discussion.

Computers

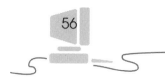

comp.dcom.cell-relay:

comp.dcom.cell-relay FAQ: ATM, SMDS, and related technologies

comp.dcom.fax:

De Facto Class2 fax modem Command Scorecard part 0 of 6
De Facto Class2 fax modem Command Scorecard part 0b of 6
De Facto Class2 fax modem Command Scorecard part 1 of 6
De Facto Class2 fax modem Command Scorecard part 2 of 6
De Facto Class2 fax modem Command Scorecard part 3 of 6
De Facto Class2 fax modem Command Scorecard part 4 of 6
De Facto Class2 fax modem Command Scorecard part 5 of 6
De Facto Class2 fax modem Command Scorecard part 6 of 6
Fax (comp.dcom.fax) Frequently Asked Questions (FAQ)
ZyXEL modem FAQ List v3.0, July 26, 1993 Edition
ZyXEL modem FAQ List v3.1, August 16, 1993 Edition

comp.dcom.modems:

Configuring the Telebit Trailblazer for Use with UNIX
De Facto Class2 fax modem Command Scorecard part 0 of 6
De Facto Class2 fax modem Command Scorecard part 0b of 6
De Facto Class2 fax modem Command Scorecard part 1 of 6
De Facto Class2 fax modem Command Scorecard part 2 of 6
De Facto Class2 fax modem Command Scorecard part 3 of 6
De Facto Class2 fax modem Command Scorecard part 4 of 6
De Facto Class2 fax modem Command Scorecard part 5 of 6
De Facto Class2 fax modem Command Scorecard part 6 of 6
The NetComm Modem FAQ v1.1
ZyXEL U1496 series modems resellers FAQ (bi-monthly)
ZyXEL modem FAQ List v3.0, July 26, 1993 Edition
ZyXEL modem FAQ List v3.1, August 16, 1993 Edition

comp.dcom.telecom:

About This Newsgroup and Telecom Digest

comp.doc.*:

comp.doc   Archived public-domain documentation.
                              (Moderated)

comp.doc.techreports   Lists of technical reports. (Moderated)

comp.doc.techreports:

Computer Science Tech Report Archive Sites [changes from last month]
Computer Science Technical Report Archive Sites

comp.dsp:

comp.dsp   Digital Signal Processing using computers.

Changes to: FAQ: Audio File Formats
FAQ: Audio File Formats (part 1 of 2)
FAQ: Audio File Formats (part 2 of 2)
comp.dsp FAQ [1 of 4]
comp.dsp FAQ [2 of 4]
comp.dsp FAQ [3 of 4]
comp.dsp FAQ [4 of 4]

comp.editors:

comp.editors   Discussions related to computer editors.

Emacs implementations, list of, regular post [long, FAQ]
Introduction to comp.editors (July 29 1993)
comp.editors - VI Archives ;

comp.edu:

comp.edu   Discussions related to computers and education.

comp.emacs:

comp.emacs   EMACS editors of different flavors.

Emacs implementations, list of, regular post [long, FAQ]

comp.fonts.*:

comp.fonts   Typefonts—design, conversion, use, etc.

comp.fonts FAQ.1A.General-Info (1 3)
comp.fonts FAQ.1B.General-Info (2 3)
comp.fonts FAQ.1C.General-Info (3 3)
comp.fonts FAQ.2.Mac-Info
comp.fonts FAQ.3.MS-DOS-Info

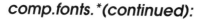

comp.fonts.*(continued):

comp.fonts FAQ.4.OS 2-Info
comp.fonts FAQ.5.Unix-Info
comp.fonts FAQ.6.Sun-Info
comp.fonts FAQ.7.NeXT-Info
comp.fonts FAQ.8.X-Info
comp.fonts FAQ.9.Utilities
comp.fonts FAQ.A.VendorList
comp.fonts FAQ: Amiga Info
comp.fonts FAQ: General Info (1 3)
comp.fonts FAQ: General Info (2 3)
comp.fonts FAQ: General Info (3 3)
comp.fonts FAQ: MS-DOS Info
comp.fonts FAQ: Macintosh Info
comp.fonts FAQ: NeXT Info
comp.fonts FAQ: OS 2 Info
comp.fonts FAQ: Sun Info
comp.fonts FAQ: Unix Info
comp.fonts FAQ: Utilities
comp.fonts FAQ: Vendor List
comp.fonts FAQ: X11 Info

comp.graphics.*:

comp.graphics	Computer graphics, art, animation,...
comp.graphics.algorithms	Computer graphic algorithms.
comp.graphics.animation	Technical aspects of computer animation.
comp.graphics.avs	The Application Visualization System.
comp.graphics.data-explorer	Discussion of the data explorer.
comp.graphics.explorer	The Explorer Modular Visualisation.
comp.graphics.gnuplot	The GNUPLOT interactive function.
comp.graphics.opengl	The OpenGL 3D application programming.
comp.graphics.research	Highly technical computer graphics research.
comp.graphics.visualization	Info on scientific visualization.

(09Aug93) comp.graphics Frequently Asked Questions (FAQ)
(18 June 93) Computer Graphics Resource Listing : WEEKLY [part 1 3]
(18 June 93) Computer Graphics Resource Listing : WEEKLY [part 2 3]

(18 June 93) Computer Graphics Resource Listing : WEEKLY [part 3 3]
(20 July 93) Computer Graphics Resource Listing : BIWEEKLY [part 1 4]
(20 July 93) Computer Graphics Resource Listing : BIWEEKLY [part 2 4]
(20 July 93) Computer Graphics Resource Listing : BIWEEKLY [part 3 4]
(20 July 93) Computer Graphics Resource Listing : BIWEEKLY [part 4 4]
(28 May 93) Computer Graphics Resource Listing : WEEKLY [part 1 3]
(28 May 93) Computer Graphics Resource Listing : WEEKLY [part 2 3]
(28 May 93) Computer Graphics Resource Listing : WEEKLY [part 3 3]
(9 June 93) Computer Graphics Resource Listing : WEEKLY [part 1 3]
(9 June 93) Computer Graphics Resource Listing : WEEKLY [part 2 3]
(9 June 93) Computer Graphics Resource Listing : WEEKLY [part 3 3]
JPEG image compression: Frequently Asked Questions

comp.graphics.gnuplot:

comp.graphics.gnuplot FAQ (Frequent Answered Questions)

comp.graphics.opengl:

comp.graphics.opengl Frequently Asked Questions (FAQ) [1 1]

comp.groupware:

comp.groupware	Software and hardware for shared interactive environments.

Introduction to comp.groupware (Periodic informational Posting)

comp.human-factors:

comp.human-factors	Issues related to human-computer interaction.

FAQ: Typing Injuries (1 5): Changes since last month [monthly posting]
FAQ: Typing Injuries (2 5): General Info [monthly posting]
FAQ: Typing Injuries (3 5): Keyboard Alternatives [monthly posting]
FAQ: Typing Injuries (4 5): Software Monitoring Tools [monthly posting]
FAQ: Typing Injuries (5 5): Furniture Information [monthly posting]

Computers

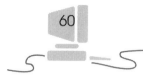
comp.infosystems.*:

comp.infosystems	Any discussion about information systems.
comp.infosystems.gis	All aspects of Geographic Information Systems.
comp.infosystems.gopher	Discussion of the gopher information search tool.
comp.infosystems.wais	The Z39.50-based WAIS full-text search tool.
comp.infosystems.www	Discussion of the World Wide Web.

comp.infosystems.gopher:

Gopher (comp.infosystems.gopher) Frequently Asked Questions (FAQ)

comp.infosystems.wais:

comp.infosystems.wais Frequently asked Questions [FAQ] (with answers)

comp.lang.*:

comp.lang	Discussion about computer languages.
comp.lang.ada	Discussion about Ada*.
comp.lang.apl	Discussion about APL.
comp.lang.asm370	Programming in IBM System/370 Assembly Language.
comp.lang.c	Discussion about C.
comp.lang.c++	The object-oriented C++ language.
comp.lang.clos	Common Lisp Object System discussions.
comp.lang.clu	The CLU language & related topics.
comp.lang.dylan	For discussion of the Dylan language.
comp.lang.eiffel	The object-oriented Eiffel language.
comp.lang.forth	Discussion about Forth.
comp.lang.fortran	Discussion about FORTRAN.
comp.lang.functional	Discussion about functional languages.
comp.lang.hermes	The Hermes language for distributed applications.
comp.lang.icon	Topics related to the ICON programming lang.

comp.lang.idl-pvwave	IDL and PV-Wave language discussions.
comp.lang.lisp	Discussion about LISP.
comp.lang.lisp.franz	The Franz Lisp programming language.
comp.lang.lisp.mcl	Discussing Apple's Macintosh Common Lisp.
comp.lang.lisp.x	The XLISP language system.
comp.lang.logo	The Logo teaching and learning language.
comp.lang.misc	Different computer languages not specified.
comp.lang.ml	
comp.lang.modula2	Discussion about Modula-2.
comp.lang.modula3	Discussion about the Modula-3 language.
comp.lang.oberon	
comp.lang.objective-c	The Objective-C language and environment.
comp.lang.pascal	Discussion about Pascal.
comp.lang.perl	Discussion of Larry Wall's Perl system.
comp.lang.pop	Pop11 and the Plug user group.
comp.lang.postscript	The PostScript Page Description Language.
comp.lang.prolog	Discussion about PROLOG.
comp.lang.rexx	The REXX command language.
comp.lang.sather	
comp.lang.scheme	The Scheme Programming language.
comp.lang.scheme.c	The Scheme language environment.
comp.lang.sigplan	Info & announcements from ACM SIGPLAN.
comp.lang.smalltalk	Discussion about Smalltalk 80.
comp.lang.tcl	The Tcl programming language and related topics.
comp.lang.verilog	Discussing Verilog and PLI.
comp.lang.vhdl	VHSIC Hardware Description Language, IEEE.
comp.lang.visual	Visual programming languages.

Computers

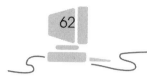

comp.lang.ada:

Public Ada Library FAQ
comp.lang.ada FAQ 1 2
comp.lang.ada FAQ 2 2

comp.lang.c:

C-FAQ-list
C-FAQ-list.abridged
C-FAQ-list.diff
Diffs to Index of free C or C++ source code for numerical computation
Part 1 of 2: Free C,C++ for numerical computation
Part 2 of 2: Free C,C++ for numerical computation
So You Want To Be A UNIX Wizard? (The Loginataka)
index

comp.lang.c++:

Diffs to Index of free C or C++ source code for numerical computation
FAQ for g++ and libg++, plain text version [Revised 15 Aug 1993]
FAQ for g++ and libg++, plain text version [Revised 31 Jul 1993]
FAQ for g++ and libg++, texinfo version [Revised 15 Aug 1993]
FAQ for g++ and libg++, texinfo version [Revised 31 Jul 1993]
Part 1 of 2: Free C,C++ for numerical computation
Part 2 of 2: Free C,C++ for numerical computation
comp.lang.c++ FAQ (part 1 of 4)
comp.lang.c++ FAQ (posting 2 of 4)
comp.lang.c++ FAQ (posting 3 of 4)
comp.lang.c++ FAQ (posting 4 of 4)

comp.lang.clos:

FAQ: Object-oriented Programming in Lisp 5 7 [Monthly posting]

comp.lang.eiffel:

comp.lang.eiffel Frequently Asked Questions (FAQ)

comp.lang.forth:

Forth FAQ: ANS Forth Standard Info. (l m 22.Jul.93)
Forth FAQ: Applications done with Forth. (l m 22.Jul.93)
Forth FAQ: CASE,OF,ENDOF,ENDCASE. (l m 30.Jan.93)
Forth FAQ: FAQ Overview. (l m 07.Aug.93)
Forth FAQ: ForthNet: What and how? (l m 19.Jun.93)
Forth FAQ: Forth Implementations. (l m 07.Aug.93)
Forth FAQ: Forth In Print. (l m 30.Jul.93)
Forth FAQ: General Internet info. (l m 30.Jan.93)
Forth FAQ: Libraries: Where and how? (l m 31.Mar.93)
Forth FAQ: Organizations and Publications. (l m 30.Jan.93)
Forth FAQ: Programmable BBS Information. (l m 05.Jun.93)
Forth FAQ: What is Forth? (l m 30.Jan.93)

comp.lang.fortran:

Fortran FAQ

comp.lang.idl-pvwave:

IDL (Interactive Data Language) FAQ

comp.lang.lisp:

FAQ: Lisp FTP Resources 6 7 [Monthly posting]
FAQ: Lisp Frequently Asked Questions 1 7 [Monthly posting]
FAQ: Lisp Frequently Asked Questions 2 7 [Monthly posting]
FAQ: Lisp Frequently Asked Questions 3 7 [Monthly posting]
FAQ: Lisp Implementations and Mailing Lists 4 7 [Monthly posting]
FAQ: Lisp Window Systems and GUIs 7 7 [Monthly posting]
FAQ: Object-oriented Programming in Lisp 5 7 [Monthly posting]
FAQ: Scheme Frequently Asked Questions 1 1 [Monthly posting]

comp.lang.misc:

Catalog of compilers, interpreters, and other language tools [p1of4]
Catalog of compilers, interpreters, and other language tools [p2of4]
Catalog of compilers, interpreters, and other language tools [p3of4]
Catalog of compilers, interpreters, and other language tools [p4of4]

comp.lang.ml:

Comp.Lang.ML FAQ [Monthly Posting]

comp.lang.modula2:

comp.lang.modula2: Answers to Common Questions - v1.5 93.06.02

comp.lang.oberon:

Comp.lang.oberon FAQ (monthly)

comp.lang.objective-c:

comp.lang.objective-c FAQ, part 1 3: Answers
comp.lang.objective-c FAQ, part 2 3: ClassWare Listing
comp.lang.objective-c FAQ, part 2 3: Classes
comp.lang.objective-c FAQ, part 3 3: A Sample Program

comp.lang.perl:

Frequently asked questions about Perl (revised 11 30 92)
comp.lang.perl FAQ (part 0 of 2)
comp.lang.perl FAQ (part 1 of 2)
comp.lang.perl FAQ (part 2 of 2)

comp.lang.postscript:

PostScript monthly FAQ v2.1 05-21-93 [01-04 of 11]
PostScript monthly FAQ v2.1 05-21-93 [05-06 of 11]
PostScript monthly FAQ v2.1 05-21-93 [07-10 of 11]
PostScript monthly FAQ v2.1 05-21-93 [11 of 11]

comp.lang.prolog:

FAQ: Prolog Implementations 2 2 [Monthly posting]
FAQ: Prolog Resource Guide 1 2 [Monthly posting]
comp.lang.prolog Frequently Asked Questions

comp.lang.scheme:

FAQ: Scheme Frequently Asked Questions 1 1 [Monthly posting]

comp.lang.smalltalk:

Smalltalk Frequently-Asked Questions (FAQ)

comp.lang.tcl:

FAQ: comp.lang.tcl Frequently Asked Questions (1 3) (Last updated: June 16, 1993)
FAQ: comp.lang.tcl Frequently Asked Questions (2 3) (Last updated: June 16, 1993)
FAQ: comp.lang.tcl Frequently Asked Questions (3 3) (Last updated: June 16, 1993)

comp.lsi.*:

comp.lsi	Large scale integrated circuits.
comp.lsi.cad	Electrical Computer Aided Design.
comp.lsi.testing	Testing of electronic circuits.

comp.lsi.cad Frequently Asked Questions With Answers (Part 1 4) [LONG]
comp.lsi.cad Frequently Asked Questions With Answers (Part 2 4) [LONG]
comp.lsi.cad Frequently Asked Questions With Answers (Part 3 4) [LONG]
comp.lsi.cad Frequently Asked Questions With Answers (Part 4 4) [LONG]

comp.lsi.cad:

comp.lsi.cad Frequently Asked Questions With Answers (Part 1 4) [LONG]
comp.lsi.cad Frequently Asked Questions With Answers (Part 2 4) [LONG]
comp.lsi.cad Frequently Asked Questions With Answers (Part 3 4) [LONG]
comp.lsi.cad Frequently Asked Questions With Answers (Part 4 4) [LONG]

comp.mail.*:

comp.mail	Discussion of electronic mail systems.
comp.mail.elm	Discussion and fixes for ELM mail system.
comp.mail.headers	Gatewayed from the Internet header-people.
comp.mail.maps	Various maps, including UUCP maps. (Moderated)
comp.mail.mh	The UCI version of the Rand Message Handler.
comp.mail.mime	Multipurpose Internet Mail Extensions.
comp.mail.misc	General discussions about computer mail.
comp.mail.multi-media	Multimedia Mail.

Computers

comp.mail.* (continued):

comp.mail.mush	The Mail User's Shell (MUSH).
comp.mail.sendmail	Configuring and using the BSD sendmail.
comp.mail.uucp	Mail in the uucp network environment.

comp.mail.elm:

Changes to the Monthly Elm Posting from the Elm Development Group
Elm Mail User Agent FAQ - monthly posting
Monthly Elm Posting from the Elm Development Group

comp.mail.maps:

UUCP map for README	*UUCP map for u.aus.1*
UUCP map for d.AProject	*UUCP map for u.aus.2*
UUCP map for d.Top	*UUCP map for u.aus.3*
UUCP map for u.are.1	*UUCP map for u.aus.act.1*
UUCP map for u.arg.1	*UUCP map for u.aus.nsw.1*
UUCP map for u.arg.ba.1	*UUCP map for u.aus.nsw.2*
UUCP map for u.arg.ba.2	*UUCP map for u.aus.nsw.3*
UUCP map for u.arg.cb.1	*UUCP map for u.aus.nsw.4*
UUCP map for u.arg.cc.1	*UUCP map for u.aus.nsw.5*
UUCP map for u.arg.ch.1	*UUCP map for u.aus.nt.1*
UUCP map for u.arg.cn.1	*UUCP map for u.aus.qld.1*
UUCP map for u.arg.ct.1	*UUCP map for u.aus.sa.1*
UUCP map for u.arg.er.1	*UUCP map for u.aus.tas.1*
UUCP map for u.arg.fm.1	*UUCP map for u.aus.vic.1*
UUCP map for u.arg.lr.1	*UUCP map for u.aus.vic.2*
UUCP map for u.arg.mn.1	*UUCP map for u.aus.vic.3*
UUCP map for u.arg.mz.1	*UUCP map for u.aus.wa.1*
UUCP map for u.arg.nq.1	*UUCP map for u.aut.0*
UUCP map for u.arg.rn.1	*UUCP map for u.aut.1*
UUCP map for u.arg.sa.1	*UUCP map for u.bel.0*
UUCP map for u.arg.se.1	*UUCP map for u.bel.1*
UUCP map for u.arg.sf.1	*UUCP map for u.bel.100*
UUCP map for u.arg.sj.1	*UUCP map for u.bgr.0*
UUCP map for u.arg.sl.1	*UUCP map for u.bgr.1*
UUCP map for u.arg.tf.1	*UUCP map for u.bra.1*
UUCP map for u.arg.tm.1	*UUCP map for u.bys.1*

UUCP map for u.can.1
UUCP map for u.can.10
UUCP map for u.can.2
UUCP map for u.can.3
UUCP map for u.can.4
UUCP map for u.can.5
UUCP map for u.can.6
UUCP map for u.can.7
UUCP map for u.can.8
UUCP map for u.can.9
UUCP map for u.can.ab.1
UUCP map for u.can.ab.2
UUCP map for u.can.bc.1
UUCP map for u.can.bc.2
UUCP map for u.can.mb.1
UUCP map for u.can.nb.1
UUCP map for u.can.nf.1
UUCP map for u.can.ns.1
UUCP map for u.can.nt.1
UUCP map for u.can.on.1
UUCP map for u.can.on.2
UUCP map for u.can.on.3
UUCP map for u.can.on.4
UUCP map for u.can.on.5
UUCP map for u.can.on.6
UUCP map for u.can.on.7
UUCP map for u.can.qc.1
UUCP map for u.can.sk.1
UUCP map for u.can.yk.1
UUCP map for u.che.0
UUCP map for u.che.1
UUCP map for u.che.10
UUCP map for u.che.100
UUCP map for u.chl.1
UUCP map for u.col.1
UUCP map for u.cri.1
UUCP map for u.csk.0
UUCP map for u.csk.1
UUCP map for u.deu.0

UUCP map for u.deu.1
UUCP map for u.deu.100
UUCP map for u.deu.101
UUCP map for u.deu.102
UUCP map for u.deu.103
UUCP map for u.deu.104
UUCP map for u.deu.105
UUCP map for u.deu.106
UUCP map for u.deu.107
UUCP map for u.deu.108
UUCP map for u.deu.2
UUCP map for u.deu.3
UUCP map for u.deu.4
UUCP map for u.deu.5
UUCP map for u.deu.6
UUCP map for u.deu.7
UUCP map for u.deu.8
UUCP map for u.deu.9
UUCP map for u.dnk.0
UUCP map for u.dnk.1
UUCP map for u.dom.1
UUCP map for u.egy.1
UUCP map for u.esp.0
UUCP map for u.esp.1
UUCP map for u.esp.100
UUCP map for u.esp.2
UUCP map for u.esp.3
UUCP map for u.esp.4
UUCP map for u.eur.0
UUCP map for u.eur.ita.1
UUCP map for u.fin.0
UUCP map for u.fin.1
UUCP map for u.fin.2
UUCP map for u.fin.3
UUCP map for u.fin.4
UUCP map for u.fin.5
UUCP map for u.fra.0
UUCP map for u.fra.1
UUCP map for u.fra.100

comp.mail.maps (continued):

UUCP map for u.fra.2	*UUCP map for u.lux.1*
UUCP map for u.fra.3	*UUCP map for u.mex.1*
UUCP map for u.fra.4	*UUCP map for u.mys.1*
UUCP map for u.gbr.0	*UUCP map for u.nic.1*
UUCP map for u.gbr.1	*UUCP map for u.nld.0*
UUCP map for u.gbr.100	*UUCP map for u.nld.1*
UUCP map for u.gbr.2	*UUCP map for u.nld.100*
UUCP map for u.gbr.3	*UUCP map for u.nld.2*
UUCP map for u.gbr.4	*UUCP map for u.nld.3*
UUCP map for u.gbr.5	*UUCP map for u.nld.4*
UUCP map for u.gbr.6	*UUCP map for u.nor.0*
UUCP map for u.gbr.7	*UUCP map for u.nor.1*
UUCP map for u.gbr.8	*UUCP map for u.nor.100*
UUCP map for u.grc.0	*UUCP map for u.nor.2*
UUCP map for u.grc.1	*UUCP map for u.nor.3*
UUCP map for u.gtm.1	*UUCP map for u.nzl.1*
UUCP map for u.hnd.1	*UUCP map for u.pak.1*
UUCP map for u.hun.0	*UUCP map for u.phl.1*
UUCP map for u.hun.1	*UUCP map for u.prt.0*
UUCP map for u.hun.100	*UUCP map for u.prt.1*
UUCP map for u.idn.1	*UUCP map for u.prt.100*
UUCP map for u.ind.1	*UUCP map for u.pry.1*
UUCP map for u.irl.0	*UUCP map for u.qat.1*
UUCP map for u.irl.1	*UUCP map for u.sau.1*
UUCP map for u.isl.0	*UUCP map for u.sgp.1*
UUCP map for u.isl.1	*UUCP map for u.sun.0*
UUCP map for u.isr.1	*UUCP map for u.sun.1*
UUCP map for u.ita.0	*UUCP map for u.sun.100*
UUCP map for u.ita.1	*UUCP map for u.sun.2*
UUCP map for u.jam.1	*UUCP map for u.sun.3*
UUCP map for u.jpn.1	*UUCP map for u.sun.4*
UUCP map for u.jpn.2	*UUCP map for u.svn.0*
UUCP map for u.jpn.3	*UUCP map for u.svn.1*
UUCP map for u.jpn.4	*UUCP map for u.swe.0*
UUCP map for u.kor.1	*UUCP map for u.swe.1*
UUCP map for u.kwt.1	*UUCP map for u.swe.2*
UUCP map for u.lka.1	*UUCP map for u.swe.3*

UUCP map for u.tha.1
UUCP map for u.tun.0
UUCP map for u.tun.1
UUCP map for u.tur.1
UUCP map for u.twn.1
UUCP map for u.ukr.1
UUCP map for u.ury.1
UUCP map for u.usa.ak.1
UUCP map for u.usa.al.1
UUCP map for u.usa.ar.1
UUCP map for u.usa.az.1
UUCP map for u.usa.ca.1
UUCP map for u.usa.ca.10
UUCP map for u.usa.ca.11
UUCP map for u.usa.ca.12
UUCP map for u.usa.ca.14
UUCP map for u.usa.ca.16
UUCP map for u.usa.ca.18
UUCP map for u.usa.ca.2
UUCP map for u.usa.ca.20
UUCP map for u.usa.ca.3
UUCP map for u.usa.ca.4
UUCP map for u.usa.ca.5
UUCP map for u.usa.ca.6
UUCP map for u.usa.ca.7
UUCP map for u.usa.ca.8
UUCP map for u.usa.ca.9
UUCP map for u.usa.co.1
UUCP map for u.usa.co.2
UUCP map for u.usa.ct.1
UUCP map for u.usa.ct.2
UUCP map for u.usa.dc.1
UUCP map for u.usa.de.1
UUCP map for u.usa.fl.1
UUCP map for u.usa.ga.0
UUCP map for u.usa.ga.1
UUCP map for u.usa.ga.2
UUCP map for u.usa.ga.3
UUCP map for u.usa.ga.4

UUCP map for u.usa.ga.5
UUCP map for u.usa.ga.6
UUCP map for u.usa.hi.1
UUCP map for u.usa.ia.1
UUCP map for u.usa.id.1
UUCP map for u.usa.il.1
UUCP map for u.usa.il.2
UUCP map for u.usa.il.3
UUCP map for u.usa.in.1
UUCP map for u.usa.is.1
UUCP map for u.usa.ks.1
UUCP map for u.usa.ky.1
UUCP map for u.usa.la.1
UUCP map for u.usa.ma.1
UUCP map for u.usa.ma.2
UUCP map for u.usa.ma.3
UUCP map for u.usa.ma.4
UUCP map for u.usa.ma.5
UUCP map for u.usa.ma.6
UUCP map for u.usa.md.1
UUCP map for u.usa.md.2
UUCP map for u.usa.me.1
UUCP map for u.usa.mi.1
UUCP map for u.usa.mi.2
UUCP map for u.usa.mi.3
UUCP map for u.usa.mn.1
UUCP map for u.usa.mn.2
UUCP map for u.usa.mo.1
UUCP map for u.usa.ms.1
UUCP map for u.usa.mt.1
UUCP map for u.usa.nc.1
UUCP map for u.usa.nd.1
UUCP map for u.usa.ne.1
UUCP map for u.usa.nh.1
UUCP map for u.usa.nh.2
UUCP map for u.usa.nj.1
UUCP map for u.usa.nj.2
UUCP map for u.usa.nj.3
UUCP map for u.usa.nm.1

comp.mail.maps (continued):

UUCP map for u.usa.nv.1	*UUCP map for u.usa.tx.1*
UUCP map for u.usa.ny.1	*UUCP map for u.usa.tx.2*
UUCP map for u.usa.ny.2	*UUCP map for u.usa.tx.3*
UUCP map for u.usa.ny.3	*UUCP map for u.usa.tx.4*
UUCP map for u.usa.ny.4	*UUCP map for u.usa.tx.5*
UUCP map for u.usa.ny.5	*UUCP map for u.usa.ut.1*
UUCP map for u.usa.oh.1	*UUCP map for u.usa.va.1*
UUCP map for u.usa.oh.2	*UUCP map for u.usa.va.2*
UUCP map for u.usa.ok.1	*UUCP map for u.usa.va.3*
UUCP map for u.usa.or.1	*UUCP map for u.usa.vi.1*
UUCP map for u.usa.or.2	*UUCP map for u.usa.vt.1*
UUCP map for u.usa.or.3	*UUCP map for u.usa.wa.1*
UUCP map for u.usa.pa.1	*UUCP map for u.usa.wa.2*
UUCP map for u.usa.pa.2	*UUCP map for u.usa.wa.3*
UUCP map for u.usa.pa.3	*UUCP map for u.usa.wi.1*
UUCP map for u.usa.pr.1	*UUCP map for u.usa.wv.1*
UUCP map for u.usa.ri.1	*UUCP map for u.usa.wy.1*
UUCP map for u.usa.sc.1	*UUCP map for u.yug.0*
UUCP map for u.usa.sd.1	*UUCP map for u.yug.1*
UUCP map for u.usa.tn.1	*UUCP map for u.zaf.1*

comp.mail.mh:

MH Frequently Asked Questions (FAQ) with Answers

comp.mail.mime:

comp.mail.mime frequently asked questions list (FAQ)

comp.mail.misc:

FAQ: How to find people s E-mail addresses
FAQ: International E-mail accessibility
Mail Archive Server software list
RIPEM Frequently Asked Questions
RIPEM Frequently Noted Vulnerabilities
UNIX Email Software Survey FAQ
Updated Inter-Network Mail Guide

comp.mail.uucp:

FAQ: International E-mail accessibility
FAQ: International E-mail accessibility
UUCP Internals Frequently Asked Questions

comp.misc:

comp.misc   General topics about computers not covered
                                   elsewhere.

Nixpub Posting (Long)
Nixpub Posting (Short)
Updated Inter-Network Mail Guide
Updated Internet Services List

comp.multimedia:

comp.multimedia   Interactive multimedia technologies of all
                                   kinds.

alt.cd-rom FAQ

comp.music:

Computer Music bibliography
Electronic and Computer Music Frequently-Asked Questions (FAQ)
FAQ: Gravis Ultrasound (GUS) FAQ v1.30
Midi files software archives on the Internet
Midi files software archives on the Internet.

comp.newprod:

comp.newprod   Announcements of new products of interest.
                                   (Moderated)

Welcome to comp.newprod [periodic posting]

comp.object.*:

comp.object   Object-oriented programming and languages.
comp.object.logic   Object-oriented programming logic.

comp.object.logic:

FAQ: Prolog Implementations 2 2 [Monthly posting]
FAQ: Prolog Resource Guide 1 2 [Monthly posting]

comp.org.*:

comp.org	Computer organizations.
comp.org.decus	The DEC Users Group related issues.
comp.org.fidonet	Fidonet organization related issues.
comp.org.usenix	USENIX organization issues.

comp.org.decus:

DECUS Questions Answered (last modified 1-Jul-93)
Monthly info posting: What is VMSnet?

comp.org.fidonet:

FidoNet Newsletter, Volume 10, # 32
FidoNet Newsletter, Volume 10, # 33

comp.org.usenix:

FAQ: SAGE, The System Administrators Guild

comp.os.*:

comp.os	Discussions related to computer operating systems.
comp.os.386bsd.announce	Announcements relating to 386bsd.
comp.os.386bsd.apps	Applications which run under 386bsd.
comp.os.386bsd.bugs	Bugs and fixes for the 386bsd.
comp.os.386bsd.development	Working on 386bsd internal development.
comp.os.386bsd.misc	General aspects of 386bsd.
comp.os.386bsd.questions	General questions about 386bsd.
comp.os.aos	Topics related to Data General systems.
comp.os.coherent	Discussion and support of Coherent products.

comp.os.cpm	Discussion about the CP/M operating system.
comp.os.cpm.amethyst	Discussion of Amethyst, ...
comp.os.linux	The free UNIX-clone.
comp.os.linux.admin	Linux administration issues.
comp.os.linux.announce	Announcements important to Linux users.
comp.os.linux.development	Linux development.
comp.os.linux.help	Help for Linux.
comp.os.linux.misc	Miscellaneous Linux discussions.
comp.os.mach	The MACH OS from CMU & other sources.
comp.os.minix	Discussion of Tanenbaum's Minix.
comp.os.misc	General OS-oriented discussion.
comp.os.ms-windows.advocacy	Speculation and debate about Windows.
comp.os.ms-windows.announce	Announcements relating to Windows.
comp.os.ms-windows.apps	Applications in the Windows.
comp.os.ms-windows.misc	General discussions about Windows.
comp.os.ms-windows.nt.misc	Windows and NT,
comp.os.ms-windows.nt.setup	Windows and NT installation and setup.
comp.os.ms-windows.-programmer.misc	Programming Microsoft Windows.
comp.os.ms-windows.-programmer.tools	Development tools in Windows.
comp.os.ms-windows.-programmer.win32	32-bit Windows programming.
comp.os.ms-windows.setup	Installing and configuring Windows.
comp.os.msdos.4dos	The 4DOS command processor.
comp.os.msdos.apps	Discussion of applications for MSDOS.
comp.os.msdos.desqview	QuarterDeck's Desqview.
comp.os.msdos.mail-news	
comp.os.msdos.misc	Miscellaneous topics about MSDOS.
comp.os.msdos.pcgeos	GeoWorks PC/GEOS and PC/G.
comp.os.msdos.programmer	Programming MS-DOS machines.

comp.os.msdos.programmer.-turbovision	O/S2 and Turbovision.
comp.os.os2	Discussion of os2.
comp.os.os2.advocacy	Supporting and flaming O/S2.
comp.os.os2.announce	O/S2 announcements.
comp.os.os2.apps	Discussions of applications for O/S2.
comp.os.os2.beta	O/S2 beta testing discussions.
comp.os.os2.bugs	O/S2 bugs.
comp.os.os2.misc	Miscellaneous topics about O/S2.
comp.os.os2.multimedia	O/S2 and multimedia.
comp.os.os2.networking	Networking in OS/2 environment.
comp.os.os2.programmer	Programming OS/2 machines.
comp.os.os2.programmer.misc	Programming O/S2.
comp.os.os2.programmer.-porting	Porting O/S2.
comp.os.os2.setup	O/S2 installation and setup.
comp.os.os2.ver1x	
comp.os.os9	Discussions about the os9.
comp.os.research	Operating systems and research.
comp.os.v	The V distributed operating system.
comp.os.vms	DEC's VAX* line of computers.
comp.os.vxworks	The VxWorks real-time operating system.
comp.os.xinu	The XINU operating system.

comp.os.386bsd.announce:

386bsd NetBSD FAQ Section 0
386bsd NetBSD FAQ Section 1
386bsd NetBSD FAQ Section 2
386bsd NetBSD FAQ Section 3
386bsd NetBSD FAQ Section 4
386bsd NetBSD FAQ Section 5
FAQ: 386BSD NetBSD Compatible tape drive list
Monthly Reminder: 386bsd news archive via ftp

comp.os.386bsd.questions:

386bsd NetBSD FAQ Section 0
386bsd NetBSD FAQ Section 1
386bsd NetBSD FAQ Section 2
386bsd NetBSD FAQ Section 3
386bsd NetBSD FAQ Section 4
386bsd NetBSD FAQ Section 5
FAQ: 386BSD NetBSD Compatible tape drive list
Monthly Reminder: 386bsd news archive via ftp

comp.os.coherent:

Coherent FAQ, Features in 4.x
Coherent FAQ, General Information
Coherent FAQ, Tech-tips for OS-rev-3.2
Coherent FAQ, Tech-tips for OS-rev-4.x

comp.os.linux:

** Linux Documents Explained for Newbies ** Weekly Post
Linux Frequently Asked Questions: TABLE OF CONTENTS [monthly posted]
Linux Frequently Asked Questions 1 6 [monthly posted]
Linux Frequently Asked Questions 2 6 [monthly posted]
Linux Frequently Asked Questions 3 6 [monthly posted]
Linux Frequently Asked Questions 4 6 [monthly posted]
Linux Frequently Asked Questions 5 6 [monthly posted]
Linux Frequently Asked Questions 6 6 [monthly posted]
Linux INFO-SHEET
Linux META-FAQ
Linux NET-2-FAQ
PC-Clone UNIX Hardware Buyer s Guide
PC-clone UNIX Software Buyer s Guide
Welcome to the comp.os.linux.* hierarchy!
[comp.os.linux.announce] Guidelines for posting
[comp.os.linux.announce] Welcome to comp.os.linux.announce!

comp.os.linux.admin:

FAQ: SAGE, The System Administrators Guild
Welcome to the comp.os.linux.* hierarchy!

Computers

comp.os.linux.announce:

Linux Frequently Asked Questions: TABLE OF CONTENTS [monthly posted]
Linux Frequently Asked Questions 1 6 [monthly posted]
Linux Frequently Asked Questions 2 6 [monthly posted]
Linux Frequently Asked Questions 3 6 [monthly posted]
Linux Frequently Asked Questions 4 6 [monthly posted]
Linux Frequently Asked Questions 5 6 [monthly posted]
Linux Frequently Asked Questions 6 6 [monthly posted]
Linux INFO-SHEET
Linux META-FAQ
Linux NET-2-FAQ
PC-Clone UNIX Hardware Buyer s Guide
PC-clone UNIX Software Buyer s Guide
Welcome to the comp.os.linux.* hierarchy!
[comp.os.linux.announce] Guidelines for posting
[comp.os.linux.announce] Welcome to comp.os.linux.announce!

comp.os.linux.development:

Welcome to the comp.os.linux.* hierarchy!

comp.os.linux.help:

Welcome to the comp.os.linux.* hierarchy!

comp.os.linux.misc:

Welcome to the comp.os.linux.* hierarchy!

comp.os.mach:

comp.os.mach Frequently Asked Questions

comp.os.minix:

MINIX Frequently Asked Questions (Last Changed: 30 June 1993)
Minix Information Sheet (Last Changed: 30 June 1993)

comp.os.ms-windows.advocacy:

Mac & IBM Info-Version 1.8.5

Computers

comp.os.ms-windows.apps:

Ye Olde Secrete Screene Cheete Sheete (long; 2000+ lines) (part 1 2)
Ye Olde Secrete Screene Cheete Sheete (long; 2000+ lines) (part 2 2)

comp.os.ms-windows.misc:

Ye Olde Secrete Screene Cheete Sheete (long; 2000+ lines) (part 1 2)
Ye Olde Secrete Screene Cheete Sheete (long; 2000+ lines) (part 2 2)

comp.os.ms-windows.programmer.tools:

Windows Programmer FAQ: How to get it

comp.os.ms-windows.programmer.win32:

Windows Programmer FAQ: How to get it

comp.os.msdos.apps:

Useful MSDOS Programs at SIMTEL20 and Garbo (Part 1 of 2)
Useful MSDOS Programs at SIMTEL20 and Garbo (Part 2 of 2)

comp.os.msdos.desqview:

DESQview QEMM Frequently Asked Questions: READ BEFORE POSTING

comp.os.msdos.misc:

Ye Olde Secrete Screene Cheete Sheete (long; 2000+ lines) (part 1 2)
Ye Olde Secrete Screene Cheete Sheete (long; 2000+ lines) (part 2 2)

comp.os.msdos.pcgeos:

PC GEOS FAQ List part 1 3—General questions
PC GEOS FAQ List part 2 3—Developers Q & A

comp.os.msdos.programmer:

comp.os.msdos.programmer FAQ diffs
comp.os.msdos.programmer FAQ part 1 of 4
comp.os.msdos.programmer FAQ part 2 of 4
comp.os.msdos.programmer FAQ part 3 of 4
comp.os.msdos.programmer FAQ part 4 of 4

comp.os.os2.advocacy:

Mac & IBM Info-Version 1.8.5

comp.os.os2.apps:

OS 2 Frequently Asked Questions List Rel. 2.1A (1 of 4)
OS 2 Frequently Asked Questions List Rel. 2.1A (2 of 4)
OS 2 Frequently Asked Questions List Rel. 2.1A (3 of 4)
OS 2 Frequently Asked Questions List Rel. 2.1A (4 of 4)

comp.os.os2.misc:

OS 2 Frequently Asked Questions List Rel. 2.1A (1 of 4)
OS 2 Frequently Asked Questions List Rel. 2.1A (2 of 4)
OS 2 Frequently Asked Questions List Rel. 2.1A (3 of 4)
OS 2 Frequently Asked Questions List Rel. 2.1A (4 of 4)

comp.os.vms:

DECUS Questions Answered (last modified 1-Jul-93)
Info-VAX: How to find VAX VMS software.
Info-VAX: Introduction to Info-VAX
Info-VAX: Advanced Common Questions
Info-VAX: Basic Common Questions
Monthly info posting: VMSnet on Bitnet
Monthly info posting: What is VMSnet?
Monthly info posting: vmsnet.sources archive sites

comp.parallel:

comp.parallel   Discussions related to parallel programming.

comp.patents:

comp.patents   Discussing patents of computer technology.
                             (Moderated)

[ADMIN] Comp.patents FAQ
[ADMIN] Comp.patents FTP Information

comp.periphs.*:

comp.periphs	Peripheral devices.
comp.periphs.printers	Information on printers.
comp.periphs.scsi	Discussion of SCSI-based peripheral devi

comp.periphs.scsi:

comp.periphs.scsi FAQ

comp.programming:

comp.programming	Programming issues that transcend languages

--- comp.programming charter: read before you post (weekly notice)

comp.protocols:

comp.protocols.appletalk	Applebus hardware & software.
comp.protocols.ibm	Networking with IBM mainframes.
comp.protocols.iso	The ISO protocol stack.
comp.protocols.iso.dev-environ	The ISO Development Environment.
comp.protocols.iso.x400	X400 mail protocol discussions.
comp.protocols.iso.x400.gateway	X400 mail gateway discussions.
comp.protocols.kerberos	The Kerberos authentication...
comp.protocols.kermit	Info about the Kermit package.
comp.protocols.misc	Various forms and types of FTP.
comp.protocols.nfs	Discussion about the Network File
comp.protocols.pcnet	Topics related to PCNET.
comp.protocols.tcp-ip	TCP and IP network protocols.
comp.protocols.tcp-ip.domains	Topics related to Domain Style.
comp.protocols.tcp-ip.ibmpc	TCP/IP for IBM(-like) personal computers.
comp.protocols.time.ntp	The network time protocol.
comp.protocols.ppp	Discussion of the Internet...
comp.protocols.snmp	The Simple Network Management protocol.
comp.protocols.dicom	

comp.protocols.iso:

Standards FAQ
comp.protocols.iso FAQ

comp.protocols.kerberos:

Kerberos Users Frequently Asked Questions 1.5

comp.protocols.ppp:

comp.protocols.ppp frequently wanted information

comp.protocols.snmp:

comp.protocols.snmp [SNMP] Frequently Asked Questions (FAQ)

comp.protocols.tcp-ip.ibmpc:

comp.protocols.tcp-ip.ibmpc Frequently Asked Questions (FAQ)

comp.realtime.*:

comp.realtime   Issues related to real-time computing.

Comp.realtime: A list of real-time operating systems and tools (LONG)
Comp.realtime: Frequently Asked Questions (FAQs)
Comp.realtime: Welcome to comp.realtime

comp.research:

comp.research   Discussions about computer research.

comp.risks:

comp.risks   Discussions about computers and risks.

comp.robotics:

comp.robotics   All aspects of robots and their applications.

comp.robotics Frequently Asked Questions (FAQ) part 1 2
comp.robotics Frequently Asked Questions (FAQ) part 2 2

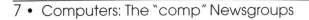
comp.security:

comp.security	Discussions about computer security.
comp.security.announce	Announcements from the CERT about security.
comp.security.misc	Security issues of computers and networks.

FAQ: Computer Security Frequently Asked Questions
RIPEM Frequently Asked Questions
RIPEM Frequently Noted Vulnerabilities

comp.simulation:

comp.simulation:	Discussions about computer simulation.

comp.society.*:

comp.society	The impact of technology on society.
comp.society.cu-digest	The Computer Underground Digest. (Moderated)
comp.society.development	Computer technology in developing countries.
comp.society.folklore	Computer folklore & culture, past & present.
comp.society.futures	Events in technology affecting future.
comp.society.privacy	Effects of technology on privacy. (Moderated)

comp.society.privacy:

Privacy & Anonymity on the Internet FAQ (1 of 3)
Privacy & Anonymity on the Internet FAQ (2 of 3)
Privacy & Anonymity on the Internet FAQ (3 of 3)
Social Security Number FAQ

comp.soft-sys:

comp.soft-sys	Discussion of software systems.

Computers

comp.software-eng:

comp.software-eng	Software Engineering and related topics.

Comp.software-eng periodic postings and archives
FAQ 1: comp.software-eng questions and answers
FAQ 2: CASE tools summary
FAQ 3: Software engineering readings

comp.software:

comp.software	Discussions about computer software.
comp.software.licensing	Software licensing technology.
comp.software.testing	Software testing issues.

comp.sources.*:

comp.sources.3b1	Source code-only postings for the AT&T.
comp.sources.acorn	Source code-only postings for the Acorn.
comp.sources.amiga	Source code-only postings for the Amiga.
comp.sources.apple2	Source code and discussion for the Apple II.
comp.sources.atari.st	Source code-only postings for the Atari.
comp.sources.bugs	Bug reports, fixes, discussion for postings.
comp.sources.d	For any discussion of source postings.
comp.sources.games	Postings of recreational software. (Moderated)
comp.sources.games.bugs	Bug reports and fixes for posted games.
comp.sources.hp48	Programs for the HP48 and HP28 calculators.
comp.sources.mac	Software for the Apple Macintosh. (Moderated)
comp.sources.misc	Posting of software. (Moderated)
comp.sources.postscript	Source code for programs written in Postscript.
comp.sources.reviewed	Source code evaluated by peer review.
comp.sources.sun	Software for Sun workstations. (Moderated)
comp.sources.testers	Finding people to test software.

comp.sources.unix	Postings of complete, UNIX-oriented solutions.
comp.sources.wanted	Requests for software and fixes.
comp.sources.x	Software for the X windows system. (Moderated)

inpaths.c (last updated Jan 28 1993)
arbitron program (v2.4.4--last updated 20 Oct 1989)
v38INF1: Introduction to comp.sources.misc

comp.sources.games:

v18INF1: intro18 - Introduction to comp.sources.games
v18INF2: num-idx18a - Index of comp.sources.games postings by volume issue number, Part1 3
v18INF3: num-idx18b - Index of comp.sources.games postings by volume issue number, Part2 3
v18INF4: num-idx18c - Index of comp.sources.games postings by volume issue number, Part3 3
v18INF5: alpha-idx18a - Index of comp.sources.games postings by name, Part1 3
v18INF6: alpha-idx18b - Index of comp.sources.games postings by name, Part2 3
v18INF7: alpha-idx18c - Index of comp.sources.games postings by name, Part3 3
v18INF8: patchlog18 - Index of patches posted to comp.sources.games
v18INF9: archivers18 - Listing of archive sites

comp.sources.misc:

v38INF1: Introduction to comp.sources.misc
v38INF2: Index for comp.sources.misc, Volume01 through Volume07
v38INF3: Index for comp.sources.misc, Volume08 through Volume14
v38INF4: Index for comp.sources.misc, Volume15 through Volume21
v38INF5: Index for comp.sources.misc, Volume22 through Volume27
v38INF6: Index for comp.sources.misc, Volume28 through Volume33
v38INF7: Index for comp.sources.misc, Volume34 through Volume37
v38INF8: Index of Patches posted to comp.sources.misc
v39INF1: Introduction to comp.sources.misc
v39INF2: Index for comp.sources.misc, Volume01 through Volume07
v39INF3: Index for comp.sources.misc, Volume08 through Volume14
v39INF4: Index for comp.sources.misc, Volume15 through Volume21

comp.sources.misc (continued):

v39INF5: Index for comp.sources.misc, Volume22 through Volume27
v39INF6: Index for comp.sources.misc, Volume28 through Volume33
v39INF7: Index for comp.sources.misc, Volume34 through Volume38
v39INF8: Index of Patches posted to comp.sources.misc

comp.sources.postscript:

v01INF2: PostScript Sources monthly FAQ v1.10 07-06-93 [1 of 3]
v01INF3: PostScript Sources monthly FAQ v1.10 07-06-93 [2 of 3]
v01INF4: PostScript Sources monthly FAQ v1.10 07-06-93 [3 of 3]

comp.sources.testers:

comp.sources.testers - Frequently Asked Questions (FAQ)

comp.sources.wanted:

How to find sources (READ THIS BEFORE POSTING)
Mail Archive Server software list
Project Management Programs - Frequently asked Questions (FAQ)

comp.specification.*:

comp.specification	Languages and methodologies for formal specification.
comp.specification.z	Discussion about the formal specification.

comp.specification.z:

comp.specification.z Frequently Asked Questions (Monthly)

comp.speech:

comp.speech	Research & applications in speech science & technology.

comp.speech FAQ (Frequently Asked Questions)

comp.std:

comp.std	Discussion about computer related standards.
comp.std.announce	Announcements about standards activities. (Moderated)
comp.std.c	Discussion about C language standards.
comp.std.c++	Discussion about C++ language, library, stan
comp.std.internat	Discussion about international standards.
comp.std.misc	Discussion about various standards.
comp.std.mumps	Discussion for the X11.1 committee on Mumps.
comp.std.unix	Discussion for the P1003 committee on UNIX.
comp.std.wireless	Discussion about wireless computing standards.

comp.std.internat:

Standards FAQ

comp.std.misc:

Standards FAQ

comp.std.unix:

Policy and Guidelines for comp.std.unix

comp.sw:

comp.sw.components	Software components and related technology.

comp.sys.:*

comp.sys.3b1	Discussion and support of AT&
comp.sys.acorn	Discussion on Acorn and ARM-b.
comp.sys.acorn.advocacy	Why Acorn computers and programs.
comp.sys.acorn.announce	Announcements for Acorn.
comp.sys.acorn.tech	Software and hardware aspects of Acorn.

comp.sys.* (continued):

comp.sys.alliant	Info and discussion about Alliant.
comp.sys.amiga	Discussion about Amiga systems.
comp.sys.amiga.announce	Announcements about the Amiga.
comp.sys.amiga.applications	Miscellaneous applications.
comp.sys.amiga.audio	Music, MIDI, speech synthesis.
comp.sys.amiga.advocacy	Why an Amiga is better.
comp.sys.amiga.datacomm	Methods of getting bytes.
comp.sys.amiga.emulations	Various hardware & software emulators.
comp.sys.amiga.games	Discussion of games for the Amiga.
comp.sys.amiga.graphics	Charts, graphs, pictures, etc.
comp.sys.amiga.hardware	Amiga computer hardware, Q&A,
comp.sys.amiga.introduction	Group for newcomers to Amigas.
comp.sys.amiga.marketplace	Where to find it, prices, etc.
comp.sys.amiga.misc	Discussions not falling in another category.
comp.sys.amiga.multimedia	Animations, video, & multimedia.
comp.sys.amiga.programmer	Developers & hobbyists discuss Amiga.
comp.sys.amiga.reviews	Reviews of Amiga software, hardare.
comp.sys.amiga.software.pirate	Pirate software for the Amiga.
comp.sys.amiga.tech	Discussion about Amiga technology.
comp.sys.apollo	Apollo computer systems.
comp.sys.apple	Apple computer systems.
comp.sys.apple2	Discussion about Apple II.
comp.sys.apple2.comm	Apple II communications.
comp.sys.apple2.gno	The AppleIIgs GNO multitasking.
comp.sys.apple2.marketplace	Apple II wanted and for sale.
comp.sys.apple2.programmer	Programming the Apple II.
comp.sys.apple2.usergroups	Users groups for the Apple II.
comp.sys.atari.8bit	Discussion about 8 bit Atari.
comp.sys.atari.advocacy	Atari advocacy.
comp.sys.atari.st	Discussion about 16 bit Atari.
comp.sys.atari.st.tech	Technical discussions of Atari.

comp.sys.att	Discussions about AT&T microcomputer.
comp.sys.cbm	Discussion about Commodore.
comp.sys.cdc	Control Data Corporation Computers.
comp.sys.concurrent	The Concurrent/Masscomp line.
comp.sys.convex	Convex computer systems hardware.
comp.sys.dec	Discussions about DEC computers.
comp.sys.dec.micro	DEC Micros.
comp.sys.encore	Encore's MultiMax computers.
comp.sys.handhelds	Handheld computers and programs.
comp.sys.harris	
comp.sys.hp	Discussion about Hewlett-Packard computers.
comp.sys.hp48	Hewlett-Packard's HP48.
comp.sys.hp48.d	HP48 discussion.
comp.sys.ibm.pc	Discussion about IBM PC computers.
comp.sys.ibm.pc.demos	Available demos for the IBM PC.
comp.sys.ibm.pc.digest	The IBM PC, PC-XT, and PC-AT.
comp.sys.ibm.pc.games	Games for IBM PCs and compatibles.
comp.sys.ibm.pc.games.action	IBM PC games.
comp.sys.ibm.pc.games.- announce	IBM PC game announcements.
comp.sys.ibm.pc.games.- adventure	Adventure games for the IBM PC.
comp.sys.ibm.pc.games.- flight-sim	Flight simulators for the IBM PC.
comp.sys.ibm.pc.games.misc	Discussion about IBM PC games.
comp.sys.ibm.pc.games.rpg	RPG IBM PC games.
comp.sys.ibm.pc.games.strategic	Strategic IBM PC games.
comp.sys.ibm.pc.misc	Discussion about IBM personal computer.
comp.sys.ibm.pc.hardware	XT/AT/EISA hardware, any vendor.
comp.sys.ibm.pc.programmer	Programming the IBM PC.
comp.sys.ibm.pc.rt	Topics related to IBM's RT computers.

comp.sys.* (continued):

comp.sys.ibm.pc.soundcard	Hardware and software aspects of soundcards.
comp.sys.ibm.ps2.hardware	Microchannel hardware, any vendor.
comp.sys.intel	Discussions about Intel systems.
comp.sys.intel.ipsc310	Anything related to Xenix...
comp.sys.isis	The ISIS distributed system.
comp.sys.laptops	Laptop (portable) computers.
comp.sys.m6809	Discussion about 6809's.
comp.sys.m68k	Discussion about 68k's.
comp.sys.m68k.pc	Discussion about 68k-based PC
comp.sys.m88k	Discussion about 88k-based computer.
comp.sys.mac	Discussion about the Macintosh.
comp.sys.mac.announce	Important notices for Macintosh.
comp.sys.mac.apps	Discussions of Macintosh applications.
comp.sys.mac.advocacy	The Macintosh computer family.
comp.sys.mac.comm	Discussion of Macintosh communications.
comp.sys.mac.databases	Database systems for the Apple Macintosh.
comp.sys.mac.digest	Apple Macintosh: info&uses, bugs,...
comp.sys.mac.games	Discussions of games on the Macintosh.
comp.sys.mac.hardware	Macintosh hardware issues & discussion.
comp.sys.mac.hypercard	The Macintosh Hypercard: info.
comp.sys.mac.misc	General discussions about the Macintosh.
comp.sys.mac.oop.macapp3	Version 3 of the MacApp object oriented prog.
comp.sys.mac.oop.misc	Object oriented programming for the Mac.
comp.sys.mac.oop.tcl	
comp.sys.mac.portables	Macintosh portables.
comp.sys.mac.programmer	Discussion by people programming the Mac.
comp.sys.mac.scitech	Issues related to Macintosh.
comp.sys.mac.system	Discussions of Macintosh systems.
comp.sys.mac.wanted	Postings of "I want XYZ for my Mac."
comp.sys.mentor	Mentor Graphics products.

comp.sys.mips	Systems based on MIPS chips.
comp.sys.misc	Discussion about computers.
comp.sys.ncr	Discussion about NCR computers.
comp.sys.next	Discussion about NeXT computers.
comp.sys.next.advocacy	The NeXT religion.
comp.sys.next.announce	Announcements related to the NeXT.
comp.sys.next.bugs	Discussion and solutions for
comp.sys.next.hardware	Discussing the physical aspects of NeXT.
comp.sys.next.marketplace	NeXT hardware, software, ...
comp.sys.next.misc	General discussion about the NeXT.
comp.sys.next.programmer	NeXT related programming issues.
comp.sys.next.software	Function, use and availability of NeXt software.
comp.sys.next.sysadmin	Discussions related to NeXT system administration.
comp.sys.northstar	Northstar microcomputer users.
comp.sys.novell	Discussion of Novell Netware.
comp.sys.nsc.32k	National Semiconductor 32000.
comp.sys.palmtops	Super-powered calculators.
comp.sys.pen	Interacting with computers.
comp.sys.prime	Prime Computer products.
comp.sys.proteon	Proteon gateway products.
comp.sys.pyramid	Pyramid 90x computers.
comp.sys.ridge	Ridge 32 computers and ROS.
comp.sys.sequent	Sequent systems.
comp.sys.sgi	Discussion about Silicon Graphic systems.
comp.sys.sgi.admin	System administration on Silicon Graphics.
comp.sys.sgi.announce	Announcements for the SGI computers.
comp.sys.sgi.apps	Applications which run on Silicon Graphics.
comp.sys.sgi.bugs	Bugs found in the IRIX operating system.
comp.sys.sgi.graphics	Graphics packages and issues.
comp.sys.sgi.hardware	Base systems and peripherals.

Computers

comp.sys.* (continued):

comp.sys.sgi.misc	General discussion about Silicon Graphics.
comp.sys.stratus	Stratus products.
comp.sys.sun	Discussion about Sun systems.
comp.sys.sun.announce	Sun announcements and Sunergy.
comp.sys.sun.apps	Software applications for Sun.
comp.sys.sun.hardware	Sun Microsystems hardware.
comp.sys.sun.misc	Miscellaneous discussions about Sun.
comp.sys.sun.admin	Sun system administration issues.
comp.sys.sun.wanted	People looking for Sun products.
comp.sys.super	Supercomputers.
comp.sys.tahoe	CCI 6/32, Harris HCX/7, & …
comp.sys.tandy	Discussion about Tandy computers.
comp.sys.ti	Discussion about Texas Instruments.
comp.sys.ti.explorer	The Texas Instruments Explorer.
comp.sys.transputer	The Transputer computer.
comp.sys.unisys	Sperry, Burroughs, Convergent products.
comp.sys.xerox	Xerox 1100 workstations.
comp.sys.zenith	Heath terminals and related issues.
comp.sys.zenith.z100	The Zenith Z-100.

comp.sys.3b1:

comp.sys.3b1 FAQ part1
comp.sys.3b1 FAQ part2

comp.sys.acorn:

Acorn ftp and mail-server archives (fortnightly posting)
Comp.Sys.Acorn FAQ List Posting (Automatic)

comp.sys.acorn.announce:

Acorn ftp and mail-server archives (fortnightly posting)
Comp.Sys.Acorn FAQ List Posting (Automatic)

comp.sys.amiga.applications:

[comp.sys.amiga.applications] Answers about Science, School, UNIX software

comp.sys.amiga.audio:

Midi files software archives on the Internet

comp.sys.amiga.datacomm:

Amiga Point Manager Frequently Asked Questions (FAQ)
ZyXEL U1496 series modems resellers FAQ (bi-monthly)
[comp.sys.amiga.datacomm]: AmigaNOS Frequently asked questions

comp.sys.amiga.games:

rec.games.int-fiction Frequently Asked Questions, part 1 of 3
rec.games.int-fiction Frequently Asked Questions, part 2 of 3
rec.games.int-fiction Frequently Asked Questions, part 3 of 3

comp.sys.apollo:

comp.sys.apollo monthly FAQ (part1 2)
comp.sys.apollo monthly FAQ (part2 2)

comp.sys.apple2:

comp.sys.apple2 - Frequently Asked Questions (and answers) part 1 of 2
comp.sys.apple2 - Frequently Asked Questions (and answers) part 2 of 2

comp.sys.apple2.comm:

ZyXEL U1496 series modems resellers FAQ (bi-monthly)

comp.sys.atari.games:

rec.games.int-fiction Frequently Asked Questions, part 1 of 3
rec.games.int-fiction Frequently Asked Questions, part 2 of 3
rec.games.int-fiction Frequently Asked Questions, part 3 of 3

comp.sys.atari.st:

Welcome to comp.sys.atari.st!
Welcome to comp.sys.atari.st! (Hardware)
Welcome to comp.sys.atari.st! (Software)

comp.sys.att:

AT&T 3B2 Frequently Asked Questions - Part 1 2
AT&T 3B2 Frequently Asked Questions - Part 1 2 DIFFS
AT&T 3B2 Frequently Asked Questions - Part 2 2
AT&T 3B2 Frequently Asked Questions - Part 2 2 DIFFS

comp.sys.dec:

DECUS Questions Answered (last modified 1-Jul-93)
Monthly info posting: What is VMSnet?
comp.unix.ultrix Common Frequently Asked Questions
comp.unix.ultrix DEC OSF 1 Frequently Asked Questions
comp.unix.ultrix ULTRIX Frequently Asked Questions

comp.sys.hp:

comp.sys.hp FAQ

comp.sys.ibm.pc.games:

ADMIN: comp.sys.ibm.pc.games - Frequently Asked Questions - Read before posting

comp.sys.ibm.pc.games.adventure:

rec.games.int-fiction Frequently Asked Questions, part 1 of 3
rec.games.int-fiction Frequently Asked Questions, part 2 of 3
rec.games.int-fiction Frequently Asked Questions, part 3 of 3

comp.sys.ibm.pc.games.flight-sim:

rec.aviation.simulators Frequently Asked Questions

comp.sys.ibm.pc.hardware:

FAQ: Gravis Ultrasound (GUS) FAQ v1.30

Mac & IBM Info-Version 1.8.5

ZyXEL U1496 series modems resellers FAQ (bi-monthly)

comp.sys.ibm.pc.misc:

Mac & IBM Info-Version 1.8.5

Useful MSDOS Programs at SIMTEL20 and Garbo (Part 1 of 2)

Useful MSDOS Programs at SIMTEL20 and Garbo (Part 2 of 2)

comp.sys.ibm.pc.rt:

COMP.SYS.IBM.PC.RT: IBM RT - Hardware - Frequently Asked Questions

comp.sys.ibm.pc.soundcard:

FAQ: Gravis Ultrasound (GUS) FAQ v1.30

Generic IBM PC Soundcard FAQ periodic posting

IBM MOD Players Compared!

Midi files software archives on the Internet

Ultrasound FTP Sites - New files validated - June 7, 93

comp.sys.intel:

Mac & IBM Info-Version 1.8.5

PC-Clone UNIX Hardware Buyer s Guide

comp.sys.mac.advocacy:

Mac & IBM Info-Version 1.8.5

comp.sys.mac.apps:

Introductory Macintosh frequently asked questions (FAQ)

Macintosh application software frequently asked questions (FAQ)

Computers

comp.sys.mac.comm:

ZyXEL U1496 series modems resellers FAQ (bi-monthly)
comp.sys.mac.comm Frequently Asked Questions [1 4]
comp.sys.mac.comm Frequently Asked Questions [2 4]
comp.sys.mac.comm Frequently Asked Questions [3 4]
comp.sys.mac.comm Frequently Asked Questions [4 4]

comp.sys.mac.games:

New Mac Games List (Full), 8 13 93
New Mac Games List (Updates), 8 13 93
rec.games.int-fiction Frequently Asked Questions, part 1 of 3
rec.games.int-fiction Frequently Asked Questions, part 2 of 3
rec.games.int-fiction Frequently Asked Questions, part 3 of 3

comp.sys.mac.hardware:

Introductory Macintosh frequently asked questions (FAQ)
Mac & IBM Info-Version 1.8.5

comp.sys.mac.misc:

Introductory Macintosh frequently asked questions (FAQ)
Miscellaneous Macintosh frequently asked questions (FAQ)

comp.sys.mac.programmer:

Comp.Sys.Mac.Programmer FAQ Part 1 2 (1 12 93)
Comp.Sys.Mac.Programmer FAQ Part 2 2 (1 12 93)

comp.sys.mac.scitech:

MacImageProc
index

comp.sys.mac.system:

Introductory Macintosh frequently asked questions (FAQ)
Macintosh system software frequently asked questions (FAQ)

comp.sys.mac.wanted:

Introductory Macintosh frequently asked questions (FAQ)

comp.sys.next.sysadmin:

FAQ: SAGE, The System Administrators Guild

comp.sys.sgi.admin:

FAQ: SAGE, The System Administrators Guild
SGI admin Frequently Asked Questions (FAQ)
SGI apps Frequently Asked Questions (FAQ)
SGI graphics Frequently Asked Questions (FAQ)
SGI hardware Frequently Asked Questions (FAQ)
SGI misc Frequently Asked Questions (FAQ)

comp.sys.sgi.apps:

SGI admin Frequently Asked Questions (FAQ)
SGI apps Frequently Asked Questions (FAQ)
SGI graphics Frequently Asked Questions (FAQ)
SGI hardware Frequently Asked Questions (FAQ)
SGI misc Frequently Asked Questions (FAQ)

comp.sys.sgi.bugs:

SGI admin Frequently Asked Questions (FAQ)
SGI apps Frequently Asked Questions (FAQ)
SGI graphics Frequently Asked Questions (FAQ)
SGI hardware Frequently Asked Questions (FAQ)
SGI misc Frequently Asked Questions (FAQ)

comp.sys.sgi.graphics:

SGI admin Frequently Asked Questions (FAQ)
SGI apps Frequently Asked Questions (FAQ)
SGI graphics Frequently Asked Questions (FAQ)
SGI hardware Frequently Asked Questions (FAQ)
SGI misc Frequently Asked Questions (FAQ)

Computers

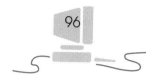
comp.sys.sgi.hardware:

SGI admin Frequently Asked Questions (FAQ)
SGI apps Frequently Asked Questions (FAQ)
SGI graphics Frequently Asked Questions (FAQ)
SGI hardware Frequently Asked Questions (FAQ)
SGI misc Frequently Asked Questions (FAQ)

comp.sys.sgi.misc:

SGI Anonymous FTP archives (monthly)
SGI Anonymous FTP archives differences (monthly)
SGI admin Frequently Asked Questions (FAQ)
SGI apps Frequently Asked Questions (FAQ)
SGI graphics Frequently Asked Questions (FAQ)
SGI hardware Frequently Asked Questions (FAQ)
SGI misc Frequently Asked Questions (FAQ)

comp.sys.sun.admin:

FAQ: SAGE, The System Administrators Guild
FAQ: Sun Computer Administration Frequently Asked Questions
Master Sun format.dat
OPEN LOOK GUI frequently asked questions
Solaris 2.1 Frequently Answered Questions (FAQ) $Revision: 1.20 $

comp.sys.sun.announce:

Comp.Sys.Sun.Announce Moderation Policies [last modified: Mar 1 1993]

comp.sys.sun.apps:

OPEN LOOK GUI frequently asked questions

comp.sys.sun.misc:

FAQ: Sun Computer Administration Frequently Asked Questions

comp.terminals.*:

comp.terminals	All sorts of terminals.
comp.terminals.bitgraph	The BB&N BitGraph Terminal.
comp.terminals.tty5620	AT&T Dot Mapped Display Terminals (562

comp.text.*:

comp.text	Text processing issues and methods.
comp.text.desktop	Technology & techniques of desktop publishing.
comp.text.frame	Desktop publishing with FrameMaker.
comp.text.interleaf	Applications and use of Interleaf software.
comp.text.sgml	ISO 8879 SGML, structured documents, markup.
comp.text.tex	Discussion about the TeX and LaTeX systems.

comp.text Frequently Asked Questions

comp.text.frame:

FrameMaker FAQ (Frequently Asked Questions)

comp.text.interleaf:

Interleaf FAQ—Frequently Asked Questions for comp.text.interleaf

comp.text.tex:

Diffs to Frequently Asked Questions about TeX and LaTeX [monthly]
TeX, LaTeX, etc.: Frequently Asked Questions with Answers [Monthly]
TeX-FAQ-supplement (part 1 of 3)
TeX-FAQ-supplement (part 2 of 3)
TeX-FAQ-supplement (part 3 of 3)
TeXhax Digest V93 #011
UKTeX Digest V93 #25

comp.unix.*:

comp.unix	Discussion about UNIX.
comp.unix.admin	Administering a Unix-based system.
comp.unix.aix	IBM's version of UNIX.
comp.unix.amiga	Minix, SYSV4 and other *nix systems.
comp.unix.appleIIgs	UNIX on the Apple II.
comp.unix.aux	The version of UNIX for...
comp.unix.bsd	Discussion of Berkeley Software.
comp.unix.cray	Cray computers and their operating system.
comp.unix.dos-under-unix	MS-DOS running under UNIX.
comp.unix.i386	Intel 386 systems and UNIX.
comp.unix.internals	Discussions on hacking UNIX.
comp.unix.large	UNIX on mainframes.
comp.unix.microport	
comp.unix.misc	Various topics that don't fit else where.
comp.unix.msdos	UNIX on MSDOS.
comp.unix.osf.misc	Various aspects of Open Software Foundation.
comp.unix.osf.osf1	The Open Software Foundation.
comp.unix.pc-clone.16bit	UNIX on 286 architectures.
comp.unix.pc-clone.32bit	UNIX on 386 and 486 architectures.
comp.unix.programmer	Q&A for people programming UNIX.
comp.unix.questions	UNIX neophytes group.
comp.unix.shell	Using and programming the UNIX shell.
comp.unix.sys3	System III UNIX discussions.
comp.unix.sys5.misc	Versions of System V.
comp.unix.sys5.r3	Discussing System V Release 3.
comp.unix.sys5.r4	Discussing System V Release 4.
comp.unix.sysv286	System V on the 286.
comp.unix.sysv386	System V on the 386.
comp.unix.ultrix	Discussions about DEC's Ultrix.
comp.unix.wizards	Questions for only true Unix wizards.

comp.unix.xenix	Xenix discussion.
comp.unix.xenix.misc	General discussions regarding Xenix.
comp.unix.xenix.sco	XENIX versions from the Santa Cruz Operations.

Computers

comp.unix.admin:

FAQ: SAGE, The System Administrators Guild
[misc.books.technical] A Concise Guide to UNIX Books

comp.unix.aix:

AIX Frequently Asked Questions (Part 1 of 3)
AIX Frequently Asked Questions (Part 2 of 3)
AIX Frequently Asked Questions (Part 3 of 3)

comp.unix.amiga:

[comp.sys.amiga.applications] Answers about Science,School,UNIX software

comp.unix.aux:

Apple A UX FAQ List (1 2)
Apple A UX FAQ List (2 2)

comp.unix.bsd:

PC-clone UNIX Software Buyer s Guide
X on Intel-based Unix Frequently Asked Questions [FAQ]

comp.unix.osf.osf1:

comp.unix.ultrix Common Frequently Asked Questions
comp.unix.ultrix DEC OSF 1 Frequently Asked Questions

comp.unix.pc-clone.32bit:

Known Bugs in the USL UNIX distribution
PC-Clone UNIX Hardware Buyer s Guide
PC-clone UNIX Software Buyer s Guide
SCO Enhanced Feature Supplements [summary of recent changes]

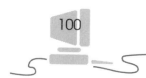

comp.unix.pc-clone.32bit (continued):

SCO Support Level Supplements [summary of recent changes]
X on Intel-based Unix Frequently Asked Questions [FAQ]
biz.sco.* newsgroups mlists FAQ (periodic posting)

comp.unix.programmer:

Csh Programming Considered Harmful

comp.unix.questions:

Csh Programming Considered Harmful
So You Want To Be A UNIX Wizard? (The Loginataka)
UNIX BBS Software FAQ with Answers
UNIX BBS Software FAQ with Answers (v 0.6)
Unix - Frequently Asked Questions (1 7) [Frequent posting]
Unix - Frequently Asked Questions (2 7) [Frequent posting]
Unix - Frequently Asked Questions (3 7) [Frequent posting]
Unix - Frequently Asked Questions (4 7) [Frequent posting]
Unix - Frequently Asked Questions (5 7) [Frequent posting]
Unix - Frequently Asked Questions (6 7) [Frequent posting]
Unix - Frequently Asked Questions (7 7) [Frequent posting]
Unix - Frequently Asked Questions (Contents) [Frequent posting]
Welcome to comp.unix.questions [Frequent posting]
[misc.books.technical] A Concise Guide to UNIX Books

comp.unix.shell:

Csh Programming Considered Harmful
Unix - Frequently Asked Questions (1 7) [Frequent posting]
Unix - Frequently Asked Questions (2 7) [Frequent posting]
Unix - Frequently Asked Questions (3 7) [Frequent posting]
Unix - Frequently Asked Questions (4 7) [Frequent posting]
Unix - Frequently Asked Questions (5 7) [Frequent posting]
Unix - Frequently Asked Questions (6 7) [Frequent posting]
Unix - Frequently Asked Questions (7 7) [Frequent posting]
Unix - Frequently Asked Questions (Contents) [Frequent posting]
Welcome to comp.unix.shell [Frequent posting]
Z-shell Frequently-Asked Questions

comp.unix.solaris:

FAQ: Sun Computer Administration Frequently Asked Questions
Solaris 2.1 Frequently Answered Questions (FAQ) $Revision: 1.20 $
Solaris 2 Porting FAQ

comp.unix.sys5.r4:

Known Bugs in the USL UNIX distribution
PC-Clone UNIX Hardware Buyer s Guide
PC-clone UNIX Software Buyer s Guide

comp.unix.ultrix:

comp.unix.ultrix Common Frequently Asked Questions
comp.unix.ultrix DEC OSF 1 Frequently Asked Questions
comp.unix.ultrix ULTRIX Frequently Asked Questions

comp.unix.wizards:

Intro to comp.unix.wizards - read before posting! (last change: Wed Jan 13 9:47:56 EST 1993)
[misc.books.technical] A Concise Guide to UNIX Books

comp.unix.xenix.sco:

SCO Enhanced Feature Supplements [summary of recent changes]
SCO Support Level Supplements [summary of recent changes]
Welcome to comp.unix.xenix.sco [changes from previous version]
Welcome to comp.unix.xenix.sco [monthly FAQ posting]
biz.sco. newsgroups mlists FAQ (periodic posting)*

comp.virus:

comp.virus   Computer viruses & security. (Moderated)

Amiga Anti-viral archive sites last changed 17 August 1992
Anti-viral Documentation archive sites last changed 18 July 1993
Apple II Anti-viral archive sites last changed 07 July 1992
Archive access without anonymous ftp last changed 11 July 1992
Atari ST Anti-viral archive sites last changed 07 July 1992
Brief guide to files formats last changed 05 February 1993

Computers

comp.virus (continued):

IBMPC Anti-viral archive sites last changed 18 July 1993
Introduction to the Anti-viral archives listing of 01 August 1993
Macintosh Anti-viral archive sites last changed 17 August 1992
Unix security archive sites last changed 21 August 1992
VIRUS-L comp.virus Frequently Asked Questions (FAQ)

comp.windows.*:

comp.windows.garnet	The Garnet user interface development.
comp.windows.interviews	The InterViews object-oriented windowing system.
comp.windows.misc	Various issues about windowing systems.
comp.windows.ms	Microsoft Windows discussion.
comp.windows.ms.programmer	Programming Microsoft Windows.
comp.windows.news	Sun Microsystems' NeWS window systems.
comp.windows.open-look	Discussion about the Open Look GUI.
comp.windows.suit	
comp.windows.x	Discussion about the X Window Systems.
comp.windows.x.apps	Getting and using, not programming,...
comp.windows.x.i386unix	The XFree86 window system and others.
comp.windows.x.intrinsics	Discussion of the X toolkit.
comp.windows.x.motif	The Motif GUI for the X Window Systems.
comp.windows.x.pex	The PHIGS extension of the X Window...

comp.windows.misc:

Comp.windows.misc Frequently Asked Questions (FAQ)

comp.windows.news:

FAQ: OPEN LOOK UI: 02 04: Sun OpenWindows DeskSet Questions
FAQ: OPEN LOOK UI: 04 04: List of programs with an OPEN LOOK UI

comp.windows.open-look:

FAQ: OPEN LOOK UI: 02 04: Sun OpenWindows DeskSet Questions
FAQ: OPEN LOOK UI: 04 04: List of programs with an OPEN LOOK UI
OPEN LOOK GUI frequently asked questions

comp.windows.x:

OPEN LOOK GUI frequently asked questions

X Terminal List - Quarterly posting (Q2 93)

X on Intel-based Unix Frequently Asked Questions [FAQ]

biz.sco.* newsgroups mlists FAQ (periodic posting)

comp.windows.x.intrinsics Frequently Asked Questions (FAQ)

comp.windows.x: Getting more performance out of X. FAQ

comp.windows.x Frequently Asked Questions (FAQ) 1 5

comp.windows.x Frequently Asked Questions (FAQ) 2 5

comp.windows.x Frequently Asked Questions (FAQ) 3 5

comp.windows.x Frequently Asked Questions (FAQ) 4 5

comp.windows.x Frequently Asked Questions (FAQ) 5 5

comp.windows.x.i386unix:

X on Intel-based Unix Frequently Asked Questions [FAQ]

comp.windows.x.intrinsics:

OPEN LOOK GUI frequently asked questions

comp.windows.x.intrinsics Frequently Asked Questions (FAQ)

comp.windows.x.motif:

Motif FAQ (Part 1 of 5)

Motif FAQ (Part 2 of 5)

Motif FAQ (Part 3 of 5)

Motif FAQ (Part 4 of 5)

Motif FAQ (Part 5 of 5)

biz.sco.* newsgroups mlists FAQ (periodic posting)

comp.windows.x.pex:

(02mar93) Welcome to comp.windows.x.pex! (FAQ)

This branch of USENET covers topics that do not neatly fit into one of the other branches. In here you will find items of interest to most everybody.

8

Miscellaneous: The "misc" Newsgroups

misc.activism:

misc.activism   Discussion about activism and related issues.

misc.answers:

misc.answers   Repository for periodic USENET articles.
(Moderated)

books	*libertarian*
consumer-credit-faq	*misc-kids-FAQ*
contract-jobs	*news-answers*
electrical-wiring	*ssn-privacy*
house-faq	*woodworking*
index	*writing*
investment-faq	

misc.books.*:

misc.books   Discussion about books.

misc.books.technical   Discussion of books about technical topics.

misc.books.technical:

[misc.books.technical] A Concise Guide to UNIX Books
misc.books.technical FREQUENTLY ASKED QUESTIONS (Periodic post)

misc.consumers.*:

misc.consumers   Consumer interests, product reviews, etc.

misc.consumers.house   Discussion about owning and maintaining a house.

misc.consumers FAQ on credit diff 1 of 4
misc.consumers FAQ on credit diff 2 of 4
misc.consumers FAQ on credit diff 3 of 4
misc.consumers FAQ on credit diff 4 of 4
misc.consumers FAQ on credit part 1 of 4
misc.consumers FAQ on credit part 2 of 4
misc.consumers FAQ on credit part 3 of 4
misc.consumers FAQ on credit part 4 of 4

misc.consumers.house:

Electrical Wiring FAQ
misc.consumers.house FAQ (frequently asked questions)
rec.woodworking Electric Motors Frequently asked Questions

misc.education.*:

misc.education	Discussion of the educational system.
misc.education.language.english	English language education.

misc.emergency-services:

misc.emerg-services	Forum for paramedics & other first response units.

misc.entrepreneurs:

misc.entrepreneurs	Discussion on operating a business.

misc.fitness:

misc.fitness	Physical fitness, exercise, etc.

misc.forsale.*:

misc.forsale	Short, tasteful postings about items for sale.
misc.forsale.computers	Computers for sale.
misc.forsale.computers.d	Discussion of misc.forsale.
misc.forsale.computers.mac	Apple Macintosh related computers.
misc.forsale.computers.other	Selling miscellaneous computers.
misc.forsale.computers.pc-clone	IBM PC related computer items.
misc.forsale.computers.-workstation	Workstation related computers.

misc.forsale.computers:

misc.forsale.computers.d FAQ

misc.forsale.computers.d:

misc.forsale.computers.d FAQ

misc.handicap:

misc.handicap   Items of interest for/about the handicapped. (Moderated)

misc.headlines:

misc.headlines   Current interest: drug testing, terrorism.

misc.headlines.unitex

The Great Usenet Piss List Monthly Posting

misc.health.*:

misc.health.alternative   Alternative, complementary and holistic approaches.

misc.health.diabetes   Discussion about diabetes.

misc.int-property:

misc.int-property   Discussion of intellectual property rights.

misc.invest.*:

misc.invest   Investments and the handling of money.

misc.invest.canada   Canadian investment discussion.

misc.invest.real-estate   Property investments.

misc.invest.technical

diffs for misc.invest general FAQ

misc.invest FAQ on general investment topics (Table of Contents)

misc.invest FAQ on general investment topics (part 1 of 3)

misc.invest FAQ on general investment topics (part 2 of 3)

misc.invest FAQ on general investment topics (part 3 of 3)

misc.jobs.*:

misc.jobs.contract	Discussions about contract labor.
misc.jobs.misc	Discussion about employment, workplace.
misc.jobs.offered	Announcements of positions available.
misc.jobs.offered.entry	Job listings only for entry-level positons.
misc.jobs.resumes	Postings of resumes and "situation wanted."

misc.jobs.contract:

Misc.jobs.contract: Frequently Asked Questions (FAQs)
Misc.jobs.contract: Text of USA IRS Section 1706; the Twenty Questions
Misc.jobs.contract: Welcome to misc.jobs.contract
The Great Usenet Piss List Monthly Posting
Welcome to misc.jobs!

misc.jobs.misc:

The Great Usenet Piss List Monthly Posting
Welcome to misc.jobs!

misc.jobs.offered:

REMINDER:put JOB-TITLE COMPANY LOCATION in subject
-->[l m 6 29 93]---->Read BEFORE posting: stylistic consensus
Welcome to misc.jobs!

misc.jobs.offered.entry:

*** READ BEFORE POSTING: SPECIAL FAQ on using m.j.o.e***
-->[l m 6 29 93]---->Read BEFORE posting: stylistic consensus

misc.jobs.resumes:

Welcome to misc.jobs!

misc.kids.*:

misc.kids	Children, their behavior and activities.
misc.kids.computer	Discussion of software for children.

Welcome to Misc.kids FAQ File Index (Updated 8 10 93)

Miscellaneous

misc.legal.*:

misc.legal	Legalities and the ethics of law.
misc.legal.computing	Discussing the legal climate of the computer world.

Libertarian Frequently Asked Questions
Libertarian Frequently Over-Exposed Postings
Libertarian Organizations
Libertarian World s Smallest Political Quiz [periodic posting]
Social Security Number FAQ

misc.misc:

USENET Readership summary for Jul 93 posted

misc.news.*:

misc.news.southasia	News from Bangladesh, India, Nepal.
misc.news.east-europe.rferl	Radio Free Europe/Radio Liberty...

misc.rural:

misc.rural	Devoted to issues concerning rural living.

misc.taxes:

misc.taxes	Tax laws and advice.

misc.test:

misc.test	For testing of network software. Very boring.

misc.wanted:

misc.wanted	Requests for things that are needed (NOT software).

misc.writers:

misc.writers	Newsgroup for writers.

the Internet Writer Resource Guide

misc.writing:

misc.writing   Discussion of writing in all of its forms.

misc.writing FAQ
misc.writing FAQ: Recommended Reading

Miscellaneous

This branch of USENET discusses items that are important to all USENET users. It contains many articles that are highly recommended for the new user to read. Announcements that affect all USENET are placed here. It also contains maps, statistics and administrative items about USENET itself.

9

Network News: The "news" Newsgroups

news.admin.*:

news.admin	Network news administration.
news.admin.misc	General topics of network news administration.
news.admin.policy	Policy issues of USENET.
news.admin.technical	Technical aspects of maintaining network news.

news.admin.misc:

Another listing of newsgroups in the alt Usenet hierarchy
Another listing of newsgroups in the alt hierarchy, Part 1 of 2
Another listing of newsgroups in the alt hierarchy, Part 2 of 2
Articles rejected at news.uu.net during the past week
BIONET BIOSCI Checkgroups message
Changes to How to Construct the Mailpaths File
Changes to How to Create a New Usenet Newsgroup
Checkgroups message (with INET groups)
Checkgroups message (without INET groups)
How to Construct the Mailpaths File
How to Create a New Usenet Newsgroup
How to become a USENET site
Known Geographic Distributions
Known University Distributions
News Administration Macros for Geographic Distributions
Public Organizational & Logical Network Distributions
Sites honoring invalid newsgroups (by group)
Sites honoring invalid newsgroups (by site)
UNIX Email Software Survey FAQ
USENET FLOW ANALYSIS REPORT FOR JUL 93
USENET READERSHIP SUMMARY REPORT FOR JUL 93
USENET Readership summary for Jul 93 posted
inpaths.c (last updated Jan 28 1993)
arbitron data from these sites has expired
arbitron program (v2.4.4--last updated 20 Oct 1989)

news.admin.technical:

News.admin.technical moderation policies [last modified: Jan 4 1993]
News.admin.technical submission guidelines [last modified: Mar 16 1993]

news.announce.*:

news.announce.conferences	Calls for papers and conference announcements.
news.announce.important	General announcements of interest to all.
news.announce.newgroups	Calls for new groups & announcements.
news.announce.newusers	Explanatory postings for new users.

news.announce.newgroups:

Alternative Newsgroup Hierarchies, Part I
Alternative Newsgroup Hierarchies, Part II
Bogus USENET Groups
Changes to Alternative Newsgroup Hierarchies, Part I
Changes to Alternative Newsgroup Hierarchies, Part II
Changes to How to Create a New Usenet Newsgroup
Changes to List of Active Newsgroups, Part I
Changes to List of Active Newsgroups, Part II
Checkgroups message (with INET groups)
Checkgroups message (without INET groups)
Current Status of USENET Newsgroup Proposals
How to Create a New Usenet Newsgroup
List of Active Newsgroups, Part I
List of Active Newsgroups, Part II
New USENET Groups

news.announce.newusers:

Alternative Newsgroup Hierarchies, Part I
Alternative Newsgroup Hierarchies, Part II
Changes to List of Periodic Informational Postings
How to Create a New Usenet Newsgroup
How to become a USENET site
Introduction to the *.answers newsgroups
List of Active Newsgroups, Part I
List of Active Newsgroups, Part II
List of Moderators for Usenet
List of Periodic Informational Postings, Part 1 6
List of Periodic Informational Postings, Part 2 6
List of Periodic Informational Postings, Part 3 6
List of Periodic Informational Postings, Part 4 6

news.announce.newusers (continued):

List of Periodic Informational Postings, Part 5 6
List of Periodic Informational Postings, Part 6 6
Publicly Accessible Mailing Lists, Part 1 5
Publicly Accessible Mailing Lists, Part 2 5
Publicly Accessible Mailing Lists, Part 3 5
Publicly Accessible Mailing Lists, Part 4 5
Publicly Accessible Mailing Lists, Part 5 5
Usenet Newsgroup Creation Companion

news.answers:

news.answers   Repository for periodic USENET articles.
                                 (Moderated)

3b1-faq	*aix-faq*
3b2-faq	*alt-buddha-short-fat-guy*
AudioFAQ	*alt-config-guide*
C-faq	*alt-hierarchies*
ForthFaq	*alt-security-faq*
GNU-Emacs-FAQ	*alt-sex*
Intel-Unix-X-faq	*alt-sources-intro*
LANs	*amiga*
Modula-2-faq	*animation-faq*
Modula-3-faq	*anime*
Oberon-FAQ	*anu-faq*
Objective-C	*apollo-faq*
PC-games-faq	*apple2*
PCsoundcards	*atheism*
Quaker-faq	*audio-fmts*
RC-flying-FAQ	*aux-faq*
SCItalian-faq	*aviation*
Satellite-TV	*backcountry-faq*
Solaris2	*bahai-faith*
Star-Trek -> star-trek	*benchmark-faq*
Turkish-FAQ	*bicycles-faq*
Xt-FAQ	*billiards-faq*
acorn	*biology*
active-newsgroups	*bisexual*
address-book	*bit*
ai-faq	*bonsai-faq*

books
brewing-faq
ca-driving-faq
canadian-football
car-audio
cats-faq
cdrom-faq
cell-relay-faq
chinese-text
clarinet
co-ops-faq
comp-lang-ada
comp-speech-faq
comp-sys-sun-faq
compilers-faq
compression-faq
computer-virus-faq
consumer-credit-faq
contract-jobs
cooking-faq
crafts-historical-costuming
crafts-textiles
crafts-textiles-books
creating-newsgroups
crossword-faq
cryonics-faq
cryptography-faq
csas-faq
culture-french-faq
dave-barry-faq
de-talk-chat-faq
dec-faq
desqview-faq
disc-faq
disney-faq
distributions
dogs-faq
douglas-adams-FAQ
drug-law-reformers

drugs
drumcorps-faq
dsp-faq
editor-faq
eiffel-faq
electrical-wiring
elm
emacs-implementations
emily-postnews
emulate-apple2-faq
epoch-faq
erotica-faq
esperanto-faq
fax-faq
feminism
finding-addresses
finding-sources
firesign-theatre
fleas-ticks
folklore-faq
fonts-faq
fortran-faq
fractal-faq
frame
free-compilers
fsp-faq
fuzzy-logic
g++-FAQ
gambling-faq
games
german-faq
gopher-faq
gothic-faq
graphics
greek-faq
groupware-intro
hockey-faq
holocaust
hongkong-faq

news.answers (continued):

house-faq	mail
howard-stern	mailpaths
hp-faq	manga
hungarian-faq	mensa
i18n-faq	meta-lang-faq
ibm-rt-faq	mexican-faq
ibmpc-tcp-ip	mh-faq
idl-faq	minix-faq
image-processing	minix-info
index	misc-kids-FAQ
index-	mlm-faq
india-faq	modems
inet-bbs-faq	moderator-list
info-vax	motif-faq
inn-faq	movies
internet-services	msdos-archives
internet-talk-radio	msdos-programmer-faq
investment-faq	music
iranian-faq	net-anonymity
irc-faq	net-privacy
japan	network-info
jpeg-faq	neural-net-faq
judaism	newprod
kerberos-faq	news-announce-intro
killfile-faq	news-answers
lebanon-faq	news-newusers-intro
lemur-faq	nn-faq
letterman	northern-exposure-faq
libertarian	nude-faq
linear-programming-faq	os2-faq
linux-faq	osi-protocols
lisp-faq	paddling-faq
locksmith-faq	paganism-faq
lsi-cad-faq	pagemaker-faq
mach-faq	pc-games-FAQ
macintosh	pc-unix
magic-faq	pcgeos-faq

pdial
periodic-postings
perl-faq
pern-intro
pets-birds-faq
pex-faq
physics-faq
pictures-faq
posting-rules
postscript
ppp-faq
pratchett
pro-wrestling
proj-plan-faq
prolog
puzzles
pyrotechnics-faq
quotations
radio
realtime-computing
rec-autos
rec-photo-faq
rec-skate-faq
red dwarf-faq
ren-n-stimpy
rhf-intro
ripem
robotics-faq
roller-coaster-faq
running-faq
sca-faq
scheme-faq
sci-lang-faq
sci-math-faq
scientology-faq
sco
scouting
scsi-faq
scuba-faq

sf
sgi
shenanigans-faq
simpsons
site-setup
skeptic-faq
skydiving-faq
smalltalk-faq
snmp-faq
social-newsgroups
software-eng
sources-test-faq
space
ssn-privacy
standards-faq
star-trek
supermodels-faq
sybase-faq
table-tennis
talk-bizarre
talk-origins
tasteless-faq
tcl-faq
techreport-sites
tennis-faq
tex-faq
tex-faq-supplement
text-faq
theatre
tiny-toon-faq
tmbg-faq
trailblazer-faq
travel
tv
typing-injury-faq
unix-faq
usenet-faq
usenet-oracle-intro
usenet-primer

Network News

news.answers (continued):

usenet-software	what-is-usenet
usenet-univ-FAQ	whistleblowing
usenet-writing-style	whitewater-addr
usl-bugs	windows-misc-faq
uucp-internals	wireless-cable
vegetarian	woodworking
volleyball-faq	writing
waffle-faq	x-faq
wais-faq	z-faq
weather-data	

news.config:

news.config   Postings of system down times and
                                interruptions.

news.future:

news.future   The future technology of network news
                                systems.

news.groups:

news.groups   Discussions and lists of newsgroups.

Alternative Newsgroup Hierarchies, Part I
Alternative Newsgroup Hierarchies, Part II
Another listing of newsgroups in the alt Usenet hierarchy
Another listing of newsgroups in the alt hierarchy, Part 1 of 2
Another listing of newsgroups in the alt hierarchy, Part 2 of 2
Bogus USENET Groups
Changes to Alternative Newsgroup Hierarchies, Part I
Changes to Alternative Newsgroup Hierarchies, Part II
Changes to How to Create a New Usenet Newsgroup
Changes to List of Active Newsgroups, Part I
Changes to List of Active Newsgroups, Part II
Changes to List of Moderators for Usenet
Creating a new alt group—guidelines
Current Status of USENET Newsgroup Proposals

How to Create a New Usenet Newsgroup
List of Active Newsgroups, Part I
List of Active Newsgroups, Part II
List of Moderators for Usenet
New USENET Groups
Sites honoring invalid newsgroups (by group)
Sites honoring invalid newsgroups (by site)
TOP 40 NEWSGROUPS IN ORDER BY AMOUNT OF CROSSPOSTING
  (JUL 93)
TOP 40 NEWSGROUPS IN ORDER BY PER-READER COST (JUL 93)
TOP 40 NEWSGROUPS IN ORDER BY POPULARITY (JUL 93)
TOP 40 NEWSGROUPS IN ORDER BY TRAFFIC VOLUME (JUL 93)
USENET FLOW ANALYSIS REPORT FOR JUL 93
USENET READERSHIP SUMMARY REPORT FOR JUL 93
USENET Readership summary for Jul 93 posted
Usenet Newsgroup Creation Companion
[l m 5 10 93] FAQ on FAQs n.g.FAQ
arbitron data from these sites has expired

news.lists. *:

news.lists	News-related statistics and lists. (Moderated)
news.lists.ps-maps	Maps relating to USENET traffic flows. (Moderated)

Alternative Newsgroup Hierarchies, Part I
Alternative Newsgroup Hierarchies, Part II
Articles rejected at news.uu.net during the past week
Changes to Alternative Newsgroup Hierarchies, Part I
Changes to Alternative Newsgroup Hierarchies, Part II
Changes to How to Construct the Mailpaths File
Changes to List of Active Newsgroups, Part I
Changes to List of Active Newsgroups, Part II
Changes to List of Moderators for Usenet
Changes to List of Periodic Informational Postings
How to Construct the Mailpaths File
Known Geographic Distributions
Known University Distributions
List of Active Newsgroups, Part I
List of Active Newsgroups, Part II

news.lists.* (continued):

List of Moderators for Usenet
List of Periodic Informational Postings, Part 1 6
List of Periodic Informational Postings, Part 2 6
List of Periodic Informational Postings, Part 3 6
List of Periodic Informational Postings, Part 4 6
List of Periodic Informational Postings, Part 5 6
List of Periodic Informational Postings, Part 6 6
News Administration Macros for Geographic Distributions
Public Organizational & Logical Network Distributions
Publicly Accessible Mailing Lists, Part 1 5
Publicly Accessible Mailing Lists, Part 2 5
Publicly Accessible Mailing Lists, Part 3 5
Publicly Accessible Mailing Lists, Part 4 5
Publicly Accessible Mailing Lists, Part 5 5
Sites honoring invalid newsgroups (by group)
Sites honoring invalid newsgroups (by site)
TOP 40 NEWSGROUPS IN ORDER BY AMOUNT OF CROSSPOSTING (JUL 93)
TOP 40 NEWSGROUPS IN ORDER BY PER-READER COST (JUL 93)
TOP 40 NEWSGROUPS IN ORDER BY POPULARITY (JUL 93)
TOP 40 NEWSGROUPS IN ORDER BY TRAFFIC VOLUME (JUL 93)
Top 25 News Groups for the last 2 weeks
Top 25 News Submitters by Site by Kbytes for the last 2 weeks
Top 25 News Submitters by Site by number of articles for the last 2 weeks
Top 25 News Submitters by User by Kbytes for the last 2 weeks
Top 25 News Submitters by User by number of articles for the last 2 weeks
Total traffic through uunet for the last 2 weeks
USENET FLOW ANALYSIS REPORT FOR JUL 93
USENET FLOW ANALYSIS for JUL 93: Top 1000 sites
USENET READERSHIP SUMMARY REPORT FOR JUL 93
USENET Readership report for Jul 93
Usenet article size statistics—June 1993
arbitron data from these sites has expired

news.lists.ps-maps:

USENET FLOW ANALYSIS REPORT FOR JUL 93
USENET FLOW ANALYSIS for JUL 93: Top 1000 sites
USENET PostScript map m.anz.ref

USENET PostScript map m.ca.bb
USENET PostScript map m.ca.flow
USENET PostScript map m.ca.ref
USENET PostScript map m.de.bb
USENET PostScript map m.de.flow
USENET PostScript map m.de.ref
USENET PostScript map m.eur.bb
USENET PostScript map m.eur.flow
USENET PostScript map m.eur.ref1
USENET PostScript map m.eur.ref2
USENET PostScript map m.maps.hdr
USENET PostScript map m.na.bb
USENET PostScript map m.na.flow1
USENET PostScript map m.na.flow2
USENET PostScript map m.na.flow3
USENET PostScript map m.na.flow4
USENET PostScript map m.na.ref1
USENET PostScript map m.na.ref2
USENET PostScript map m.nena.bb
USENET PostScript map m.nena.flow1
USENET PostScript map m.nena.flow2
USENET PostScript map m.nena.ref
USENET PostScript map m.uk.flow
USENET PostScript map m.uk.ref
USENET PostScript map m.wld.bb
USENET PostScript map m.wld.flow1
USENET PostScript map m.wld.flow2
USENET PostScript map m.wld.flow3
USENET PostScript map m.wld.ref1
USENET PostScript map m.wld.ref2
USENET PostScript map misc. files
inpaths.c (last updated Jan 28 1993)
notes about the contents of this newsgroup

news.misc:

news.misc   Discussions of USENET itself.

Changes to Alternative Newsgroup Hierarchies, Part I
Changes to Alternative Newsgroup Hierarchies, Part II
Changes to How to Create a New Usenet Newsgroup

Network News

news.misc (continued):

Changes to List of Active Newsgroups, Part I
Changes to List of Active Newsgroups, Part II
Changes to List of Moderators for Usenet
USENET Readership summary for Jul 93 posted

news.newsites:

news.newsites	Postings of new site announcements.

news.newusers.*:

news.newusers	Newsgroup for new users.
news.newusers.questions	Q & A for users new to the Usenet.

news.newusers.questions:

FAQ: How to find people s E-mail addresses
FAQ: International E-mail accessibility
FAQ: International E-mail accessibility
Welcome to news.newusers.questions! (weekly posting)
rn KILL file FAQ

news.software.*:

news.software.anu-news	VMS B-news software from Australia.
news.software.b	Discussion about B-news-compatible software.
news.software.nn	Discussion about the "nn" news reader.
news.software.nntp	The Network News Transfer Protocol.
news.software.notes	Notesfile software from the Univ. of Illinois.
news.software.readers	Discussion of software used to read network news.

news.software.anu-news:

FAQ: news.software.anu-news

news.software.b:

Changes to FAQ: FAQ: Norman s INN quick-start guide (Part 3 of 3)

Changes to FAQ: INN General Information (and compiling) (Part 1 of 3)

Changes to FAQ: The INN Tutorial (plus Debugging FAQ) (Part 2 of 3)

Changes to INN FAQ Part 1 3: General Information, how to compile, how to operate

Changes to INN FAQ Part 2 3: Tutorial on installing

Changes to INN FAQ Part 3 3: Tutorial on debugging and adding options

FAQ: INN General Information (and compiling) (Part 1 of 3)

FAQ: Norman s INN quick-start guide (Part 3 of 3)

FAQ: The INN Tutorial (plus Debugging FAQ) (Part 2 of 3)

INN FAQ Part 1 3: General Information, how to compile, how to operate

INN FAQ Part 2 3: Tutorial on installing

INN FAQ Part 3 3: Tutorial on debugging and adding options

news.software.nn:

NN Frequently Asked Questions (FAQ) with Answers

news.software.nntp:

Changes to FAQ: FAQ: Norman s INN quick-start guide (Part 3 of 3)

Changes to FAQ: INN General Information (and compiling) (Part 1 of 3)

Changes to FAQ: The INN Tutorial (plus Debugging FAQ) (Part 2 of 3)

Changes to INN FAQ Part 1 3: General Information, how to compile, how to operate

Changes to INN FAQ Part 2 3: Tutorial on installing

Changes to INN FAQ Part 3 3: Tutorial on debugging and adding options

FAQ: INN General Information (and compiling) (Part 1 of 3)

FAQ: Norman s INN quick-start guide (Part 3 of 3)

FAQ: The INN Tutorial (plus Debugging FAQ) (Part 2 of 3)

INN FAQ Part 1 3: General Information, how to compile, how to operate

INN FAQ Part 2 3: Tutorial on installing

INN FAQ Part 3 3: Tutorial on debugging and adding options

news.software.readers:

rn KILL file FAQ

Network News

This is a branch of the USENET newsgroup tree that is a favorite among many people. It is where you can find others who enjoy doing what you enjoy doing when you are not working. Hobbies and recreational activities of all sorts can be found here.

Recreation: The "rec" Newsgroups

rec.answers:

rec.answers

Repository for periodic USENET articles. (Moderated)

AudioFAQ
PC-games-faq
PCsoundcards
RC-flying-FAQ
Satellite-TV
Star-Trek
animation-faq
anime
aviation
backcountry-faq
bicycles-faq
billiards-faq
bonsai-faq
books
canadian-football
car-audio
cats-faq
cooking-faq
crafts-historical-costuming
crafts-textiles
crafts-textiles-books
crossword-faq
disc-faq
disney-faq
dogs-faq
drumcorps-faq
electrical-wiring
erotica-faq
fleas-ticks
gambling-faq
games
gothic-faq
hockey-faq

index
index-
manga
mensa
movies
music
news-answers
nude-faq
pc-games-FAQ
pets-birds-faq
pictures-faq
pro-wrestling
puzzles
radio
rec-photo-faq
rec-skate-faq
roller-coaster-faq
running-faq
sca-faq
scouting
scuba-faq
sf
skydiving-faq
star-trek
tennis-faq
theatre
travel
tv
usenet-oracle-intro
vegetarian
wireless-cable
woodworking
writing

Recreation

rec.antiques:

rec.antiques   Discussing antiques and vintage items.

rec.aquaria:

rec.aquaria   Keeping fish and aquaria as a hobby.
FAQ: Beginner topics and books
FAQ: Filters
FAQ: Magazines and mail order
FAQ: Plants
FAQ: README and administrivia
FAQ: Water quality

rec.arts.*:

rec.arts.animation   Discussion of various kinds of animation.

rec.arts.anime   Japanese animation fen discussion.

rec.arts.anime.info   Japanese animation.

rec.arts.anime.marketplace   Market place for Japanese animation.

rec.arts.anime.stories   Stories in Japanese animation.

rec.arts.bodyart   Tattoos and body decoration discussion.

rec.arts.books   Books of all genres.

rec.arts.books.tolkien   Discussion of things Tolkien.

rec.arts.bonsai   The art of Bonsai.

rec.arts.cinema   Discussion of the art of cinema. (Moderated)

rec.arts.comics   Comic books.

rec.arts.comics.info   Reviews, convention information...

rec.arts.comics.marketplace   The exchange of comics.

rec.arts.comics.misc   Comic books, graphic novels,...

rec.arts.comics.strips   Discussion of short-form comics.

rec.arts.comics.xbooks   The Mutant Universe of Marvel Comics.

rec.arts.dance   Any aspects of dance not covered elsewhere.

rec.arts.disney   Discussion of any Disney-related items.

rec.arts.drwho   Discussion about Dr. Who.

rec.arts.erotica   Erotic fiction and verse. (Moderated)

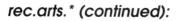

rec.arts.* (continued):

rec.arts.fine	Fine arts & artists.
rec.arts.int-fiction	Discussions about interactive fiction.
rec.arts.manga	All aspects of the Japanese storytelling.
rec.arts.marching.drumcorps	Drum and bugle corps.
rec.arts.marching.misc	Marching-related performance activities.
rec.arts.misc	Discussions about the arts not in other groups.
rec.arts.movies	Discussions of movies and movie making.
rec.arts.movies.reviews	Reviews of movies. (Moderated)
rec.arts.poems	For the posting of poems.
rec.arts.prose	Discussion pf prose.
rec.arts.sf.announce	Major announcements of the SF world.
rec.arts.sf.fandom	Discussions of SF fan activities.
rec.arts.sf.misc	Science fiction lovers' newsgroup.
rec.arts.sf-lovers	For science fiction lovers.
rec.arts.sf.movies	Discussing SF motion pictures.
rec.arts.sf.marketplace	Personal forsale notices of SF material.
rec.arts.sf.reviews	Reviews of science fiction/fantasy.
rec.arts.sf.science	Real and speculative aspects of SF.
rec.arts.sf.starwars	Discussion of the Star Wars universe.
rec.arts.sf.tv	Discussing general television SF.
rec.arts.sf.written	Discussion of written science fiction.
rec.arts.startrek	For the followers of Star Trek.
rec.arts.startrek.current	New Star Trek shows, movies and books.
rec.arts.startrek.fandom	Star Trek conventions and memorabilia.
rec.arts.startrek.info	Information about the universe of StarTrek.
rec.arts.startrek.misc	General discussions of Star Trek.
rec.arts.startrek.reviews	Reviews of Star Trek books, episodes.
rec.arts.startrek.tech	Star Trek's depiction of future technology.
rec.arts.theatre	Discussion of all aspects of stage.
rec.arts.tv	The boob tube, its history, ...

rec.arts.tv.soaps	Postings about soap operas.
rec.arts.tv.tiny-toon	Tiny Toon discussion.
rec.arts.tv.uk	Discussions of telly shows from the UK.
rec.arts.wobegon	"A Prairie Home Companion" radio.

rec.arts.animation:

[rec.arts.animation] Frequently Asked Questions v. 1.22

rec.arts.anime:

rec.arts.anime: Anime Primer
rec.arts.anime: Anime Resources List
rec.arts.anime: FAQ Availability Info
rec.arts.anime: Frequently Asked Questions
rec.arts.anime: Welcome to rec.arts.anime!

rec.arts.anime.info:

Anime Manga Convention List
National Anime BBS Watch
rec.arts.anime: Anime Primer
rec.arts.anime: Anime Resources List
rec.arts.anime: FAQ Availability Info
rec.arts.anime: Frequently Asked Questions
rec.arts.anime: Welcome to rec.arts.anime!

rec.arts.bodyart:

rec.arts.bodyart: Tattoo FAQ
rec.arts.bodyart piercing FAQ part 1 --- address list

rec.arts.bonsai:

The rec.arts.bonsai alt.bonsai FAQ: Part1
The rec.arts.bonsai alt.bonsai FAQ: Part2
The rec.arts.bonsai alt.bonsai FAQ: Part3
The rec.arts.bonsai alt.bonsai FAQ: Part4
The rec.arts.bonsai alt.bonsai FAQ: Part5

Recreation

rec.arts.books:

Arthurian Booklist (rec.arts.books)
Basement Full of Books
Book Catalogues and Book Clubs List (rec.arts.books)
Bookstores in Eastern North American Cities (rec.arts.books)
Bookstores in New York City (NYC) List (rec.arts.books)
Bookstores in Northern North American Cities (rec.arts.books)
Bookstores in San Francisco Bay Area (SF) List (rec.arts.books)
Bookstores in Various European Cities List (rec.arts.books)
Bookstores in Western North American Cities (rec.arts.books)
Changes to Holmes Booklist (rec.arts.books)
FAQ for alt.books.reviews
Holmes Booklist (rec.arts.books)
LIST: Sherlock Holmes Illustrated
R.A.B BOOKSTORES LIST: CAMBRIDGE BOSTON
Robin Hood Booklist (rec.arts.books)
rec.arts.books Frequently Asked Questions

rec.arts.books.tolkien:

Monthly posting: TolkLang - mailing list on Tolkien s languages.

rec.arts.comics.info:

WELCOME TO REC.ARTS.COMICS (part 1 of 6: introduction)
WELCOME TO REC.ARTS.COMICS (part 1 of 6; introduction)
WELCOME TO REC.ARTS.COMICS (part 4 of 6: netiquette)
WELCOME TO REC.ARTS.COMICS (parts 2-3 of 6: the r.a.c FAQ)
WELCOME TO REC.ARTS.COMICS (parts 5-6 of 6: other net sources)

rec.arts.disney:

Disneyland FAQ
Disneyland FAQ; last revised Jun 2 1993
rec.arts.disney FAQ, part 1a
rec.arts.disney FAQ, part 1b
rec.arts.disney FAQ, part 1c
rec.arts.disney FAQ, part 2

rec.arts.erotica:

ADMIN: rec.arts.erotica introduction

rec.arts.fine:

fine art digitized groups general info, welcome and FAQ

rec.arts.int-fiction:

Adventure Authoring Systems FAQ
rec.games.int-fiction Frequently Asked Questions, part 1 of 3
rec.games.int-fiction Frequently Asked Questions, part 2 of 3
rec.games.int-fiction Frequently Asked Questions, part 3 of 3

rec.arts.manga:

rec.arts.manga: FAQ Availability Info
rec.arts.manga: Frequently Asked Questions
rec.arts.manga: Manga Guide Part 1 2
rec.arts.manga: Manga Guide Part 2 2
rec.arts.manga: Manga Resources
rec.arts.manga: Welcome to rec.arts.manga

rec.arts.marching.drumcorps:

rec.arts.marching.drumcorps FAQ 1 6 Contents and General Info
rec.arts.marching.drumcorps FAQ 2 6 1993 Tour and Music Info
rec.arts.marching.drumcorps FAQ 3 6 Historical Information
rec.arts.marching.drumcorps FAQ 4 6 Addresses for corps, etc.
rec.arts.marching.drumcorps FAQ 5 6 Joining a Corps, etc.
rec.arts.marching.drumcorps FAQ 6 6 DCA - senior corps info

rec.arts.movies:

BLADE RUNNER Frequently Asked Questions (FAQ)
LIST: MOVIE TRIVIA: in-jokes, cameos, signatures
rec.arts.movies Frequently Asked Questions

rec.arts.prose:

ADMIN: rec.arts.erotica introduction
the Internet Writer Resource Guide

rec.arts.sf.announce:

Rec.arts.sf groups, an introduction

rec.arts.sf.misc:

Rec.arts.sf groups, an introduction
SF-references-in-music List
rec.arts.sf.written FAQ

rec.arts.sf.movies:

BLADE RUNNER Frequently Asked Questions (FAQ)
LIST: MOVIE TRIVIA: in-jokes, cameos, signatures
rec.arts.sf.movies Frequently Asked Questions

rec.arts.sf.reviews:

Welcome to rec.arts.sf.reviews

rec.arts.sf.written:

Bookstores in Eastern North American Cities (rec.arts.books)
Bookstores in New York City (NYC) List (rec.arts.books)
Bookstores in Northern North American Cities (rec.arts.books)
Bookstores in San Francisco Bay Area (SF) List (rec.arts.books)
Bookstores in Various European Cities List (rec.arts.books)
Bookstores in Western North American Cities (rec.arts.books)
alt history
index
rec.arts.sf.written FAQ
the Internet Writer Resource Guide

rec.arts.startrek.current:

DSN Promos for: IN THE HANDS OF THE PROPHETS (#420)
FAQL: FREQUENTLY ASKED QUESTIONS LIST for rec.arts.startrek.current
FAQL: diff listing (changes since last posting of rasc FAQL)
R.A.S.* NETIQUETTE LIST (8 15 93 version)
R.A.S.* SPOILER LIST (8 15 93 version)
Star Trek DSN List of Lists (July, 1993)

Star Trek TNG List of Lists [1 3] (July, 1993)
Star Trek TNG List of Lists [2 3] (July, 1993)
Star Trek TNG List of Lists [3 3] (July, 1993)
TNG Promos for: DESCENT (#252)

rec.arts.startrek.fandom:

R.A.S.* NETIQUETTE LIST (8 15 93 version)
R.A.S.* SPOILER LIST (8 15 93 version)

rec.arts.startrek.info:

DSN Promos for: IN THE HANDS OF THE PROPHETS (#420)
Guidelines For Submitting Articles
Introduction to rec.arts.startrek.info
List of Upcoming Conventions
TNG Promos for: DESCENT (#252)

rec.arts.startrek.misc:

DSN Promos for: IN THE HANDS OF THE PROPHETS (#420)
FAQ: Star Trek Spelling List v5.0 [1 2]
FAQL: ACRONYMS USED IN THE REC.ARTS.STARTREK.* NEWS-
GROUPS
FAQL: FREQUENTLY ASKED QUESTIONS LIST for rec.arts.startrek.misc
FAQL: HOW TO SUBMIT CREATIVE MATERIAL
FAQL: LIST OF PERIODIC POSTINGS TO r.a.s.* NEWSGROUPS
FAQL: NAMES, RANKS, AND SERIAL NUMBERS (AND CREW DATA)
FAQL: PILOT EPISODES AND UNAIRED EPISODES
FAQL: SNAFUs
FAQL: STAR TREK MUSIC
FAQL: TIME LOOPS, YESTERDAY S ENTERPRISE, AND TASHA YAR EX-
PLAINED
FAQL: diff listing (changes since last posting of rasm FAQL)
R.A.S.* NETIQUETTE LIST (8 15 93 version)
R.A.S.* SPOILER LIST (8 15 93 version)
STAR TREK:DSN FIRST SEASON PROMO SUMMARY
STAR TREK:TNG FIFTH SEASON PROMO SUMMARY
STAR TREK:TNG FOURTH SEASON PROMO SUMMARY
STAR TREK:TNG SIXTH SEASON PROMO SUMMARY

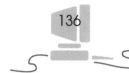
rec.arts.startrek.misc (continued):

STAR TREK LOCATIONS [Updated: Aug 17, 1993]
STAR TREK LOCATIONS [Updated: Jul 16, 1993]
STAR TREK SHIPS [Updated: Aug 17, 1993]
STAR TREK SHIPS [Updated: Jul 16, 1993]
Star Trek Actors Other Roles FAQ [02 07]
Star Trek Actors Other Roles FAQ [03 07]
Star Trek Actors Other Roles FAQ [04 07]
Star Trek Actors Other Roles FAQ [05 07]
Star Trek Actors Other Roles FAQ [06 07]
Star Trek Actors Other Roles FAQ [07 07]
Star Trek Actors Other Roles FAQ [INTRO] [01 07]
Star Trek Books-On-Tape
Star Trek Comics Checklist, Part 1 2
Star Trek Comics Checklist, Part 2 2
Star Trek Comics Checklist, README
Star Trek DSN List of Lists (July, 1993)
Star Trek Spelling List v5.0 [2 2]
Star Trek TMS List of Lists (April, 1993)
Star Trek TNG List of Lists [1 3] (July, 1993)
Star Trek TNG List of Lists [2 3] (July, 1993)
Star Trek TNG List of Lists [3 3] (July, 1993)
Star Trek TOS TAS List of Lists (April, 1993)
Star Trek story archive (weekly FAQ—automated posting)
Syndicated Ratings for week ending 5 16 93
TNG Promos for: DESCENT (#252)
TOS Novels Compendium [01 11]
TOS Novels Compendium [02 11]
TOS Novels Compendium [03 11]
TOS Novels Compendium [04 11]
TOS Novels Compendium [05 11]
TOS Novels Compendium [06 11]
TOS Novels Compendium [07 11]
TOS Novels Compendium [08 11]
TOS Novels Compendium [09 11]
TOS Novels Compendium [10 11]
TOS Novels Compendium [11 11]
TOS Novels Compendium [Changes since last release]
TOS Novels Compendium [Intro]

TOS Novels Compendium [Update]
TREK RATE ballot
TREK RATE results (BOOKS)
TREK RATE results (DS9)
TREK RATE results (MOVIES)
TREK RATE results (TAS)
TREK RATE results (TNG)
TREK RATE results (TOS)

rec.arts.startrek.tech:

FAQL: FREQUENTLY ASKED QUESTIONS LIST for rec.arts.startrek.tech
Not the Technical Manual
R.A.S.* NETIQUETTE LIST (8 15 93 version)
R.A.S.* SPOILER LIST (8 15 93 version)
Relativity and FTL Travel
STAR TREK LOCATIONS [Updated: Aug 17, 1993]
STAR TREK LOCATIONS [Updated: Jul 16, 1993]
STAR TREK SHIPS [Updated: Aug 17, 1993]
STAR TREK SHIPS [Updated: Jul 16, 1993]

rec.arts.theatre:

rec.arts.theatre Frequently Asked Questions (FAQ): part 1 2
rec.arts.theatre Frequently Asked Questions (FAQ): part 2 2

rec.arts.tv:

MARRIED WITH CHILDREN PROGRAM GUIDE (Part 1 5)
MARRIED WITH CHILDREN PROGRAM GUIDE (Part 2 5)
MARRIED WITH CHILDREN PROGRAM GUIDE (Part 3 5)
MARRIED WITH CHILDREN PROGRAM GUIDE (Part 4 5)
MARRIED WITH CHILDREN PROGRAM GUIDE (Part 5 5)
Mystery Science Theater 3000 Episode Guide
Mystery Science Theater 3000 FAQ
Mystery Science Theater 3000 Songs
Syndicated Ratings for week ending 5 16 93
ALF EPISODE GUIDE
BOB PROGRAM GUIDE
FLYING BLIND PROGRAM GUIDE

rec.arts.tv (continued):

GET A LIFE PROGRAM GUIDE
HERMAN S HEAD PROGRAM GUIDE
SHAKY GROUND PROGRAM GUIDE
The Simpsons Air Dates (*)

rec.arts.tv.soaps:

ALL: rec.arts.tv.soaps Monthly FAQ (Frequently Asked Questions)

rec.audio.*:

rec.audio	High fidelity audio.
rec.audio.car	Discussions of automobile audio systems.
rec.audio.high-end	High-end audio systems. (Moderated)
rec.audio.pro	Professional audio recording and studio engineering.

FAQ: rec.audio (part 1 of 4)
FAQ: rec.audio (part 2 of 4)
FAQ: rec.audio (part 3 of 4)
FAQ: rec.audio (part 4 of 4)
rec.audio FAQ (part 1 of 4)
rec.audio FAQ (part 2 of 4)
rec.audio FAQ (part 3 of 4)
rec.audio FAQ (part 4 of 4)

rec.audio.car:

rec.audio.car FAQ
rec.audio.car FAQ (part 1 1)

rec.autos:

rec.autos	Automobiles, automotive products,...
rec.autos.antique	Discussing all aspects of old automobiles.
rec.autos.driving	Driving automobiles.
rec.autos.rod-n-custom	Customization.
rec.autos.sport	Discussion of organized, legal auto competition.

rec.autos.tech	Technical aspects of automobiles, et al.
rec.autos.vw	Issues pertaining to Volkswagen products.

rec.aviation.*:

rec.aviation	
rec.aviation.announce	Events of interest to the aviation communty.
rec.aviation.answers	Frequently asked questions about aviation.
rec.aviation.ifr	Flying under Instrument Flight Rules.
rec.aviation.homebuilt	Selecting, designing, building, ...
rec.aviation.military	Military aircraft of the past, present and future.
rec.aviation.misc	Miscellaneous topics in aviation.
rec.aviation.owning	Information on owning airplanes.
rec.aviation.piloting	General discussion for aviators.
rec.aviation.products	Reviews and discussion of products used.
rec.aviation.simulators	Flight simulation on all levels.
rec.aviation.soaring	All aspects of sailplanes and hang-gliders.
rec.aviation.stories	Anecdotes of flight experiences. (Moderated)
rec.aviation.student	Learning to fly.

rec.aviation.answers:

aviation
index

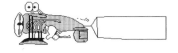

rec.aviation.simulators:

r.a.s F A Q
rec.aviation.simulators Frequently Asked Questions

rec.backcountry:

rec.backcountry	Activities in the Great Outdoors.

[l m 12 7 92] summary of past topics Distilled non-wisdom (5 28) XYZ
[l m 1 26 93] Lyme Disease: Distilled Wisdom (19 28) XYZ

Recreation

rec.backcountry (continued):

[l m 2 11 93] Rachel Carson s Words: Distilled Wisdom (10 28) XYZ

[l m 4 14 93] Leopold s Land Ethic Distilled Wisdom (14 28) XYZ

[l m 4 15 91] Netiquette: Distilled Wisdom (12 28) XYZ

[l m 4 15 92] Eco-warriors Distilled Wisdom (22 28) XYZ

[l m 4 15 92] High tech employment, a romantic notion DW (25 28) XYZ

[l m 4 15 92] Information on bears: Distilled Wisdom (17 28) XYZ

[l m 4 15 92] Oak Ivy Distilled Wisdom (18 28) XYZ

[l m 4 15 92] Words from Colin Fletcher Distilled Wisdom (8 28) XYZ

[l m 4 22 93] rec.backC DISCLAIMER—Distilled wisdom (1 28) XYZ

[l m 4 23 93] Related news groups: Distilled Wisdom (26 28) XYZ

[l m 4 27 93] Questions on conditions and travel DW (13 28) XYZ

[l m 5 11 93] Water filters & Giardia Distilled Wisdom (9 28) XYZ

[l m 5 14 93] Snake bite: Distilled Wisdom (11 28) XYZ

[l m 5 17 93] Telling questions r.b. Turing test DW: (20 28) XYZ

[l m 5 18 1993] Morbid backcountry memorial: Distilled Wisdom (16 28) XYZ

[l m 5 24 93] Song Distilled Wisdom (23 28) XYZ

[l m 5 31 93] Film Cinema Distilled wisdom (27 28) XYZ

[l m 6 20 91] Leopold s post Distilled Wisdom (15 28) XYZ

[l m 6 29 93] References Distilled Wisdom (28 28) XYZ

[l m 6 2 92] Backcountry Ethics Distilled Wisdom (2 28) XYZ

[l m 6 7 93] summary of one past topic Not Distilled wisdom (6 28) XYZ

[l m 6 8 93] learning (2) Distilled wisdom (4 28) XYZ

[l m 7 23 93] Phone address list Distilled Wisdom (7 28) XYZ

[l m 8 29 92] What is natural? Distilled Wisdom (24 28) XYZ

[l m 9 17 92] learning (I) Distilled wisdom (3 28) XYZ

[l m 9 18 92] AMS Distilled Wisdom (21 28) XYZ

rec.bicycles.*:

rec.bicycles	
rec.bicycles.marketplace	Buying, selling & reviewing items for bicycles.
rec.bicycles.misc	General discussion of bicycling.
rec.bicycles.racing	Bicycle racing techniques, rules,...
rec.bicycles.rides	Discussions of tours and training.
rec.bicycles.soc	Societal issues of bicycling.
rec.bicycles.tech	Cycling product design, construction.

rec.bicycles.misc:

Rec.Bicycles Frequently Asked Questions Posting Part 1 5
Rec.Bicycles Frequently Asked Questions Posting Part 2 5
Rec.Bicycles Frequently Asked Questions Posting Part 3 5
Rec.Bicycles Frequently Asked Questions Posting Part 4 5
Rec.Bicycles Frequently Asked Questions Posting Part 5 5

rec.birds:

rec.birds	Hobbyists interested in bird watching.

rec.boats.*:

rec.boats	Hobbyists interested in boating.
rec.boats.paddle	Talk about any boats with oars, paddles, etc.

rec.boats.paddle:

Whitewater outfitter dealer address list
rec.boats.paddle frequently asked questions and answers

rec.climbing:

rec.climbing	Climbing techniques, competition announcements,...

[l m 4 15 91] Netiquette: Distilled Wisdom (12 28) XYZ
[l m 5 18 1993] Morbid backcountry memorial: Distilled Wisdom (16 28) XYZ

rec.collecting.*:

rec.collecting	Discussion among collectors of many things.
rec.collecting.cards	Collecting all sorts of sport and non-sports cards.

rec.crafts.*:

rec.crafts.brewing	The art of making beers and meads.
rec.crafts.metalworking	All aspects of working with metal.
rec.crafts.misc	Handiwork arts not covered elsewhere.
rec.crafts.textiles	Sewing, weaving, knitting and others.

Recreation

rec.crafts.brewing:

rec.crafts.brewing Frequently Asked Questions (FAQ)

rec.crafts.textiles:

Historical Costuming FAQ
Textile Related Books FAQ: Part 1 of 2
Textile Related Books FAQ: Part 2 of 2
Textiles FAQ

rec.equestrian:

rec.equestrian	Discussion of things equestrian.

rec.folk-dancing:

rec.folk-dancing	Folk dances, dancers, and dancing.

rec.food.*:

rec.food.cooking	Food, cooking, cookbooks, and recipes.
rec.food.drink	Wines and spirits.
rec.food.historic	The history of food making arts.
rec.food.recipes	Recipes for interesting food and drink. (Moderated)
rec.food.restaurants	Discussion of dining out.
rec.food.sourdough	Making and baking with sourdough.
rec.food.veg	Vegetarians.

rec.food.cooking:

rec.food.cooking FAQ and conversion file

rec.food.recipes:

rec.food.cooking FAQ and conversion file

rec.food.veg:

rec.food.veg FREQUENTLY ASKED QUESTIONS LIST (FAQ)

rec.food.veg World Guide to Vegetarianism - California1
rec.food.veg World Guide to Vegetarianism - California2
rec.food.veg World Guide to Vegetarianism - Canada1
rec.food.veg World Guide to Vegetarianism - Canada2
rec.food.veg World Guide to Vegetarianism - Europe
rec.food.veg World Guide to Vegetarianism - Other
rec.food.veg World Guide to Vegetarianism - USA1
rec.food.veg World Guide to Vegetarianism - USA2
rec.food.veg World Guide to Vegetarianism - USA3

rec.gambling:

rec.gambling	Articles on games of chance & betting.

rec.gambling Changes to Frequently Asked Questions
rec.gambling Frequently Asked Questions

rec.games:

rec.games.abstract	Perfect information, pure strategy.
rec.games.backgammon	Discussion of the game of backgammon.
rec.games.board	Discussion and hints on board games.
rec.games.board.ce	The Cosmic Encounter board game.
rec.games.bridge	Hobbyists interested in bridge.
rec.games.chess	Chess & computer chess.
rec.games.corewar	The Core War computer challenge.
rec.games.cyber	Cyberspace.
rec.games.design	Discussion of game design.
rec.games.diplomacy	The conquest game Diplomacy.
rec.games.empire	Discussion and hints about Empire.
rec.games.frp	Fantasy role playing.
rec.games.frp.advocacy	Flames and rebuttals about various FRP games.
rec.games.frp.announce	Announcements of happenings in the FRP world.
rec.games.frp.archives	Archivable fantasy stories and other...
rec.games.frp.cyber	Discussions of cyberpunk related role playing.
rec.games.frp.dnd	Fantasy role-playing with TSR's...
rec.games.frp.marketplace	Role-playing game materials wanted.
rec.games.frp.misc	General discussions of role-playing.
rec.games.go	Discussion about Go.
rec.games.hack	Discussion, hints, etc.
rec.games.int-fiction	All aspects of interactive fiction.

Recreation

rec.games (continued):

rec.games.mecha	Giant robot games.
rec.games.miniatures	Miniatures.
rec.games.misc	Games and computer games.
rec.games.moria	Comments, hints, and info about the Moria game.
rec.games.mud	Multiuser games.
rec.games.mud.admin	Administrative issues of multiuser games.
rec.games.mud.announce	Informational articles about multiuser games.
rec.games.mud.diku	All about DikuMuds.
rec.games.mud.lp	Discussions of the LPMUD computer game.
rec.games.mud.misc	Various aspects of multiuser computer games.
rec.games.mud.tiny	Discussion about Tiny muds, ...
rec.games.netrek	Discussion of the X window system.
rec.games.pbm	Discussion about Play by Mail game.
rec.games.pinball	Discussing pinball-related issues.
rec.games.programmer	Discussion of adventure game programming.
rec.games.rogue	Discussion and hints about Rogue.
rec.games.rpg	Role playing games.
rec.games.trivia	Discussion about trivia.
rec.games.vectrex	The Vectrex game system.
rec.games.video	Discussion about video games.
rec.games.video.arcade	Discussions about coin-operated video games.
rec.games.video.classic	Classic video games.
rec.games.video.marketplace	Video games for sale.
rec.games.video.misc	Video game discussion that doesn't fit elsewhere.
rec.games.video.nintendo	Nintendo games.
rec.games.video.sega	Sega games.
rec.games.xtank.play	Strategy and tactics.
rec.games.xtank.programmer	Coding the Xtank game and its...

rec.games.board:

Scrabble FAQ - Club and Tournament Supplement
Scrabble FAQ - General Information
Talisman boardgame FAQ (Frequently Asked Questions)
rec.games.board FAQ and intro

rec.games.bridge:

rec.games.bridge style guide

rec.games.chess:

rec.games.chess Answers to Frequently Asked Questions [1 2]
rec.games.chess Answers to Frequently Asked Questions [1 2] 93 07 01
rec.games.chess Answers to Frequently Asked Questions [2 2]
rec.games.chess Answers to Frequently Asked Questions [2 2] 93 07 01

rec.games.corewar:

Core War Frequently Asked Questions (rec.games.corewar FAQ)

rec.games.design:

rec.games.design FAQ

rec.games.diplomacy:

rec.games.diplomacy FAQ

rec.games.empire:

versions of empire—monthly posting

rec.games.frp.announce:

[rec.games.frp.] BBSes of interest to roleplayers*
[rec.games.frp.] Frequently asked questions Part 1*
[rec.games.frp.] Frequently asked questions Part 2*
[rec.games.frp.] Roleplaying mailing lists and digests part 1 2*
[rec.games.frp.] Roleplaying mailing lists and digests part 2 2*
[rec.games.frp.] Roleplaying net.*.books,faq keepers*
[rec.games.frp.] Welcome to the roleplaying discussion groups!*
[rec.games.frp.] archive sites with roleplaying material*

rec.games.go:

Go Players Address List
Go Related Files for Anonymous FTP
The Game Go—Frequently Asked Questions

rec.games.int-fiction:

rec.games.int-fiction Frequently Asked Questions, part 1 of 3
rec.games.int-fiction Frequently Asked Questions, part 2 of 3
rec.games.int-fiction Frequently Asked Questions, part 3 of 3

rec.games.misc:

ADMIN: comp.sys.ibm.pc.games - Frequently Asked Questions - Read before posting
PC GAMES FAQ <- Guide To The Gaming World (Part 1 of 2)
PC GAMES FAQ <- Guide To The Gaming World (Part 2 of 2)
rec.games.int-fiction Frequently Asked Questions, part 1 of 3
rec.games.int-fiction Frequently Asked Questions, part 2 of 3
rec.games.int-fiction Frequently Asked Questions, part 3 of 3

rec.games.moria:

rec.games.moria Frequently Asked Questions

rec.games.mud.announce:

The Totally Unofficial List of Internet Muds
[rec.games.mud]: FAQ #1 3: MUDs and MUDding
[rec.games.mud]: FAQ #2 3: MUD Clients and Servers
[rec.games.mud]: FAQ #3 3: RWHO and mudwho

rec.games.mud.diku:

rec.games.mud.diku FAQ (frequently asked questions)
rec.games.mud.diku FAQ 01 02
rec.games.mud.diku FAQ 02 02

rec.games.mud.misc:

The Totally Unofficial List of Internet Muds
[rec.games.mud]: FAQ #1 3: MUDs and MUDding

[rec.games.mud]: FAQ #2 3: MUD Clients and Servers
[rec.games.mud]: FAQ #3 3: RWHO and mudwho

rec.games.netrek:

Netrek FTP list.
Netrek Server List
rec.games.netrek FAQ List

rec.games.pbm:

FAQ: rec.games.pbm Frequently Asked Questions

rec.games.pinball:

monthly rec.games.pinball FAQ, one of two
monthly rec.games.pinball FAQ, two of two

rec.games.video:

rec.games.video Frequently Asked Questions
rec.games.video Frequently Asked Questions (part 1 of 2)
rec.games.video Frequently Asked Questions (part 2 of 2)

rec.games.video.arcade:

rec.games.video.arcade Frequently Asked Questions
rec.games.video.arcade Mailserver and FTP information

rec.games.video.classic:

rec.games.video.arcade Frequently Asked Questions

rec.games.video.misc:

Turbo-Grafx 16 Frequently Asked Questions
Turbo-Grafx 16 Product & Price list
rec.games.video Frequently Asked Questions
rec.games.video Frequently Asked Questions (part 1 of 2)
rec.games.video Frequently Asked Questions (part 2 of 2)

Recreation

rec.games.video.nintendo:

rec.games.video Frequently Asked Questions
rec.games.video Frequently Asked Questions (part 1 of 2)
rec.games.video Frequently Asked Questions (part 2 of 2)

rec.games.video.sega:

rec.games.video Frequently Asked Questions
rec.games.video Frequently Asked Questions (part 1 of 2)
rec.games.video Frequently Asked Questions (part 2 of 2)

rec.gardens:

rec.gardens	Gardening, methods and results.

rec.guns:

rec.guns	Discussions about firearms. (Moderated)
charter for rec.guns	

rec.heraldry:

rec.heraldry	Discussion of coats of arms.

rec.humor.*:

rec.humor	Jokes and the like. May be somewhat offensive.
rec.humor.d	Discussions on the content of rec.humor articles.
rec.humor.funny	Jokes that are funny (in the moderator's opinion).
rec.humor.flame	A place to flame.
rec.humor.oracle	Sagacious advice from the USENET Oracle. (Moderated)
rec.humor.oracle.d	Comments about the USENET Oracle's comments.

rec.humor.funny:

Editorial Policy on Offensive Jokes—Monthly Posting
Guidelines for Submissions—Monthly Posting
Introduction to REC.HUMOR.FUNNY—Monthly Posting

rec.humor.oracle:

[rec.humor.oracle] Intro to the Usenet Oracle (Monthly Posting)

rec.hunting:

rec.hunting	Discussions about hunting. (Moderated)

rec.juggling:

rec.juggling	Juggling techniques, equipment and events.

rec.kites:

rec.kites	Talk about kites and kiting.

rec.mag:

rec.mag	Magazine summaries, tables of contents, et
rec.mag.fsfnet	A Science Fiction "fanzine." (Moderated)
rec.mag.otherrealms	More magazine discussion.

rec.martial-arts:

rec.martial-arts	Discussion of the various martial art forms.

rec.misc:

rec.misc	General topics about recreational/participant sports.

rec.models.*:

rec.models.rc	Radio-controlled models for hobbyists.
rec.models.rockets	Model rockets for hobbyists.
rec.models.railroad	Model railroads of all scales.
rec.models.scale	Construction of models.

rec.models.railroad:

rec.models.railroad Fortnightly FAQ (GENERAL)

rec.models.railroad Fortnightly FAQ (INFO)

rec.models.railroad Fortnightly FAQ (INTRO)

rec.models.railroad Fortnightly FAQ (OPERATIONS)

rec.models.railroad Fortnightly FAQ (PROTOTYPE)

rec.models.railroad Fortnightly FAQ (PROTOTYPE Part 1 of 2)

rec.models.railroad Fortnightly FAQ (PROTOTYPE Part 2 of 2)

rec.models.railroad Fortnightly FAQ (TECHNIQUE)

rec.models.railroad Fortnightly FAQ (TECHNIQUE - PART 1 of 2)

rec.models.railroad Fortnightly FAQ (TECHNIQUE - PART 2 of 2)

rec.models.rc:

R C Flying: Part 1 of 2 rec.models.rc FAQ

R C Flying: Part 2 of 2 rec.models.rc FAQ

rec.motorcycles:

rec.motorcycles	Motorcycles and related products.
rec.motorcycles.dirt	Riding motorcycles and ATVs off-road.
rec.motorcycles.harley	All aspects of Harley-Davidson motorcycles.
rec.motorcycles.racing	Discussion of all aspects of racing motorcycles.

Beginner Motorcycle Info: Periodic Post

FAQ - What is the DoD?

What is the DoD? - Weekly Micro-FAQ

rec.motorcycles FAQ of 93.05.01 (Part 4 of 6)

rec.motorcycles FAQ of 93.08.01 (Part 1 of 6)

rec.motorcycles FAQ of 93.08.01 (Part 2 of 6)

rec.motorcycles FAQ of 93.08.01 (Part 3 of 6)

rec.motorcycles FAQ of 93.08.01 (Part 5 of 6)

rec.motorcycles FAQ of 93.08.01 (Part 6 of 6)

rec.motorcycles.dirt:

FAQ - What is the DoD?

rec.motorcycles.harley:

FAQ - What is the DoD?

rec.motorcycles.racing:

FAQ - What is the DoD?

rec.music.*:

rec.music.a-cappella	
rec.music.afro-latin	Music with afro-latin, African influence.
rec.music.beatles	Postings about the Fab Four.
rec.music.bluenote	Discussion of jazz, blues, ...
rec.music.cd	CDs—availability and other issues.
rec.music.christian	Christian music, both contempory.
rec.music.classical	Discussion about classical music.
rec.music.classical.guitar	Discussion about classical guitar music.
rec.music.classical.performing	Discussion about performing classical music.
rec.music.compose	Creating musical and lyrical pieces.
rec.music.country.western	C&W music, performers, performances, ...
rec.music.dementia	Discussion of comedy and novel creations.
rec.music.dylan	Discussion of Bob's works...
rec.music.early	Discussion of pre-classical music.
rec.music.folk	Folks discussing folk music.
rec.music.funky	Funk, rap, hip-hop, house, ...
rec.music.gaffa	Discussion of Kate Bush & others.
rec.music.gdead	A group for (Grateful) Dead-heads.
rec.music.indian.classical	Hindustani and Carnatic Indian music.
rec.music.indian.misc	Discussing Indian music in general.
rec.music.industrial	Discussion of all industrial ...
rec.music.info	News and announcements on music.

rec.music.* (continued):

rec.music.makers	For performers...
rec.music.makers.bass	Upright bass and bass guitar.
rec.music.makers.guitar	Electric and acoustic guitar.
rec.music.makers.guitar.tablature	Guitar tablature/chords.
rec.music.makers.marketplace	Marketplace for music makers.
rec.music.makers.percussion	Drum & other percussion...
rec.music.makers.synth	Synthesizers and computer music.
rec.music.marketplace	Records, tapes, and CDs: wanted.
rec.music.misc	Music lovers' group.
rec.music.newage	"New Age" music discussions.
rec.music.phish	Discussing the musical groups.
rec.music.reggae	The melodies of the Caribbean.
rec.music.reviews	Reviews of music of all genres.
rec.music.synth	Synthesizer music discussion.
rec.music.video	Discussion of music videos.

rec.music.a-cappella:

rec.music.a-cappella Frequently Asked Questions list - August 93

rec.music.bluenote:

FAQ: Rec.music.bluenote: Frequently Asked Questions (FAQs)
FAQ: Rec.music.bluenote: Further sources of information
FAQ: Rec.music.bluenote: Welcome to rec.music.bluenote!
Listing of open musical jam sessions

rec.music.classical:

rec.music.classical FAQ

rec.music.classical.performing:

Welcome to rec.music.classical.performing!
rec.music.classical.performing - FAQ

rec.music.compose:

Electronic and Computer Music Frequently-Asked Questions (FAQ)

rec.music.dylan:

Guide to Frequently Asked Questions (1 of 2)
Guide to Frequently Asked Questions (2 of 2)

rec.music.folk:

Listing of open musical jam sessions

rec.music.funky:

CHART: Dutch Dance

rec.music.industrial:

rec.music.industrial FAQ Part 1 2—Questions and History
rec.music.industrial FAQ Part 2 2—Mailorder Sources and Zines

rec.music.info:

CHART: Austrian Top 20 Singles
CHART: Bavarian Top 15 (singles), 08 06 93
CHART: Bavarian Top 15 (singles), 08 13 93
CHART: Dutch Albums
CHART: Dutch Dance
CHART: Dutch Singles
CHART: European Top 20
CHART: German Top 10 (singles), thirty-first week
CHART: German Top 10 (singles), thirty-second week
CHART: Vancouver BC Canada
CHART: Vancouver BC Canada: 05 Aug 93
FAQ: Rec.music.bluenote: Frequently Asked Questions (FAQs)
FAQ: Rec.music.bluenote: Further sources of information
FAQ: Rec.music.bluenote: Welcome to rec.music.bluenote!
FAQ: Ska (alt.music.ska) Frequently Asked Questions
FAQ: rec.audio (part 1 of 4)
FAQ: rec.audio (part 2 of 4)

rec.music.info (continued):

FAQ: rec.audio (part 3 of 4)
FAQ: rec.audio (part 4 of 4)
FAQ alt.gothic Frequently Asked Questions
REC.MUSIC.INFO: List of Internet Musical FTP Sites
REC.MUSIC.INFO: List of Internet Musical Resources
REC.MUSIC.INFO: List of Music-Oriented Fan Clubs
REC.MUSIC.INFO: List of Usenet Musical Newsgroups
REC.MUSIC.INFO: Submission Guidelines for rec.music.info
REC.MUSIC.INFO: Welcome to rec.music.info!
rec.music.industrial FAQ Part 1 2—Questions and History
rec.music.industrial FAQ Part 2 2—Mailorder Sources and Zines

rec.music.makers:

Electronic and Computer Music Frequently-Asked Questions (FAQ)
Listing of open musical jam sessions
Music Equipment Mail Phone List

rec.music.makers.bass:

Music Equipment Mail Phone List

rec.music.makers.guitar:

Music Equipment Mail Phone List

rec.music.makers.guitar.tablature:

guitar tab Frequently Asked Questions (FAQ) version 1.0b

rec.music.makers.percussion:

Music Equipment Mail Phone List

rec.music.makers.synth:

Computer Music bibliography
Electronic and Computer Music Frequently-Asked Questions (FAQ)
Midi files software archives on the Internet
Midi files software archives on the Internet.
Music Equipment Mail Phone List

rec.music.misc:

CHART: Austrian Top 20 Singles
CHART: European Top 20
CHART: The ARIA top 60 singles chart - Australia
CHART: Top 10 albums -> Australia.
CHART: Top 10 singles -> Australia.
CHART: Top 10 singles -> The U.K.
CHART: Top 10 singles -> The U.S.A.
REC.MUSIC.INFO: List of Internet Musical FTP Sites
REC.MUSIC.INFO: List of Internet Musical Resources
REC.MUSIC.INFO: List of Music-Oriented Fan Clubs
REC.MUSIC.INFO [Monthly pointer]
SF-references-in-music List

rec.music.newage:

REC.MUSIC.INFO [Monthly pointer]

rec.music.phish:

REC.MUSIC.INFO [Monthly pointer]

rec.music.reggae:

Caribana 93 - Frequently Asked Questions (FAQ)

rec.music.synth:

Electronic and Computer Music Frequently-Asked Questions (FAQ)
FAQ: Gravis Ultrasound (GUS) FAQ v1.28

rec.nude:

rec.nude   Hobbyists interested in naturist/nudist
                            activities.

REC.NUDE FAQ--Clubs and Publications, Part II of III
REC.NUDE FAQ--Electronic Access, Part III of III
REC.NUDE FAQ--The Questions, Part I of III
REC.NUDE FAQ: Naturist Site Reports: Australasia
REC.NUDE FAQ: Naturist Site Reports: California

rec.nude (continued):

REC.NUDE FAQ: Naturist Site Reports: Europe
REC.NUDE FAQ: Naturist Site Reports: North America
REC.NUDE Frequently Asked Questions, Part II of II
REC.NUDE Frequently Asked Questions, Part I of II
REC.NUDE Nude Beaches Etc. FAQ: California
REC.NUDE Nude Beaches Etc. FAQ: Not California

rec.org:

rec.org.sca	Society for Creative Anachronism.
rec.org.mensa	Talking with members of the high IQ society Mensa.

rec.org.mensa:

Mensa - FAQ: Do I qualify for Mensa? How do I Join? [BiWeekly]
Mensa - FAQ: Do I qualify for Mensa? How do I Join? [Weekly]
Mensa - FAQ: What famous people are members of Mensa? [Monthly]
Mensa - FAQ: What is Mensa? [BiWeekly]
Mensa - FAQ: What is Mensa? [Weekly]
Mensa - FAQ: What is the Mensa test like? [Monthly]
Mensa - FAQ: What other high-IQ societies are there? [Bi-Weekly]

rec.org.sca:

Come on in--the water s fine
Historical Costuming FAQ
rec.org.sca Rialto Frequently Asked Questions - part01 04
rec.org.sca Rialto Frequently Asked Questions - part02 04
rec.org.sca Rialto Frequently Asked Questions - part03 04
rec.org.sca Rialto Frequently Asked Questions - part04 04

rec.outdoors:

rec.outdoors.fishing	All aspects of sport and commercial fishing.

rec.pets:

rec.pets	Pets, pet care, and household animals in general.
rec.pets.birds	The culture and care of indoor birds.
rec.pets.cats	Discussion about domestic cats.
rec.pets.dogs	Any and all subjects relating to dogs as pets.
rec.pets.herp	Reptiles, amphibians and other exotic vivarium.

Fleas, Ticks, and Your Pet: FAQ

rec.pets.birds:

rec.pets.birds FAQ: Monthly Posting (1 3)
rec.pets.birds FAQ: Monthly Posting (2 3)
rec.pets.birds FAQ: Monthly Posting (3 3)

rec.pets.cats:

Fleas, Ticks, and Your Pet: FAQ
rec.pets.cats FAQ (part 1 4)
rec.pets.cats FAQ (part 2 4)
rec.pets.cats FAQ (part 3 4)
rec.pets.cats FAQ (part 4 4)

rec.pets.dogs:

Complete List of rec.pets.dogs FAQ s
Fleas, Ticks, and Your Pet: FAQ
rec.pets.dogs: Breed Rescue Organizations FAQ Part 1 2
rec.pets.dogs: Breed Rescue Organizations FAQ Part 2 2
rec.pets.dogs: American Kennel Club FAQ
rec.pets.dogs: Assorted Topics [Part 1] FAQ
rec.pets.dogs: Assorted Topics [Part II] FAQ
rec.pets.dogs: Behavior: Understanding and Modifying FAQ
rec.pets.dogs: Breeding Your Dog FAQ
rec.pets.dogs: Canine Medical Information FAQ
rec.pets.dogs: Cavalier King Charles Spaniels Breed-FAQ
rec.pets.dogs: Getting A Dog FAQ
rec.pets.dogs: Havanese Breed-FAQ

rec.pets.dogs (continued):

rec.pets.dogs: Health Care Issues FAQ
rec.pets.dogs: Introduction FAQ
rec.pets.dogs: Publications FAQ
rec.pets.dogs: Resources FAQ
rec.pets.dogs: Service Dogs FAQ
rec.pets.dogs: Training Your Dog FAQ
rec.pets.dogs: Working Dogs FAQ
rec.pets.dogs: Your New Dog FAQ
rec.pets.dogs: Your New Puppy FAQ

rec.photo:

rec.photo   Hobbyists interested in photography.

Nikon FAQ
Photographic Mail Order Survey
[Periodic Posting]: Medium Format Digest Info
rec.photo FAQ and answers

rec.puzzles.*:

rec.puzzles   Puzzles, problems, and quizzes.

rec.puzzles.crosswords   Making and playing gridded word puzzles.

index
puzzles
rec.puzzles Archive (Instructions), part 01 of 35
rec.puzzles Archive (analysis), part 02 of 35
rec.puzzles Archive (arithmetic), part 03 of 35
rec.puzzles Archive (arithmetic), part 04 of 35
rec.puzzles Archive (combinatorics), part 05 of 35
rec.puzzles Archive (competition), part 06 of 35
rec.puzzles Archive (competition), part 07 of 35
rec.puzzles Archive (competition), part 08 of 35
rec.puzzles Archive (competition), part 09 of 35
rec.puzzles Archive (competition), part 10 of 35
rec.puzzles Archive (cryptology), part 11 of 35
rec.puzzles Archive (decision), part 12 of 35
rec.puzzles Archive (geometry), part 13 of 35
rec.puzzles Archive (geometry), part 14 of 35

rec.puzzles Archive (group), part 15 of 35
rec.puzzles Archive (induction), part 16 of 35
rec.puzzles Archive (language), part 17 of 35
rec.puzzles Archive (language), part 18 of 35
rec.puzzles Archive (language), part 19 of 35
rec.puzzles Archive (language), part 20 of 35
rec.puzzles Archive (language), part 21 of 35
rec.puzzles Archive (logic), part 22 of 35
rec.puzzles Archive (logic), part 23 of 35
rec.puzzles Archive (logic), part 24 of 35
rec.puzzles Archive (logic), part 25 of 35
rec.puzzles Archive (logic), part 26 of 35
rec.puzzles Archive (physics), part 27 of 35
rec.puzzles Archive (pickover), part 28 of 35
rec.puzzles Archive (pickover), part 29 of 35
rec.puzzles Archive (pickover), part 30 of 35
rec.puzzles Archive (probability), part 31 of 35
rec.puzzles Archive (real-life), part 32 of 35
rec.puzzles Archive (references), part 33 of 35
rec.puzzles Archive (series), part 34 of 35
rec.puzzles Archive (trivia), part 35 of 35

rec.puzzles.crosswords:

Scrabble FAQ - Club and Tournament Supplement
Scrabble FAQ - General Information

rec.pyrotechnics:

rec.pyrotechnics	Fireworks, rocketry, safety, & other topics.
rec.pyrotechnics FAQ	

rec.radio.*:

rec.radio.amateur.antenna	Antenna discussion.
rec.radio.amateur.digital.misc	Digital discussion.
rec.radio.amateur.equipment	Amateur radio equipment discussion.
rec.radio.amateur.homebrew	
rec.radio.amateur.misc	Amateur radio practices, contests,...

rec.radio.* (continued):

rec.radio.amateur.packet	Discussion about packet radio.
rec.radio.amateur.policy	Radio use & regulation policy.
rec.radio.amateur.space	Issues related to space.
rec.radio.broadcasting	Local area broadcast radio. (Moderated)
rec.radio.cb	Citizen-band radio.
rec.radio.info	Informational postings related to radio.
rec.radio.noncomm	Topics relating to noncommercial radio.
rec.radio.shortwave	Shortwave radio enthusiasts.
rec.radio.swap	Offers to trade and swap radio equipment.

rec.radio.amateur.antenna:

Guide to the Personal Radio Newsgroups

rec.radio.amateur.digital.misc:

Guide to the Personal Radio Newsgroups
Welcome to rec.radio.info!
rec.radio.amateur.digital.misc Frequently Asked Questions

rec.radio.amateur.equipment:

Guide to the Personal Radio Newsgroups

rec.radio.amateur.homebrew:

Guide to the Personal Radio Newsgroups
My List of Mail Order Electronics Companies

rec.radio.amateur.misc:

Amateur Radio Elmers List Info and Administrivia
Amateur Radio Elmers Resource Directory
Changes to Amateur Radio Elmers Resource Directory
Examination Opportunities Scheduled 7 22 93 to 10 25 93
Guide to the Personal Radio Newsgroups
How to find the answers to frequently-asked questions about Ham Radio

Index to the rec.radio.amateur.* Supplemental Archives
My List of Mail Order Electronics Companies
Radio Amateurs on USENET List Jul 1993 Part 1 of 6
Radio Amateurs on USENET List Jul 1993 Part 2 of 6
Radio Amateurs on USENET List Jul 1993 Part 3 of 6
Radio Amateurs on USENET List Jul 1993 Part 4 of 6
Radio Amateurs on USENET List Jul 1993 Part 5 of 6
Radio Amateurs on USENET List Jul 1993 Part 6 of 6
Welcome to rec.radio.info!
rec.radio.amateur.misc Frequently Asked Questions (Part 1 of 3)
rec.radio.amateur.misc Frequently Asked Questions (Part 2 of 3)
rec.radio.amateur.misc Frequently Asked Questions (Part 3 of 3)

rec.radio.amateur.packet:

Guide to the Personal Radio Newsgroups
Welcome to rec.radio.info!
rec.radio.amateur.digital.misc Frequently Asked Questions
rec.radio.amateur.packet Frequently Asked Questions

rec.radio.amateur.policy:

Guide to the Personal Radio Newsgroups
Welcome to rec.radio.info!

rec.radio.amateur.space:

Guide to the Personal Radio Newsgroups
Welcome to rec.radio.info!

rec.radio.cb:

Guide to the Personal Radio Newsgroups
Welcome to rec.radio.info!
rec.radio.cb Frequently Asked Questions (Part 1 of 4)
rec.radio.cb Frequently Asked Questions (Part 2 of 4)
rec.radio.cb Frequently Asked Questions (Part 3 of 4)
rec.radio.cb Frequently Asked Questions (Part 4 of 4)

rec.radio.info:

(PKT): Daily Solar Geophysical Data Broadcast for 12 August
(PKT): Daily Solar Geophysical Data Broadcast for 13 August
(PKT): Daily Solar Geophysical Data Broadcast for 14 August
(PKT): Daily Solar Geophysical Data Broadcast for 15 August
(PKT): Daily Solar Geophysical Data Broadcast for 16 August
(PKT): Daily Solar Geophysical Data Broadcast for 17 August
(PKT): Daily Summary of Ionospheric Data (1 2) for 12 August
(PKT): Daily Summary of Ionospheric Data (1 2) for 14 August
(PKT): Daily Summary of Ionospheric Data (1 2) for 15 August
(PKT): Daily Summary of Ionospheric Data (1 2) for 16 August
(PKT): Daily Summary of Ionospheric Data (1 2) for 17 August
(PKT): Daily Summary of Ionospheric Data (1 3) for 13 August
(PKT): Daily Summary of Ionospheric Data (2 2) for 12 August
(PKT): Daily Summary of Ionospheric Data (2 2) for 14 August
(PKT): Daily Summary of Ionospheric Data (2 2) for 15 August
(PKT): Daily Summary of Ionospheric Data (2 2) for 16 August
(PKT): Daily Summary of Ionospheric Data (2 2) for 17 August
(PKT): Daily Summary of Ionospheric Data (2 3) for 13 August
(PKT): Daily Summary of Ionospheric Data (3 3) for 13 August
A Guide to Buying and Selling on Usenet
Amateur Radio Elmers List Info and Administrivia
Amateur Radio Elmers Resource Directory
Changes to Amateur Radio Elmers Resource Directory
Daily IPS Report - 13 Aug 93
Daily IPS Report - 14 Aug 93
Daily IPS Report - 15 Aug 93
Daily IPS Report - 16 Aug 93
Daily IPS Report - 17 Aug 93
Daily IPS Report - 18 Aug 93
Daily IPS Report - 19 Aug 93
Daily Summary of Ionospheric Data for 12 August
Daily Summary of Ionospheric Data for 13 August
Daily Summary of Ionospheric Data for 14 August
Daily Summary of Ionospheric Data for 15 August
Daily Summary of Ionospheric Data for 16 August
Daily Summary of Ionospheric Data for 17 August
Daily Summary of Solar Geophysical Activity for 12 August
Daily Summary of Solar Geophysical Activity for 13 August

Recreation

Daily Summary of Solar Geophysical Activity for 14 August

Daily Summary of Solar Geophysical Activity for 15 August

Daily Summary of Solar Geophysical Activity for 16 August

Daily Summary of Solar Geophysical Activity for 17 August

Examination Opportunities Scheduled 7 22 93 to 10 25 93

Guide to the Personal Radio Newsgroups

How to find the answers to frequently-asked questions about Ham Radio

Index to the rec.radio.amateur.* Supplemental Archives

My List of Mail Order Electronics Companies

Radio Amateurs on USENET List Jul 1993 Part 1 of 6

Radio Amateurs on USENET List Jul 1993 Part 2 of 6

Radio Amateurs on USENET List Jul 1993 Part 3 of 6

Radio Amateurs on USENET List Jul 1993 Part 4 of 6

Radio Amateurs on USENET List Jul 1993 Part 5 of 6

Radio Amateurs on USENET List Jul 1993 Part 6 of 6

Weekly IPS Report - 13 Aug 93

Welcome to rec.radio.info!

Welcome to rec.radio.shortwave

Welcome to rec.radio.shortwave (AM FM DXing)

Welcome to rec.radio.shortwave (Scanning)

Welcome to rec.radio.shortwave (Shortwave)

nic.funet.fi: pub dx new files [week 31]

nic.funet.fi: pub dx new files [week 32]

rec.radio.amateur.digital.misc Frequently Asked Questions

rec.radio.amateur.misc Frequently Asked Questions (Part 1 of 3)

rec.radio.amateur.misc Frequently Asked Questions (Part 2 of 3)

rec.radio.amateur.misc Frequently Asked Questions (Part 3 of 3)

rec.radio.amateur.packet Frequently Asked Questions

rec.radio.cb Frequently Asked Questions (Part 1 of 4)

rec.radio.cb Frequently Asked Questions (Part 2 of 4)

rec.radio.cb Frequently Asked Questions (Part 3 of 4)

rec.radio.cb Frequently Asked Questions (Part 4 of 4)

rec.radio.info Submission Guidelines

rec.radio.noncomm:

Welcome to rec.radio.info!

rec.radio.shortwave:

Handy Shortwave Chart
Phone line as SW antenna
Welcome to rec.radio.info!
Welcome to rec.radio.shortwave
Welcome to rec.radio.shortwave (AM FM DXing)
Welcome to rec.radio.shortwave (Scanning)
Welcome to rec.radio.shortwave (Shortwave)
nic.funet.fi: pub dx new files [week 31]
nic.funet.fi: pub dx new files [week 32]

rec.radio.swap:

A Guide to Buying and Selling on Usenet

rec.railroad:

rec.railroad   Real and model train fans' newsgroup.

rec.roller-coaster:

rec.roller-coaster   Roller coasters and other amusement park ri
rec.roller-coaster FAQ, part 1 3: General info & introduction
rec.roller-coaster FAQ, part 2 3: Coaster info, orgs, and refs
rec.roller-coaster FAQ, part 3 3: lists and statistics

rec.running:

rec.running   Running for enjoyment, sport, exercise, etc.
rec.running FAQ part 1 of 3
rec.running FAQ part 2 of 3
rec.running FAQ part 3 of 3

rec.scouting:

rec.scouting   Scouting youth organizations worldwide.
rec.scouting FAQ#1: Skits, Yells & Creative Campfires (1 2)
rec.scouting FAQ#1: Skits, Yells & Creative Campfires (2 2)
rec.scouting FAQ #0: Welcome to rec.scouting - General questions
rec.scouting FAQ #2: Scouting around the World

rec.scouting FAQ #3: Games (1 3)
rec.scouting FAQ #3: Games (2 3)
rec.scouting FAQ #3: Games (3 3)
rec.scouting FAQ #4: Unit Administration
rec.scouting FAQ #5: Silk Screen Techniques
rec.scouting FAQ #6: Cub Scout Leader Hints
rec.scouting FAQ #7: Fund Raising Ideas
rec.scouting FAQ #8: BSA GSUSA official policies (gays in scouting)

rec.scuba:

rec.scuba   Hobbyists interested in SCUBA diving.

[rec.scuba] FAQ: Frequently Asked Questions about Scuba, Monthly Posting

rec.skate:

rec.skate   Ice skating and roller skating.

Rec.skate FAQ: (Roller)Hockey (3 8)
Rec.skate FAQ: In-line Skate reviews (5 8)
Rec.skate FAQ: What and Where to Buy (4 8)
Rec.skate FAQ: Where to Skate (Indoors) (6 8)
Rec.skate FAQ: Where to Skate (Outdoors) Sec. 1 (7 8)
Rec.skate FAQ: Where to Skate (Outdoors) Sec. 2 (8 8)
Rec.skate FAQ: Wheels, Bearings, and Brakes (2 8)
Rec.skate Frequently-Asked Questions: General Info (1 8)

rec.skiing:

rec.skiing   Hobbyists interested in snow skiing.

rec.skydiving:

rec.skydiving   Hobbyists interested in skydiving.

rec.skydiving FAQ (Frequently Asked Questions)

rec.sport.*:

rec.sport.baseball   Discussion about baseball.

rec.sport.baseball.college   Baseball on the collegiate level.

rec.sport.baseball.fantasy   Rotisserie (fantasy) baseball playing.

rec.sport.* (continued):

rec.sport.basketball	Discussion about basketball.
rec.sport.basketball.college	Hoops on the collegiate level.
rec.sport.basketball.misc	Discussion about basketball.
rec.sport.basketball.pro	Talk of professional basketball.
rec.sport.cricket	Discussion about the sport of cricket.
rec.sport.cricket.scores	Scores from cricket matches around the world.
rec.sport.disc	Discussion of flying disc based objects.
rec.sport.fencing	All aspects of swordplay.
rec.sport.football	Discussion of football.
rec.sport.football.australian	Discussion of Australian (Rules).
rec.sport.football.canadian	Discussion of Canadian (Rules).
rec.sport.football.college	US-style college football.
rec.sport.football.misc	Discussion about American-style football.
rec.sport.football.pro	US-style professional football.
rec.sport.golf	Discussion about all aspects of golf.
rec.sport.hockey	Discussion about ice hockey.
rec.sport.hockey.field	Discussion of the sport of field hockey.
rec.sport.midget.tossing	Discussion of the sport of midget tossing.
rec.sport.misc	Spectator sports.
rec.sport.olympics	All aspects of the Olympic Games.
rec.sport.paintball	Discussing all aspects...
rec.sport.pro-wrestling	Discussion about professional wrestling.
rec.sport.rowing	Crew for competition or fitness.
rec.sport.rugby	Discussion about the game of rugby.
rec.sport.snowboarding	Discussion about snowboarding.
rec.sport.soccer	Discussion about soccer.
rec.sport.swimming	Training for and competing in swimming events.
rec.sport.table-tennis	Things related to table tennis.
rec.sport.tennis	Things related to the sport of tennis.

| rec.sport.triathlon | Discussing all aspects. |
| rec.sport.volleyball | Discussion about volleyball. |

rec.sport.disc:

rec.sport.disc FAQ - Part 1
rec.sport.disc FAQ - Part 2

rec.sport.fencing:

Fencing FAQ

rec.sport.football.misc:

Canadian Football League (CFL) - Frequently Asked Questions (FAQ)

rec.sport.football.pro:

Canadian Football League (CFL) - Frequently Asked Questions (FAQ)

rec.sport.hockey:

rec.sport.hockey FAQ Part 1 of 2
rec.sport.hockey FAQ Part 2 of 2
rec.sport.hockey Frequently Asked Questions

rec.sport.misc:

Pool & Billiards Frequently Asked Questions (FAQ)

rec.sport.pro-wrestling:

[rec.sport.pro-wrestling] FAQ: Wrestling Relations
[rec.sport.pro-wrestling] FAQ (part 01 02)
[rec.sport.pro-wrestling] FAQ (part 02 02)

rec.sport.tennis:

FAQ for rec.sport.tennis (1 4) - Tournaments
FAQ for rec.sport.tennis (2 4) - Rankings
FAQ for rec.sport.tennis (3 4) - Player Information
FAQ for rec.sport.tennis (4 4) - Miscellaneous

rec.sport.volleyball:

rec.sport.volleyball Frequently Asked Questions

rec.travel.*:

rec.travel	Traveling all over the world.
rec.travel.air	Airline travel around the world.
rec.travel.marketplace	Tickets and accomodations wanted and for sale.

Directory of tourist information offices worldwide
Directory of travel information available via internet
Index to rec.travel ftp archive
Simple suggestions for travel (net reminders really)

rec.travel.air:

FAQ: How to Get Cheap Airtickets 1 2 [Monthly posting]
FAQ: How to Get Cheap Airtickets 2 2 [Monthly posting]

rec.video:

rec.video	Video and video components.
rec.video.cable-tv	Technical and regulatory issues of cable television.
rec.video.production	Making professional quality video products.
rec.video.releases	Pre-recorded video releases on laserdisc.
rec.video.satellite	Getting shows via satellite.

rec.video.satellite:

Satellite TV Frequently Asked Questions List
rec.video.satellite: Pointer to the South Scanner Satellite Services Chart
rec.video.satellite: Pointer to the South Scanner Satellite Services Chart

rec.windsurfing:

rec.windsurfing	Riding the waves as a hobby.

rec.woodworking:

rec.woodworking   Hobbyists interested in woodworking.

Electrical Wiring FAQ
rec.woodworking Changes to Frequently Asked Questions
rec.woodworking Changes to Frequently Requested Addresses
rec.woodworking Electric Motors Frequently asked Questions
rec.woodworking Frequently Asked Questions
rec.woodworking Frequently Requested Addresses
rec.woodworking Frequently Requested Tool Reviews

Recreation

Issues of a scientific nature are discussed in this branch of the USENET newsgroup tree. In here you can find current happenings on NASA's latest scientific endeavor as well as a picture from your local weather satellite.

11

Science: The "sci" Newsgroups

sci.aeronautics.*:

sci.aeronautics	The science of aeronautics & related issues.
sci.aeronautics.airliners	Airliner technology. (Moderated)

sci.answers:

sci.answers	Repository for periodic USENET articles. (Moderated)

biology	*news-answers*
cryonics-faq	*physics-faq*
cryptography-faq	*sci-lang-faq*
fractal-faq	*sci-math-faq*
image-processing	*shamanism-overview*
index	*skeptic-faq*
index-	*space*
linear-programming-faq	*typing-injury-faq*
net-privacy	*weather-data*

sci.anthropology:

sci.anthropology	All aspects of studying humankind.

Shamanism-General Overview-Frequently Asked Questions (FAQ)

sci.aquaria:

sci.aquaria	Only scientifically-oriented postings.

FAQ: Beginner topics and books
FAQ: Filters
FAQ: Magazines and mail order
FAQ: Plants
FAQ: README and administrivia
FAQ: Water quality

sci.archaeology:

sci.archaeology	Studying antiquities of the world.

sci.astro.*:

sci.astro	Astronomy discussions and information.
sci.astro.fits	Issues related to the Flexible Image Transport.
sci.astro.hubble	Processing Hubble Space Telescope data. (Moderated)

Astro Space Frequently Seen Acronyms
Daily Solar Geophysical Data Broadcast for 06 August
Daily Solar Geophysical Data Broadcast for 15 August
Diffs to sci.space sci.astro Frequently Asked Questions
Earth and Sky - Week of August 9-13, 1993
*Electronic Journal of the ASA (EJASA) - August 1993 * FOURTH YEAR!*
NRAO RAP unRAPsheet #93-17, 20 August 1993
Purchasing Amateur Telescopes FAQ (part 1 2)
Purchasing Amateur Telescopes FAQ (part 2 2)
Sky & Telescope Weekly News Bulletin: 07Aug93
Sky & Telescope Weekly News Bulletin: 14Aug93
Space Calendar - 06 27 93
Space Calendar - 07 28 93
Space FAQ 01 13 - Introduction
Space FAQ 02 13 - Network Resources
Space FAQ 03 13 - Data Sources
Space FAQ 04 13 - Calculations
Space FAQ 05 13 - References
Weekly reminder for Frequently Asked Questions list

sci.astro.fits:

FITS basics and information (periodic posting)

sci.bio:

sci.bio	Biology and related sciences.
sci.bio.ecology	

A Biologist s Guide to Internet Resources

sci.chem.*:

sci.chem	Chemistry and related sciences.
sci.chem.organomet	Organometallic chemistry.

Science

sci.classics:

sci.classics   Studying classical history, languages, art,...

sci.classics FAQ

sci.cognitive:

sci.cognitive   Perception, memory, judgement and
                                      reasoning.

sci.comp-aided:

sci.comp-aided   The use of computers as tools in scientific
                                      research.

Diffs to Index of free C or C++ source code for numerical computation
Part 1 of 2: Free C,C++ for numerical computation
Part 2 of 2: Free C,C++ for numerical computation

sci.cryonics:

sci.cryonics   Theory and practice of biostasis, suspended
                                      animation.

Cryonics FAQ 1: Index
Cryonics FAQ 2: Science Technology
Cryonics FAQ 3: Philosophy Religion
Cryonics FAQ 4: Controversy surrounding Cryonics
Cryonics FAQ 5: Neurosuspension
Cryonics FAQ 6: Suspension Arrangements
Cryonics FAQ 7: Cost of Cryonics
Cryonics FAQ 8: Communications
Cryonics FAQ 9: Glossary

sci.crypt:

sci.crypt   Different methods of data en/decryption.

Cryptography FAQ (01 10: Overview; last mod 19930504)
Cryptography FAQ (02 10: Net Etiquette; last mod 19930504)
Cryptography FAQ (03 10: Basic Cryptology; last mod 19930504)
Cryptography FAQ (04 10: Mathematical Cryptology; last mod 19930504)
Cryptography FAQ (05 10: Product Ciphers; last mod 19930504)

Cryptography FAQ (06 10: Public Key Cryptography; last mod 19930504)
Cryptography FAQ (07 10: Digital Signatures; last mod 19930504)
Cryptography FAQ (08 10: Technical Miscellany; last mod 19930504)
Cryptography FAQ (09 10: Other Miscellany; last mod 19930504)
Cryptography FAQ (10 10: References; last mod 19930504)
Privacy & Anonymity on the Internet FAQ (1 of 3)
Privacy & Anonymity on the Internet FAQ (2 of 3)
Privacy & Anonymity on the Internet FAQ (3 of 3)
RIPEM Frequently Asked Questions
RIPEM Frequently Noted Vulnerabilities

sci.data.*

sci.data	Discussion of data.
sci.data.formats	Discussion of data formats.

sci.data.formats:

FITS basics and information (periodic posting)

sci.econ.*:

sci.econ	The science of economics.
sci.econ.research	

sci.edu:

sci.edu	The science of education.

sci.electronics:

sci.electronics	Circuits, theory, electrons and discussions.

My List of Mail Order Electronics Companies

sci.energy:

sci.energy	Discussions about energy, science & technology.

Science

sci.engr.*:

sci.engr	Technical discussions about engineering
sci.engr.biomed	Discussing the field of biomedical engi
sci.engr.chem	All aspects of chemical engineering.
sci.engr.civil	Topics related to civil engineering.
sci.engr.control	The engineering of control systems.
sci.engr.manufacturing	The engineering of manufacturing.
sci.engr.mech	The field of mechanical engineering.

sci.environment:

sci.environment	Discussions about the environment and ecology.

Electronic Journal of the ASA (EJASA) - August 1993 * FOURTH YEAR!

sci.fractals:

sci.fractals	Objects of non-integral dimension and other chaos.

Fractal FAQ

sci.geo.*:

sci.geo.fluids	Discussion of geophysical fluid dynamics.
sci.geo.geology	Discussion of solid earth sciences.
sci.geo.meteorology	Discussion of meteorology and related topi

sci.geo.geology:

Earth and Sky - Week of August 9-13, 1993
Electronic Journal of the ASA (EJASA) - August 1993 * FOURTH YEAR!

sci.geo.meteorology:

Sources of Meteorological Data FAQ
Tropical Cyclone Weekly Summary #105 (August 1 - 8, 1993)
Tropical Cyclone Weekly Summary #106 (August 8 - 15, 1993)

sci.image:

sci.image	Scientific image study.
sci.image.processing	Scientific image processing and analysis.

sci.image.processing:

MacImageProc
index

sci.lang.*:

sci.lang	Natural languages, communication, etc.
sci.lang.japan	The Japanese language, both spoken and written.

Monthly posting: TolkLang - mailing list on Tolkien s languages.
sci.lang FAQ (Frequently Asked Questions)

sci.logic:

sci.logic	Logic—math, philosophy & computational aspects.

sci.materials:

sci.materials	All aspects of materials engineering.

sci.math.*:

sci.math	Mathematical discussions and pursuits.
sci.math.num-analysis	Numerical Analysis.
sci.math.stat	Statistics discussion.
sci.math.symbolic	Symbolic algebra discussion.
sci.math.research	Discussion of current mathematical research.

sci.math: Frequently Asked Questions

sci.math.num-analysis:

Diffs to Index of free C or C++ source code for numerical computation
Linear Programming FAQ
Part 1 of 2: Free C,C++ for numerical computation
Part 2 of 2: Free C,C++ for numerical computation

Science

sci.med.*:

sci.med	Medicine and its related products.
sci.med.aids	AIDS: treatment, pathology/biology of HIV.
sci.med.dentistry	Dentally related topics; all about teeth.
sci.med.nutrition	Physiological impacts of diet.
sci.med.occupational	Preventing, detecting & treating occupational injuries.
sci.med.pharmacy	Pharmaceutical discussion.
sci.med.physics	Issues of physics in medical testing/care.
sci.med.telemedicine	

FAQ: Typing Injuries (1 5): Changes since last month [monthly posting]
FAQ: Typing Injuries (2 5): General Info [monthly posting]
FAQ: Typing Injuries (3 5): Keyboard Alternatives [monthly posting]
FAQ: Typing Injuries (4 5): Software Monitoring Tools [monthly posting]
FAQ: Typing Injuries (5 5): Furniture Information [monthly posting]

sci.med.occupational:

FAQ: Typing Injuries (1 5): Changes since last month [monthly posting]
FAQ: Typing Injuries (2 5): General Info [monthly posting]
FAQ: Typing Injuries (3 5): Keyboard Alternatives [monthly posting]
FAQ: Typing Injuries (4 5): Software Monitoring Tools [monthly posting]
FAQ: Typing Injuries (5 5): Furniture Information [monthly posting]

sci.military:

sci.military	Discussion about science & the military. (Moderated)

sci.misc:

sci.misc	Short-lived discussions on subjects in the sciences.

*Electronic Journal of the ASA (EJASA) - August 1993 * FOURTH YEAR!*

sci.nanotech:

sci.nanotech	Self-reproducing molecular-scale machines. (Moderated)

sci.optics:

sci.optics	Discussion relating to the science of optics.

sci.philosophy.*:

sci.philosophy.meta	Discussions within the scope of "MetaPhilosophy."
sci.philosophy.tech	Technical philosophy: math, science, logic.

sci.physics:

sci.physics	Physical laws, properties.
sci.physics.accelerators	Accelerators.
sci.physics.fusion	Info on fusion.
sci.physics.research	Current physics research.

Sci.physics Frequently Asked Questions - July 1993 - Part 1 2
Sci.physics Frequently Asked Questions - July 1993 - Part 2 2

sci.research:

sci.research	Research methods, funding, ethics, ...
sci.research.careers	Issues relevant to careers in scientific

sci.skeptic:

sci.skeptic	Skeptics discussing pseudo-science.

Blue Star LSD-laced tattoo transfer rumor FAQ
sci.skeptic FAQ: The Frequently Questioned Answers

sci.space.*:

sci.space	Space, space programs, space related research.
sci.space.news	Announcements of space-related news items. (Moderated)
sci.space.shuttle	The space shuttle and the STS program.

Astro Space Frequently Seen Acronyms
Diffs to sci.space sci.astro Frequently Asked Questions
*Electronic Journal of the ASA (EJASA) - August 1993 * FOURTH YEAR!*

Science

sci.space.* (continued):

Space Calendar - 06 27 93
Space Calendar - 07 28 93
Space FAQ 01 13 - Introduction
Space FAQ 02 13 - Network Resources
Space FAQ 03 13 - Data Sources
Space FAQ 04 13 - Calculations
Space FAQ 05 13 - References
Space FAQ 06 13 - Addresses
Space FAQ 07 13 - Mission Schedules
Space FAQ 08 13 - Planetary Probe History
Space FAQ 09 13 - Upcoming Planetary Probes
Space FAQ 10 13 - Controversial Questions
Space FAQ 11 13 - Interest Groups & Publications
Space FAQ 12 13 - How to Become an Astronaut
Space FAQ 13 13 - Orbital and Planetary Launch Services
Weekly reminder for Frequently Asked Questions list

sci.space.new:

Earth and Sky - Week of August 9-13, 1993

sci.space.shuttle:

Astro Space Frequently Seen Acronyms
Space Calendar - 07 28 93
Weekly reminder for Frequently Asked Questions list

sci.systems:

sci.systems   The theory and application of systems
                               science.

sci.virtual:

sci.virtual-worlds   Modeling the universe. (Moderated)

All things of a social nature are discussed in this branch of USENET. In here you will find newsgroups devoted to specific cultures and special interest groups. This is the place to look for a pen pal.

12

Society: The "soc" Newsgroups

soc.answers:

soc.answers	Repository for periodic USENET articles. (Moderated)

Quaker-faq	*holocaust*
SCItalian-faq	*hungarian-faq*
Turkish-FAQ	*index*
address-book	*index-*
bahai-faith	*india-faq*
bisexual	*iranian-faq*
culture-french-faq	*judaism*
esperanto-faq	*lebanon-faq*
feminism	*mail*
finding-addresses	*mexican-faq*
german-faq	*news-answers*
greek-faq	*shamanism-overview*

soc.bi:

soc.bi	Discussions of bisexuality.

Bisexual Resource List (monthly posting)
Gay & Lesbian BBS List - June 1993
soc.bi FAQ

soc.college.*:

soc.college	College, college activities, campus, ...
soc.college.grad	General issues related to graduate school.
soc.college.gradinfo	Information about graduate schools.
soc.college.teaching-asst	

FAQ: College Email Addresses 1 3 [Monthly posting]
FAQ: College Email Addresses 2 3 [Monthly posting]
FAQ: College Email Addresses 3 3 [Monthly posting]

soc.couples:

soc.couples	Discussions for couples (cf. soc.singles).

soc.culture.*:

soc.culture.afghanistan	Discussion of the Afghan society.
soc.culture.african	Discussions about Africa & things related.
soc.culture.african.american	Discussions about Afro-American.
soc.culture.arabic	Technological & cultural issues.
soc.culture.argentina	Discussion about things Argentine.
soc.culture.asean	Countries of the Assoc. of SE Asia.
soc.culture.asian.american	Issues & discussion about Asian-American.
soc.culture.australian	Australian culture and society.
soc.culture.austria	Austria culture and society.
soc.culture.baltics	People of the Baltic states.
soc.culture.bangladesh	Issues & discussion about Bangladesh.
soc.culture.bosna-herzgvna	The indepedent state of Bosnia...
soc.culture.brazil	Talking about the people and country of Brazil.
soc.culture.british	Issues about Britain & those of British decent.
soc.culture.bulgaria	Discussing Bulgarian society.
soc.culture.canada	Discussions of Canada and its people.
soc.culture.caribbean	Life in the Caribbean.
soc.culture.celtic	Irish, Scottish, Breton, Cornish,
soc.culture.china	About China and Chinese culture.
soc.culture.cis	
soc.culture.croatia	The lives of people of Croatia.
soc.culture.czecho-slovak	Bohemian, Slovak, Moravian and ...
soc.culture.esperanto	The neutral international language.
soc.culture.europe	Discussing all aspects of all-Europe.
soc.culture.filipino	Group about the Filipino culture.
soc.culture.french	French culture, history, and ...
soc.culture.german	Discussions about German culture.
soc.culture.greek	Group about Greeks.
soc.culture.hongkong	Discussions pertaining to Hong Kong.
soc.culture.indian	Group for discussion about India.

soc.culture. (continued):*

soc.culture.indian.american	Discussion about American Indian culture.
soc.culture.indian.telugu	The culture of the Telugu people.
soc.culture.indonesia	The culture of Indonesia.
soc.culture.iranian	Discussions about Iran and things Iranian.
soc.culture.italian	The Italian people and their culture.
soc.culture.japan	Everything Japanese...
soc.culture.jewish	Jewish culture & religion.
soc.culture.korean	Discussions about Korean & things.
soc.culture.latin-america	Topics about Latin-America.
soc.culture.lebanon	Discussion about things Lebanese.
soc.culture.maghreb	Discussion about things Moroccan.
soc.culture.magyar	The Hungarian people & their culture.
soc.culture.malaysia	All about Malaysian society.
soc.culture.mexican	Discussion of Mexico's society.
soc.culture.misc	Group for discussion about other cultures.
soc.culture.native	Aboriginal people around the world.
soc.culture.nepal	Discussion of people and things in Nepal.
soc.culture.netherlands	People from the Netherlands.
soc.culture.new-zealand	Discussion of topics related to New Zealand.
soc.culture.nordic	Discussion about culture up north.
soc.culture.pakistan	Topics of discussion about Pakistan.
soc.culture.peru	Discussion about Peruvian culture.
soc.culture.polish	Polish culture, Polish past, and Polish future.
soc.culture.portuguese	Discussion of the people of Portugal.
soc.culture.romanian	Discussion of Romanian and Moldavian.
soc.culture.singapore	The past, present and future of Singapore.
soc.culture.soviet	Topics relating to Russian or Soviet Union.
soc.culture.spain	Discussion of culture on the Iberian...
soc.culture.sri-lanka	Things & people from Sri Lanka.
soc.culture.taiwan	Discussion about things Taiwanese.
soc.culture.tamil	Tamil language, history and culture.

soc.culture.thai	Thai people and their culture.
soc.culture.turkish	Discussion about things Turkish.
soc.culture.ukrainian	Discussion about things Ukrainian.
soc.culture.usa	The culture of the United States.
soc.culture.venezuela	The culture of Venezuela.
soc.culture.vietnamese	Issues and discussions of Vietnam.
soc.culture.yugoslavia	Discussions of Yugoslavia.

soc.culture.african.american:

Caribana 93 - Frequently Asked Questions (FAQ)

soc.culture.asian.american:

soc.culture.asian.american FAQ

soc.culture.caribbean:

Caribana 93 - Frequently Asked Questions (FAQ)

soc.culture.china:

soc.culture.hongkong FAQ, Part II

soc.culture.esperanto:

soc.culture.esperanto Frequently Asked Questions (Oftaj Demandoj)

soc.culture.esperanto.news.answers:

esperanto-faq
index

soc.culture.europe:

Hungarian electronic resources FAQ

Society

soc.culture.french:

FAQ: soc.culture.french - Changes since last posting [monthly]
FAQ: soc.culture.french - Contents [monthly]
FAQ: soc.culture.french - French language [monthly]
FAQ: soc.culture.french - Intro [monthly]
FAQ: soc.culture.french - Medias [monthly]
FAQ: soc.culture.french - Misc. 1 1 [monthly]
FAQ: soc.culture.french - Networking 1 2 [monthly]
FAQ: soc.culture.french - Networking 2 2 [monthly]
FAQ: soc.culture.french - Restaurants [monthly]
FAQ: soc.culture.french 1 2 [monthly]
FAQ: soc.culture.french 2 2 [monthly]

soc.culture.german:

FAQ: soc.culture.german Frequently Asked Questions (posted monthly)

soc.culture.greek:

(20 July 93) Soc.Culture.Greek FAQ - Culture
(20 July 93) Soc.Culture.Greek FAQ - Linguistics
(20 July 93) Soc.Culture.Greek FAQ - Technical Information
(20 July 93) Soc.Culture.Greek FAQ - Tourist Information

soc.culture.hongkong:

Chinese BIG5 environment: FAQ of alt.chinese.text.big5
soc.culture.hongkong FAQ, Part I
soc.culture.hongkong FAQ, Part II
soc.culture.hongkong FAQ, Part III
soc.culture.hongkong FAQ, Part IV

soc.culture.indian:

[soc.culture.indian] FREQUENTLY ASKED QUESTIONS

soc.culture.iranian:

soc.culture.iranian: Frequently Asked Questions [monthly posting]

soc.culture.italian:

s.c.italian Frequently Asked Questions (FAQ) [1 3]
s.c.italian Frequently Asked Questions (FAQ) [2 3]
s.c.italian Frequently Asked Questions (FAQ) [3 3]

soc.culture.japan:

Soc.culture.japan references [Monthly Posting]

soc.culture.jewish:

Judaism Reading List: Antisemitism and Christian Relations (Pt. IX)
Judaism Reading List: Conservative Judaism (Pt. V)
Judaism Reading List: Humanistic Judaism (Pt. VII)
Judaism Reading List: Intermarriage (Pt. X)
Judaism Reading List: Introduction and General (Pt. I)
Judaism Reading List: Kabbalah and Chasidism (Pt. III)
Judaism Reading List: Periodicals (Pt. XI)
Judaism Reading List: Reconstructionist Judaism (Pt. VI)
Judaism Reading List: Reform Judaism (Pt. IV)
Judaism Reading List: Trad. Lit. and Practice (Pt. II)
Judaism Reading List: Zionism (Pt. VIII)
soc.culture.jewish FAQ: Holocaust, Antisemitism, Missionaries (9 10)
soc.culture.jewish FAQ: Introduction to the FAQ and s.c.j (1 10)
soc.culture.jewish FAQ: Jewish Thought (6 10)
soc.culture.jewish FAQ: Jews As A Nation (7 10)
soc.culture.jewish FAQ: Jews and Israel (8 10)
soc.culture.jewish FAQ: Miscellaneous and References (10 10)
soc.culture.jewish FAQ: Observance, Marriage, Women in Judaism (4 10)
soc.culture.jewish FAQ: Torah and Halachic Authority (3 10)
soc.culture.jewish FAQ: Who We Are (2 10)
soc.culture.jewish FAQ: Worship, Conversion, Intermarriage (5 10)

soc.culture.latin-america:

soc.culture.mexican FAQ (Monthly Reposting)
soc.culture.mexican FAQ (Periodic Posting)

soc.culture.lebanon:

soc.culture.lebanon FAQ, part 1 2
soc.culture.lebanon FAQ, part 2 2

soc.culture.magyar:

Hungarian electronic resources FAQ

soc.culture.mexican:

soc.culture.mexican FAQ (Monthly Reposting)
soc.culture.mexican FAQ (Periodic Posting)

soc.culture.native:

Shamanism-General Overview-Frequently Asked Questions (FAQ)

soc.culture.netherlands:

CHART: Dutch Albums
CHART: Dutch Singles

soc.culture.taiwan:

Chinese BIG5 environment: FAQ of alt.chinese.text.big5
soc.culture.hongkong FAQ, Part II

soc.culture.turkish:

[FAQ] Soc.Culture.Turkish Frequently Answered Questions

soc.feminism:

soc.feminism   Discussion of feminism & feminist issues.
                                      (Moderated)

soc.feminism Information
soc.feminism References (part 1 of 3)
soc.feminism References (part 2 of 3)
soc.feminism References (part 3 of 3)
soc.feminism Resources
soc.feminism Terminologies

soc.history:

soc.history   Discussions of things historical.

HOLOCAUST FAQ: Auschwitz-Birkenau: Layman s Guide (1 2)
HOLOCAUST FAQ: Auschwitz-Birkenau: Layman s Guide (2 2)
HOLOCAUST FAQ: Operation Reinhard: A Layman s Guide (1 2)
HOLOCAUST FAQ: Operation Reinhard: A Layman s Guide (2 2)
HOLOCAUST FAQ: The Leuchter Report (1 2)
HOLOCAUST FAQ: The Leuchter Report (2 2)
HOLOCAUST FAQ: Willis Carto & The Institute for Historical Review (1 2)
HOLOCAUST FAQ: Willis Carto & The Institute for Historical Review (2 2)

soc.libraries.*:

soc.libraries   Library discussion.

soc.libraries.talk   Discussing all aspects of libraries.

soc.men:

soc.men   Issues related to men, their problems & relationships.

soc.misc:

soc.misc   Socially-oriented topics not in other groups.

soc.motss:

soc.motss   Issues pertaining to homosexuality.

Bisexual Resource List (monthly posting)
Gay & Lesbian BBS List - June 1993
rec.scouting FAQ #8: BSA GSUSA official policies (gays in scouting)

soc.net-people:

soc.net-people   Announcements, requests, etc. about people.

FAQ: College Email Addresses 1 3 [Monthly posting]
FAQ: College Email Addresses 2 3 [Monthly posting]
FAQ: College Email Addresses 3 3 [Monthly posting]
FAQ: How to find people s E-mail addresses
Tips on using soc.net-people [l.m. 10 04 92]

Society

soc.penpals:

soc.penpals   In search of net.friendships.

Email-Pal Address Book [US list][A-M]
Email-Pal Address Book [US list][N-W]
Email-Pal Address Book [US list][N-Z]
Email-Pal Address Book [non-US list][A-M]
Email-Pal Address Book [non-US list][N-U]

soc.politics.*:

soc.politics   Political problems, systems, solutions. (Moderated)

soc.politics.arms-d   Arms discussion digest. (Moderated)

soc.religion.*:

soc.religion.bahai   Discussion of the Baha'i.

soc.religion.christian   Christianity and related issues.

soc.religion.christian.bible-study   Examining the Holy Bible. (Moderated)

soc.religion.eastern   Discussions of Eastern religions.

soc.religion.islam   Discussions of the Islamic religion.

soc.religion.quaker   The Religious Society of ...

soc.religion.bahai:

Baha i Faith Annotated Bibliography
Baha i Faith Introduction
Welcome to soc.religion.bahai

soc.religion.quaker:

soc.religion.quaker Answers to Frequently Asked Questions

Some topics are subject to prolonged discussion. This branch of USENET is the place for just such topics. Philosophy, politics and religion are a few of the topics you will find in here.

13

Talk: The "talk" Newsgroups

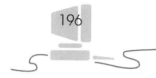

talk.abortion:

talk.abortion

All sorts of discussions and arguments on abortion.

talk.answers:

talk.answers

Repository for periodic USENET articles. (Moderated)s

drug-law-reformers
drugs
index
libertarian

news-answers
talk-bizarre
talk-origins

talk.bizarre.*:

talk.bizarre

The unusual, bizarre, curious,...

talk.bizarre.rabbit

Welcome to talk.bizarre! (Monthly Posting)

talk.environment:

talk.environment

Discussion on the state of the environment.

*Electronic Journal of the ASA (EJASA) - August 1993 * FOURTH YEAR!*

talk.origins:

talk.origins

Evolution versus creationism (sometimes hot!).

talk.origins Welcome FAQ v.1.1

talk.philosophy.*:

talk.philosophy

Discussion about philosophy.

talk.philosophy.misc

Philosophical musings on all topics.

talk.politics.*:

talk.politics.animals

The use and/or abuse of animals.

talk.politics.china

Discussion of political issues related to China.

talk.politics.cis

talk.politics.drugs	The politics of drug issues.
talk.politics.guns	The politics of firearm ownership...
talk.politics.medicine	The politics and ethics involved with health.
talk.politics.mideast	Discussion & debate over Middle Eastern topics.
talk.politics.misc	Political discussions and ravings of all sorts.
talk.politics.space	Non-technical issues affecting space.
talk.politics.soviet	Discussion of Soviet politics, domestic and international.
talk.politics.theory	Theory of politics and political systems.

talk.politics.drugs:

GROUPS: *Anti War-on-Drugs Activists List*
The Great Usenet Piss List Monthly Posting

talk.politics.misc:

Libertarian Frequently Asked Questions
Libertarian Organizations
Libertarian World s Smallest Political Quiz [periodic posting]

talk.politics.space:

*Electronic Journal of the ASA (EJASA) - August 1993 * FOURTH YEAR!*

talk.rape:

| talk.rape | Discussions on stopping rape; not to be crossposted. |

talk.religion.*:

| talk.religion.misc | Religious, ethical, & moral implications. |
| talk.religion.newage | Esoteric and minority religions & philosophies. |

talk.rumors:

| talk.rumors | For the posting of rumors. |

USENET's core newsgroup hierarchies are a way for discriminating computer system administrators to limit the quantity of the newsgroups their sites receive. Restricting subscriptions to just the core newsgroups is also a way of providing an (almost) certain level of quality of the content of the newsgroups. The "alt.*" hierarchy is a place to put your discussion if the discussion doesn't fit within USENET's core hierarchies. Unabashed anarchy is what takes place within this set of newsgroups.

In this chapter we look at four of the high volume subgroups of the alternative USENET hierarchy: alt.binaries.*, alt.fan.*, alt.sex.* and alt.tv.*.

14

Worthy Mentions from the Alternative Set

Binary Files

The alt.binaries.* set of newsgroups is a place to put files that contain material that can not be directly viewed by human eyes. These are files that require special processing to put them in their usable form. Some contain pictures. Other contain computer programs. Most take up a lot of disk space.

alt.binaries.:*

alt.binaries.multimedia

alt.binaries.pictures

alt.binaries.pictures.d

alt.binaries.pictures.erotica

alt.binaries.pictures.erotica.blondes

alt.binaries.pictures.erotica.children

alt.binaries.pictures.erotica.d

alt.binaries.pictures.erotica.female

alt.binaries.pictures.erotica.male

alt.binaries.pictures.erotica.orientals

alt.binaries.pictures.fine-art.d

alt.binaries.pictures.fine-art.graphics

alt.binaries.pictures.fine-art.digitized

alt.binaries.pictures.fractals

alt.binaries.pictures.furniture

alt.binaries.pictures.misc

alt.binaries.pictures.supermodels

alt.binaries.pictures.tasteless

alt.binaries.pictures.utilities

alt.binaries.sounds-armpit.noises

alt.binaries.sounds.d

alt.binaries.sounds.misc

alt.binaries.sounds.music

alt.binaries.pictures.d:

JPEG image compression: Frequently Asked Questions
alt.binaries.pictures FAQ - General Etiquette
alt.binaries.pictures FAQ - General info
alt.binaries.pictures FAQ - OS specific info

alt.binaries.pictures.erotica:

JPEG image compression: Frequently Asked Questions
THE WHAT WHERE WHY HOW FOR PICTURES
alt.binaries.pictures FAQ - General Etiquette
alt.binaries.pictures FAQ - General info
alt.binaries.pictures FAQ - OS specific info

alt.binaries.pictures.erotica.d:

JPEG image compression: Frequently Asked Questions
THE WHAT WHERE WHY HOW FOR PICTURES
alt.binaries.pictures FAQ - General Etiquette
alt.binaries.pictures FAQ - General info
alt.binaries.pictures FAQ - OS specific info

alt.binaries.pictures.fine-art.d:

alt.binaries.pictures FAQ - General Etiquette
alt.binaries.pictures FAQ - General info
alt.binaries.pictures FAQ - OS specific info
fine art digitized groups general info, welcome and FAQ

alt.binaries.pictures.fine-art.digitized:

fine art digitized groups general info, welcome and FAQ

alt.binaries.pictures.fine-art.graphics:

fine art digitized groups general info, welcome and FAQ

alt.binaries.pictures.fractals:

alt.binaries.pictures FAQ - General Etiquette
alt.binaries.pictures FAQ - General info
alt.binaries.pictures FAQ - OS specific info

alt.binaries.pictures.misc:

alt.binaries.pictures FAQ - General Etiquette
alt.binaries.pictures FAQ - General info
alt.binaries.pictures FAQ - OS specific info

alt.binaries.pictures.tasteless:

THE WHAT WHERE WHY HOW FOR PICTURES
alt.binaries.pictures FAQ - General Etiquette
alt.binaries.pictures FAQ - General info
alt.binaries.pictures FAQ - OS specific info

alt.binaries.pictures.utilities:

JPEG image compression: Frequently Asked Questions
alt.binaries.pictures FAQ - General Etiquette
alt.binaries.pictures FAQ - General info
alt.binaries.pictures FAQ - OS specific info

alt.binaries.sounds.d:

Changes to: FAQ: Audio File Formats
FAQ: Audio File Formats (part 1 of 2)
FAQ: Audio File Formats (part 2 of 2)

alt.binaries.sounds.misc:

Changes to: FAQ: Audio File Formats
FAQ: Audio File Formats (part 1 of 2)
FAQ: Audio File Formats (part 2 of 2)

Rabid Fandom

The alt.fan.* set of newsgroups is included here to give you a feel for the range of things people are talking about in USENET's alternative hierarchy. If a person or character has a fan club, chances are they also have a USENET newsgroup devoted to them.

alt.fan.*:

alt.fan.albedo

alt.fan.alok.vijayvargia

alt.fan.amy-fisher

alt.fan.andrew-beal

alt.fan.asprin

alt.fan.bgcrisis

alt.fan.BIFF

alt.fan.bill-fenner

alt.fan.bill-gates

alt.fan.bruce-becker

alt.fan.bruce.woodcock

alt.fan.buaf

alt.fan.bugtown

alt.fan.charles-lasner

alt.fan.chris-elliott

alt.fan.dale-bass

alt.fan.dall-agata

alt.fan.dall-agata.ctl

alt.fan.dan-quayle

alt.fan.dan-wang

alt.fan.dave-williams

alt.fan.dave_barry

alt.fan.devo

alt.fan.dick-depew

alt.fan.disney.afternoon

alt.fan.don.no-soul.simmons

alt.fan.douglas-adams

alt.fan.ecsd

alt.fan.eddings

alt.fan.enya

alt.fan.eric-dynamic

alt.fan.frank-zappa

alt.fan.furry

alt.fan.g-gordon-liddy

alt.fan.gene-scott

alt.fan.gooley

alt.fan.goons

alt.fan.greaseman

alt.fan.harry-mandel

alt.fan.hofstadter

alt.fan.holmes

alt.fan.howard-stern

alt.fan.howard-stern.fartman

alt.fan.hurricane.yip

alt.fan.itchy-n-scratchy

alt.fan.jai-maharaj

alt.fan.james-bond

alt.fan.jeff-witty

alt.fan.jen-coolest

alt.fan.jik

alt.fan.* (continued):

alt.fan.jimmy-buffett	alt.fan.ren-and-stimpy
alt.fan.jiro-nakamura	alt.fan.riscos
alt.fan.joel-furr	alt.fan.robbie.pink.tutu
alt.fan.john-palmer	alt.fan.robert-whaley
alt.fan.jokke	alt.fan.robert.mcelwaine
alt.fan.karl-malden.nose	alt.fan.roger.david.carasso
alt.fan.karla-homolka	alt.fan.ronald-reagan
alt.fan.ken-johnson	alt.fan.rumpole
alt.fan.kent-montana	alt.fan.run-dmc
alt.fan.kevin-darcy	alt.fan.rush-limbaugh
alt.fan.kevin-walsh	alt.fan.schwaben
alt.fan.laurie.anderson	alt.fan.scott
alt.fan.lemurs	alt.fan.scott-tai
alt.fan.lemurs.cooked	alt.fan.sean.corey.dewme
alt.fan.letterman	alt.fan.serdar-argic
alt.fan.lightbulbs	alt.fan.skinny
alt.fan.madonna	alt.fan.spinal-tap
alt.fan.maria-callas	alt.fan.steve-zellers
alt.fan.matt.welsh	alt.fan.suicide-squid
alt.fan.mike-jittlov	alt.fan.tania.bedrax
alt.fan.monty-python	alt.fan.tank-girl
alt.fan.mst3k	alt.fan.thunder-thumbs
alt.fan.naked-guy	alt.fan.TinyTIM
alt.fan.nathan.brazil	alt.fan.tna
alt.fan.oingo-boingo	alt.fan.tom-robbins
alt.fan.pern	alt.fan.tom_peterson
alt.fan.peter.hammill	alt.fan.TTBS
alt.fan.piers-anthony	alt.fan.tuan
alt.fan.poris	alt.fan.vic-reeves
alt.fan.pratchett	alt.fan.wang-chung
alt.fan.Priss.and.- the.Replicants	alt.fan.warlord
	alt.fan.warren.burstein

alt.fan.wodehouse
alt.fan.woody-allen

alt.fandom.cons
alt.fandom.misc

alt.fan.chris-elliot:

GET A LIFE PROGRAM GUIDE

alt.fan.dave_barry:

alt.fan.dave barry Frequently Asked Questions

alt.fan.douglas-adams:

alt.fan.douglas-adams FAQ

alt.fan.firesign-theatre:

Firesign Theatre: Frequently Asked Questions
Firesign Theatre: Introduction and Table of Contents
Firesign Theatre: Lexicon
Firesign Theatre: Lyrics to Songs

alt.fan.holmes:

Changes to Holmes Booklist (rec.arts.books)
Holmes Booklist (rec.arts.books)
LIST: Sherlock Holmes Illustrated

alt.fan.howard-stern:

[alt.fan.howard-stern] FAQ: Frequently Asked Questions about Howard Stern, Monthly Posting

alt.fan.lemurs:

index
lemur-faq

alt.fan.letterman:

FAQ: alt.fan.letterman FAQ changes since last posting
FAQ: alt.fan.letterman Frequently Asked Questions (read before posting)

alt.fan.pern:

Welcome to alt.fan.pern (Semi-monthly posting) (Part 1 of 2)
Welcome to alt.fan.pern (Semi-monthly posting) (Part 2 of 2)

alt.fan.pratchett:

Terry Pratchett Bibliography
alt.fan.pratchett FAQ

alt.fan.ren-and-stimpy:

The Ren & Stimpy Show: Encyclopedia
The Ren & Stimpy Show: Episode Guide
The Ren & Stimpy Show: Frequently Asked Questions (FAQ)

alt.fan.tolkien:

Monthly posting: TolkLang - mailing list on Tolkien s languages.

The Finer Aspects of Reproduction

This set of newsgroups is probably the most highly read set in the entire USENET newsgroup tree. Whatever your preferences, there is a newsgroup here that will cater to you.

alt.sex.*:

alt.sex	alt.sex.bondage
alt.sex.aluminum.baseball.bat	alt.sex.bondage.particle.physics
alt.sex.bestiality	alt.sex.boredom
alt.sex.bestiality.barney	alt.sex.carasso
alt.sex.bestiality.hamster.duct-tape	alt.sex.carasso.snuggles

alt.sex.* (continued):

alt.sex.fetish.amputee

alt.sex.extropians

alt.sex.fetish.feet

alt.sex.fetish.fa

alt.sex.fetish.hair

alt.sex.fetish.orientals

alt.sex.fetish.watersports

alt.sex.graphics

alt.sex.homosexual

alt.sex.motss

alt.sex.movies

alt.sex.NOT

alt.sex.nudels.me.too

alt.sex.pictures

alt.sex.pictures.d

alt.sex.pictures.female

alt.sex.pictures.male

alt.sex.prevost.derbeck

alt.sex.sonja

alt.sex.sounds

alt.sex.stories

alt.sex.stories.d

alt.sex.trans

alt.sex.voyeurism

alt.sex.wanted

alt.sex.wanted.me-too

alt.sex.watersports

alt.sex.wizards

alt.sex.woody-allen

alt.sexual.abuse.recovery

alt.sexual.abuse.recovery.d

alt.sexy.bald.captains

ADMIN: rec.arts.erotica introduction
Welcome to alt.sex.
[alt.sex] FAQ (1 4)
[alt.sex] FAQ (2 4)
[alt.sex] FAQ (3 4)
[alt.sex] FAQ (4 4)

Alternative Set

alt.sex.bondage:

The alt.sex.bondage FAQ list (part 1 of 2)
The alt.sex.bondage FAQ list (part 2 of 2)

alt.sex.homosexual:

Gay & Lesbian BBS List - June 1993

alt.sex.motss:

Gay & Lesbian BBS List - June 1993

alt.sex.pictures:

THE WHAT WHERE WHY HOW FOR PICTURES

alt.sex.pictures.d:

THE WHAT WHERE WHY HOW FOR PICTURES

alt.sex.stories.d:

ADMIN: rec.arts.erotica introduction

alt.sex.wizards:

[alt.sex.wizards] FAQ (1 2)

[alt.sex.wizards] FAQ (2 2)

Couch Potatoes Unite!

If your favorite television show doesn't quite make it to the "rec.arts.tv.*" set of newsgroups, you may be able to find it here.

alt.tv.*:

alt.tv.90210

alt.tv.animaniacs

alt.tv.antagonists

alt.tv.babylon-5

alt.tv.beakmans-world

alt.tv.bh90210

alt.tv.dinosaurs

alt.tv.fifteen

alt.tv.infomercials

alt.tv.la-law
alt.tv.liquid-tv
alt.tv.mash
alt.tv.melrose-place
alt.tv.mst3k
alt.tv.muppets
alt.tv.mwc
alt.tv.northern-exp
alt.tv.prisoner
alt.tv.twin-peaks
alt.tv.red-dwarf

alt.tv.ren-n-stimpy
alt.tv.rockford-files
alt.tv.saved-bell
alt.tv.seinfeld
alt.tv.simpsons
alt.tv.simpsons.itchy-scratchy
alt.tv.time-traxx
alt.tv.tiny-toon
alt.tv.tiny-toon.fandom
alt.tv.tiny-toon.plucky-duck

alt.tv.mst3k:

Mystery Science Theater 3000 Episode Guide
Mystery Science Theater 3000 FAQ
Mystery Science Theater 3000 Songs

alt.tv.northern-exp:

a.t.n-e F A Q
alt.tv.northern-exp FAQ reminder
alt.tv.northern-exp Frequently Asked Questions

alt.tv.prisoner:

THE PRISONER FAQ Part I (no spoilers)

alt.tv.red-dwarf:

Red Dwarf FAQ, version 3.5

alt.tv.ren-n-stimpy:

The Ren & Stimpy Show: Encyclopedia
The Ren & Stimpy Show: Episode Guide
The Ren & Stimpy Show: Frequently Asked Questions (FAQ)

Alternative Set

alt.tv.seinfeld:

alt.tv.seinfeld FAQ List and Info File (part 01 03)
alt.tv.seinfeld FAQ List and Info File (part 02 03)
alt.tv.seinfeld FAQ List and Info File (part 03 03)

alt.tv.simpsons:

The Simpsons Air Dates (*)
alt.tv.simpsons Changes to Frequently Asked Questions
alt.tv.simpsons Frequently Asked Questions

alt.tv.tiny-toon:

alt.tv.tiny-toon Frequently Asked Questions

USENET is the name that is used to refer to a recognized set of newsgroups. There are other recognized sets of newsgroups aimed at specific audiences that are not part of USENET. This chapter highlights some of them.

15

Other Available Hierarchies

214

bionet.*:

This newsgroup hierarchy is a place for biologists to discuss issues of a biological nature.

bionet.agroforestry	Discussion of Agroforestry.
bionet.announce	Announcements of widespread interest to biologists. (Moderated)
bionet.biology.computational	Computer and mathematical applications. (Moderated)
bionet.biology.n2-fixation	Research issues on biological nitrogen fixation.
bionet.biology.tropical	Discussions about tropical biology.
bionet.cellbiol	Disucssions about cell biology.
bionet.chlamydomonas	Discussions about the green alga Chlamydomonas.
bionet.drosophila	Discussions about the biology of fruit flies.
bionet.general	General BIOSCI discussion.
bionet.genome.arabidopsis	Information about the Arabidopsis project.
bionet.genome.chrom22	Discussion of Chromosome 22.
bionet.genome.chromosomes	Mapping and sequencing of eucaryote chromosomes.
bionet.immunology	Discussions about research in immunology.
bionet.info-theory	Discussions about biological information theory.
bionet.jobs	Scientific Job opportunities.
bionet.journals.contents	Contents of biology journal publications. (Moderated)
bionet.journals.note	Advice on dealing with journals in biology.
bionet.molbio.ageing	Discussions of cellular and organismal ageing.
bionet.molbio.bio-matrix	Computer applications to biological databases.
bionet.molbio.embldatabank	Info about the EMBL Nucleic acid database.
bionet.molbio.evolution	How genes and proteins have evolved.
bionet.molbio.gdb	Messages to and from the GDB database staff.

bionet.molbio.genbank	Info about the GenBank Nucleic acid database.
bionet.molbio.genbank.updates	Hot off the presses! (Moderated)
bionet.molbio.gene-linkage	Discussions about genetic linkage analysis.
bionet.molbio.genome-program	Discussion of Human Genome Project issues.
bionet.molbio.hiv	Discussions about the molecular biology of HIV.
bionet.molbio.methds-reagnts	Requests for information and lab reagents.
bionet.molbio.proteins	Research on proteins and protein databases.
bionet.molbio.rapd	Research on Randomly Amplified Polymorphic DNA.
bionet.molbio.yeast	The molecular biology and genetics of yeast.
bionet.n2-fixation	Research issues on biological nitrogen fixation.
bionet.neuroscience	Research issues in the neurosciences.
bionet.photosynthesis	Discussions about research on photosynthesis.
bionet.plants	Discussion about all aspects of plant biology.
bionet.population-bio	Technical discussions about population biology.
bionet.sci-resources	Information about funding agencies, etc. (Moderated)
bionet.software	Information about software for biology.
bionet.software.acedb	Discussions by users of genome DBs using ACEDB.
bionet.software.gcg	Discussions about using the ACEDB software.
bionet.software.sources	Software Sources relating to biology. (Moderated)
bionet.users.addresses	Who's who in Biology.
bionet.virology	Discussions about research in virology.
bionet.women-in-bio	Discussions about women in biology.
bionet.xtallography	Discussions about protein crystallography.

bionet.announce:

BIOSCI bionet Frequently Asked Questions

bionet.general:

A Biologist s Guide to Internet Resources

bionet.info-theory:

Biological Information Theory and Chowder Society FAQ

bit.*:

This set of newsgroups is an alternative hierarchy with a technical slant.

bit.admin	bit.* Newgroups Discussions.
bit.general	Discussions Relating to BitNet/Usenet.
bit.lang.neder-l	Dutch Language and Literature List. (Moderated)
bit.listserv.3com-l	3Com Products Discussion List.
bit.listserv.9370-l	IBM 9370 and VM/IS specific topics List.
bit.listserv.ada-law	ADA Law Discussions.
bit.listserv.advanc-l	Geac Advanced Integrated Library System Users.
bit.listserv.advise-l	User Services List.
bit.listserv.aix-l	IBM AIX Discussion List.
bit.listserv.allmusic	Discussions on all forms of Music.
bit.listserv.appc-l	APPC Discussion List.
bit.listserv.apple2-l	Apple II List.
bit.listserv.applicat	Applications under BITNET.
bit.listserv.arie-l	RLG Ariel Document Transmission Group.
bit.listserv.ashe-l	Higher Ed Policy and Research.
bit.listserv.asm370	IBM 370 Assembly Programming Discussions.
bit.listserv.autism	Autism and Developmental Disabilities List.
bit.listserv.banyan-l	Banyan Vines Network Software Discussions.

bit.listserv.big-lan	Campus-Size LAN Discussion Group. (Moderated)
bit.listserv.billing	Chargeback of computer resources.
bit.listserv.biosph-l	Biosphere, ecology, Discussion List.
bit.listserv.bitnews	BITNET News.
bit.listserv.blindnws	Blindness Issues and Discussions. (Moderated)
bit.listserv.buslib-l	Business Libraries List.
bit.listserv.c+health	Computers and Health Discussion List.
bit.listserv.c18-l	18th Century Interdisciplinary Discussion.
bit.listserv.c370-l	C/370 Discussion List.
bit.listserv.candle-l	Candle Products Discussion List.
bit.listserv.catala	Catalan Discussion List.
bit.listserv.catholic	Free Catholics Mailing List.
bit.listserv.cdromlan	CD-ROM on Local Area Networks.
bit.listserv.cfs.newsletter	Chronic Fatigue Syndrome Newsletter. (Moderated)
bit.listserv.christia	Practical Christian Life. (Moderated)
bit.listserv.cics-l	CICS Discussion List.
bit.listserv.cinema-l	Discussions on all forms of Cinema.
bit.listserv.circplus	Circulation Reserve and Related Library Issues.
bit.listserv.cmspip-l	VM/SP CMS Pipelines Discussion List.
bit.listserv.commed	Communication education.
bit.listserv.csg-l	Control System Group Network.
bit.listserv.cumrec-l	CUMREC-L Administrative computer use.
bit.listserv.cw-email	Campus-Wide E-mail Discussion List.
bit.listserv.cwis-l	Campus-Wide Information Systems.
bit.listserv.cyber-l	CDC Computer Discussion.
bit.listserv.dasig	Database Administration.
bit.listserv.db2-l	DB2 Data Base Discussion List.
bit.listserv.dbase-l	Discussion on the use of the dBase IV.
bit.listserv.deaf-l	Deaf List.

Other Hierarchies

bit.* (continued):

bit.listserv.decnews	Digital Equipment Corporation News List.
bit.listserv.dectei-l	DECUS Education Software Library Discussions.
bit.listserv.devel-l	Technology Transfer in International Development.
bit.listserv.disarm-l	Disarmament Discussion List.
bit.listserv.domain-l	Domains Discussion Group.
bit.listserv.earntech	EARN Technical Group.
bit.listserv.ecolog-l	Ecological Society of America List.
bit.listserv.edi-l	Electronic Data Interchange Issues.
bit.listserv.edpolyan	Professionals and Students Discuss Education.
bit.listserv.edstat-l	Statistics Education Discussion List.
bit.listserv.edtech	EDTECH - Educational Technology. (Moderated)
bit.listserv.edusig-l	EDUSIG Discussions.
bit.listserv.emusic-l	Electronic Music Discussion List.
bit.listserv.endnote	Bibsoft Endnote Discussions.
bit.listserv.envbeh-l	Forum on Environment and Human Behavior.
bit.listserv.erl-l	Educational Research List.
bit.listserv.ethics-l	Discussion of Ethics in Computing.
bit.listserv.ethology	Ethology List.
bit.listserv.euearn-l	Computers in Eastern Europe.
bit.listserv.film-l	Film making and reviews List.
bit.listserv.fnord-l	New Ways of Thinking List.
bit.listserv.frac-l	FRACTAL Discussion List.
bit.listserv.free-l	Fathers Rights and Equality Discussion List.
bit.listserv.games-l	Computer Games List.
bit.listserv.gaynet	GayNet Discussion List. (Moderated)
bit.listserv.gddm-l	The GDDM Discussion List.
bit.listserv.geodesic	List for the Discussion of Buckminster Fuller.

bit.listserv.gguide	BITNIC GGUIDE List.
bit.listserv.govdoc-l	Discussion of Government Document Issues.
bit.listserv.gutnberg	GUTNBERG Discussion List.
bit.listserv.hellas	The Hellenic Discussion List. (Moderated)
bit.listserv.help-net	Help on BitNet and the Internet.
bit.listserv.hindu-d	Hindu Digest. (Moderated)
bit.listserv.history	History List.
bit.listserv.hp3000-l	HP-3000 Computer Systems Discussion List.
bit.listserv.hytel-l	HYTELNET Discussions. (Moderated)
bit.listserv.i-amiga	Info-Amiga List.
bit.listserv.ibm-hesc	IBM Higher Education Consortium.
bit.listserv.ibm-main	IBM Mainframe Discussion List.
bit.listserv.ibm-nets	BITNIC IBM-NETS List.
bit.listserv.ibm7171	Protocol Converter List.
bit.listserv.ibmtcp-l	IBM TCP/IP List.
bit.listserv.india-d	India Interest Group. (Moderated)
bit.listserv.info-gcg	INFO-GCG: GCG Genetics Software Discussion.
bit.listserv.ingrafx	Information Graphics.
bit.listserv.innopac	Innovative Interfaces Online Public Access.
bit.listserv.ioob-l	Industrial Psychology.
bit.listserv.ipct-l	Interpersonal Computing and Technology List. (Moderated)
bit.listserv.isn	ISN Data Switch Technical Discussion Group.
bit.listserv.jes2-l	JES2 Discussion group.
bit.listserv.jnet-l	BITNIC JNET-L List.
bit.listserv.l-hcap	Handicap List. (Moderated)
bit.listserv.l-vmctr	VMCENTER Components Discussion List.
bit.listserv.lawsch-l	Law School Discussion List.
bit.listserv.liaison	BITNIC LIAISON.
bit.listserv.libref-l	Library Reference Issues. (Moderated)

bit.* (continued):

bit.listserv.libres	Library and Information Science Research. (Moderated)
bit.listserv.license	Software Licensing List.
bit.listserv.linkfail	Link failure announcements.
bit.listserv.literary	Discussions about Literature.
bit.listserv.lstsrv-l	Forum on LISTSERV.
bit.listserv.mail-l	BITNIC MAIL-L List.
bit.listserv.mailbook	MAIL/MAILBOOK subscription List.
bit.listserv.mba-l	MBA Student curriculum Discussion.
bit.listserv.mbu-l	Megabyte University - Computers and Writing.
bit.listserv.mdphd-l	Dual Degree Programs Discussion List.
bit.listserv.medforum	Medical Student Discussions. (Moderated)
bit.listserv.medlib-l	Medical Libraries Discussion List.
bit.listserv.mednews	Health Info-Com Network Newsletter. (Moderated)
bit.listserv.mideur-l	Middle Europe Discussion List.
bit.listserv.netnws-l	NETNWS-L Netnews List.
bit.listserv.nettrain	Network Trainers List.
bit.listserv.new-list	NEW-LIST - New List Announcements. (Moderated)
bit.listserv.next-l	NeXT Computer List.
bit.listserv.nodmgt-l	Node Management.
bit.listserv.notabene	Nota Bene List.
bit.listserv.notis-l	NOTIS/DOBIS Discussion group List.
bit.listserv.novell	Novell LAN Interest Group.
bit.listserv.omrscan	OMR Scanner Discussion.
bit.listserv.os2-l	OS/2 Discussion.
bit.listserv.ozone	OZONE Discussion List.
bit.listserv.pacs-l	Public-Access Computer System Forum. (Moderated)

bit.listserv.page-l	IBM 3812/3820 Tips and Problems Discussion List.
bit.listserv.pagemakr	PageMaker for Desktop Publishers.
bit.listserv.physhare	K-12 Physics List.
bit.listserv.pmdf-l	PMDF Distribution List.
bit.listserv.politics	Forum for the Discussion of Politics.
bit.listserv.postcard	Postcard Collectors Discussion Group.
bit.listserv.power-l	POWER-L IBM RS/6000 POWER Family.
bit.listserv.powerh-l	PowerHouse Discussion List.
bit.listserv.psycgrad	Psychology Grad Student Discussions.
bit.listserv.qualrs-l	Qualitative Research of the Human Sciences.
bit.listserv.relusr-l	Relay Users Forum.
bit.listserv.rhetoric	Rhetoric, social movements, persuasion.
bit.listserv.rra-l	Romance Readers Anonymous. (Moderated)
bit.listserv.rscs-l	VM/RSCS Mailing List.
bit.listserv.rscsmods	The RSCS modifications List.
bit.listserv.s-comput	SuperComputers List.
bit.listserv.sas-l	SAS Discussion.
bit.listserv.script-l	IBM vs Waterloo SCRIPT Discussion Group.
bit.listserv.scuba-l	Scuba diving Discussion List.
bit.listserv.seasia-l	Southeast Asia Discussion List.
bit.listserv.seds-l	Interchapter SEDS Communications.
bit.listserv.sfs-l	VM Shared File System Discussion List.
bit.listserv.sganet	Student Government Global Mail Network.
bit.listserv.simula	The SIMULA Language List.
bit.listserv.slart-l	SLA Research and Teaching.
bit.listserv.slovak-l	Slovak Discussion List.
bit.listserv.snamgt-l	SNA Network Management Discussion.
bit.listserv.sos-data	Social Science Data List.
bit.listserv.spires-l	SPIRES Conference List.
bit.listserv.sportpsy	Exercise and Sports Psychology.
bit.listserv.spssx-l	SPSSX Discussion.

Other Hierarchies

bit.* (continued):

bit.listserv.sqlinfo	Forum for SQL/DS and Related Topics.
bit.listserv.stat-l	STATISTICAL CONSULTING.
bit.listserv.tech-l	BITNIC TECH-L List.
bit.listserv.techwr-l	Technical Writing List.
bit.listserv.tecmat-l	Technology in Secondary Math.
bit.listserv.test	Test Newsgroup.
bit.listserv.tex-l	The TeXnical topics List.
bit.listserv.tn3270-l	tn3270 protocol Discussion List.
bit.listserv.toolb-l	Asymetrix Toolbook List.
bit.listserv.trans-l	BITNIC TRANS-L List.
bit.listserv.travel-l	Tourism Discussions.
bit.listserv.tsorexx	REXX for TSO List.
bit.listserv.ucp-l	University Computing Project Mailing List.
bit.listserv.ug-l	Usage Guidelines.
bit.listserv.uigis-l	User Interface for Geographical Info Systems.
bit.listserv.urep-l	UREP-L Mailing List.
bit.listserv.usrdir-l	User Directory List.
bit.listserv.uus-l	Unitarian-Universalist List.
bit.listserv.valert-l	Virus Alert List. (Moderated)
bit.listserv.vfort-l	VS-Fortran Discussion List.
bit.listserv.vm-util	VM Utilities Discussion List.
bit.listserv.vmesa-l	VM/ESA Mailing List.
bit.listserv.vmslsv-l	VAX/VMS LISTSERV Discussion List.
bit.listserv.vmxa-l	VM/XA Discussion List.
bit.listserv.vnews-l	VNEWS Discussion List.
bit.listserv.vpiej-l	Electronic Publishing Discussion List.
bit.listserv.win3-l	Microsoft Windows Version 3 Forum.
bit.listserv.words-l	English Language Discussion Group.
bit.listserv.wpcorp-l	WordPerfect Corporation Products Discussions.
bit.listserv.wpwin-l	WordPerfect for Windows.

bit.listserv.wx-talk	Weather Issues Discussions.
bit.listserv.x400-l	x.400 Protocol List.
bit.listserv.xcult-l	International Intercultural Newsletter.
bit.listserv.xedit-l	VM System Editor List.
bit.listserv.xerox-l	The Xerox Discussion List.
bit.listserv.xmailer	Crosswell Mailer.
bit.listserv.xtropy-l	Extopian List.
bit.mailserv.word-mac	Word Processing on the Macintosh.
bit.mailserv.word-pc	Word Processing on the IBM PC.
bit.org.peace-corps	International Volunteers Discussion Group.
bit.software.international	International Software List. (Moderated)

bit.admin:

Mailing Lists Available in Usenet
NetNews Listserv Gateway Policy
bit.** Moderator List
bit.** Newsgroup List

bit.listserv.emusic-l:

Computer Music bibliography
Midi files software archives on the Internet
Midi files software archives on the Internet.

bit.listserv.pagemakr:

Pagemaker Frequently Asked Questions, part 1 2
Pagemaker Frequently Asked Questions, part 2 2

bit.listserv.win3-l:

Windows Programmer FAQ: How to get it
Ye Olde Secrete Screene Cheete Sheete (long; 2000+ lines) (part 1 2)
Ye Olde Secrete Screene Cheete Sheete (long; 2000+ lines) (part 2 2)

bit.software.international:

bit.international.software FAQ

Other Hierarchies

biz.*:

Topics related to business products are discussed in this set of newsgroups.

biz.americast	AmeriCast announcements.
biz.americast.samples	Samples of AmeriCast. (Moderated)
biz.books.technical	Technical bookstore & publisher advertising & info.
biz.clarinet	Announcements about ClariNet.
biz.clarinet.sample	Samples of ClariNet newsgroups for the outside world.
biz.comp.hardware	Generic commercial hardware postings.
biz.comp.services	Generic commercial service postings.
biz.comp.software	Generic commercial software postings.
biz.comp.telebit	Support of the Telebit modem.
biz.comp.telebit.netblazer	The Telebit Netblazer.
biz.config	Biz Usenet configuration and administration.
biz.control	Control information and messages.
biz.dec	DEC equipment & software.
biz.dec.decathena	DECathena discussions.
biz.dec.decnews	The DECNews newsletter. (Moderated)
biz.dec.ip	IP networking on DEC machines.
biz.dec.workstations	DEC workstation discussions & info.
biz.digex.announce	Announcements from Digex. (Moderated)
biz.jobs.offered	Position announcements.
biz.misc	Miscellaneous postings of a commercial nature.
biz.next.newprod	New product announcements for the NeXT.
biz.pagesat	For discussion of the Pagesat Satellite Usenet Newsfeed.
biz.sco.announce	SCO and related product announcements. (Moderated)
biz.sco.binaries	Binary packages for SCO Xenix, UNIX, or ODT. (Moderated)

biz.sco.general	Q&A, discussions and comments on SCO products.
biz.sco.magazine	To discuss SCO Magazine and its contents.
biz.sco.opendesktop	ODT environment and applications tech info, q&a.
biz.sco.sources	Source code ported to an SCO operating environment.
biz.stolen	Postings about stolen merchandise.
biz.tadpole.sparcbook	Discussions on the Sparcbook portable computer.
biz.test	Biz newsgroup test messages.
biz.zeos.announce	Zeos Product Announcements. (Moderated)
biz.zeos.general	Zeos technical support and general information.

biz.books.technical:

[misc.books.technical] A Concise Guide to UNIX Books

biz.comp.services:

Updated Internet Services List

biz.config:

biz.sco.* newsgroups mlists FAQ (periodic posting)

biz.sco.general:

SCO Mailing List Administrative FAQ
SCO Mailing List Technical FAQ
biz.sco.* newsgroups mlists FAQ (periodic posting)

biz.sco.opendesktop:

biz.sco.* newsgroups mlists FAQ (periodic posting)

Other Hierarchies

clari.*:

The articles in this set of newsgroups have been *gatewayed* from commercials, news services and other "official" sources.

clari.biz.commodity	Commodity news and price reports. (Moderated)
clari.biz.courts	Lawsuits and business related legal matters. (Moderated)
clari.biz.economy	Economic news and indicators. (Moderated)
clari.biz.economy.world	Economy stories for non-US countries. (Moderated)
clari.biz.features	Business feature stories. (Moderated)
clari.biz.finance	Finance, currency, Corporate finance. (Moderated)
clari.biz.finance.earnings	Earnings & dividend reports. (Moderated)
clari.biz.finance.personal	Personal investing & finance. (Moderated)
clari.biz.finance.services	Banks and financial industries. (Moderated)
clari.biz.invest	News for investors. (Moderated)
clari.biz.labor	Strikes, unions and labor relations. (Moderated)
clari.biz.market	General stock market news. (Moderated)
clari.biz.market.amex	American Stock Exchange reports & news. (Moderated)
clari.biz.market.dow	Dow Jones NYSE reports. (Moderated)
clari.biz.market.ny	NYSE reports. (Moderated)
clari.biz.market.otc	NASDAQ reports. (Moderated)
clari.biz.market.report	General market reports, S&P, etc. (Moderated)
clari.biz.mergers	Mergers and acquisitions. (Moderated)
clari.biz.misc	Other business news. (Moderated)
clari.biz.products	Important new products & services. (Moderated)
clari.biz.top	Top business news. (Moderated)
clari.biz.urgent	Breaking business news. (Moderated)
clari.canada.biz	Canadian Business Summaries. (Moderated)

227

clari.canada.briefs	Regular updates of Canadian News in Brief. (Moderated)
clari.canada.briefs.ont	News briefs for Ontario and Toronto. (Moderated)
clari.canada.briefs.west	News briefs for Alberta, the Prairies & B.C. (Moderated)
clari.canada.features	Alamanac, Ottawa Special, Arts. (Moderated)
clari.canada.general	Short items on Canadian News stories. (Moderated)
clari.canada.gov	Government related news (all levels). (Moderated)
clari.canada.law	Crimes, the courts and the law. (Moderated)
clari.canada.newscast	Regular newscast for Canadians. (Moderated)
clari.canada.politics	Political and election items. (Moderated)
clari.canada.trouble	Mishaps, accidents and serious problems. (Moderated)
clari.feature.dave_barry	Columns of humourist Dave Barry. (Moderated)
clari.feature.mike_royko	Chicago Opinion Columnist Mike Royko. (Moderated)
clari.feature.miss_manners	Judith Martin's Humourous Etiquette Advice. (Moderated)
clari.local.alberta.briefs	Local news Briefs. (Moderated)
clari.local.arizona	Local news. (Moderated)
clari.local.arizona.briefs	Local news Briefs. (Moderated)
clari.local.bc.briefs	Local news Briefs. (Moderated)
clari.local.california	Local news. (Moderated)
clari.local.california.briefs	Local news Briefs. (Moderated)
clari.local.chicago	Local news. (Moderated)
clari.local.chicago.briefs	Local news Briefs. (Moderated)
clari.local.florida	Local news. (Moderated)
clari.local.florida.briefs	Local news Briefs. (Moderated)
clari.local.georgia	Local news. (Moderated)
clari.local.georgia.briefs	Local news Briefs. (Moderated)

clari.* (continued):

clari.local.headlines	Various local headline summaries. (Moderated)
clari.local.illinois	Local news. (Moderated)
clari.local.illinois.briefs	Local news Briefs. (Moderated)
clari.local.indiana	Local news. (Moderated)
clari.local.indiana.briefs	Local news Briefs. (Moderated)
clari.local.iowa	Local news. (Moderated)
clari.local.iowa.briefs	Local news Briefs. (Moderated)
clari.local.los_angeles	Local news. (Moderated)
clari.local.los_angeles.briefs	Local news Briefs. (Moderated)
clari.local.louisiana	Local news. (Moderated)
clari.local.manitoba.briefs	Local news Briefs. (Moderated)
clari.local.maritimes.briefs	Local news Briefs. (Moderated)
clari.local.maryland	Local news. (Moderated)
clari.local.maryland.briefs	Local news Briefs. (Moderated)
clari.local.massachusetts	Local news. (Moderated)
clari.local.massachusetts.briefs	Local news Briefs. (Moderated)
clari.local.michigan	Local news. (Moderated)
clari.local.michigan.briefs	Local news Briefs. (Moderated)
clari.local.minnesota	Local news. (Moderated)
clari.local.minnesota.briefs	Local news Briefs. (Moderated)
clari.local.missouri	Local news. (Moderated)
clari.local.missouri.briefs	Local news Briefs. (Moderated)
clari.local.nebraska	Local news. (Moderated)
clari.local.nebraska.briefs	Local news Briefs. (Moderated)
clari.local.nevada	Local news. (Moderated)
clari.local.nevada.briefs	Local news Briefs. (Moderated)
clari.local.new_england	Local news. (Moderated)
clari.local.new_hampshire	Local news. (Moderated)
clari.local.new_jersey	Local news. (Moderated)
clari.local.new_jersey.briefs	Local news Briefs. (Moderated)

clari.local.new_york	Local news. (Moderated)
clari.local.new_york.briefs	Local news Briefs. (Moderated)
clari.local.nyc	Local news (New York City). (Moderated)
clari.local.nyc.briefs	Local news Briefs. (Moderated)
clari.local.ohio	Local news. (Moderated)
clari.local.ohio.briefs	Local news Briefs. (Moderated)
clari.local.ontario.briefs	Local news Briefs. (Moderated)
clari.local.oregon	Local news. (Moderated)
clari.local.oregon.briefs	Local news Briefs. (Moderated)
clari.local.pennsylvania	Local news. (Moderated)
clari.local.pennsylvania.briefs	Local news Briefs. (Moderated)
clari.local.saskatchewan.briefs	Local news Briefs. (Moderated)
clari.local.sfbay	Stories datelined San Francisco Bay Area. (Moderated)
clari.local.texas	Local news. (Moderated)
clari.local.texas.briefs	Local news Briefs. (Moderated)
clari.local.utah	Local news. (Moderated)
clari.local.utah.briefs	Local news Briefs. (Moderated)
clari.local.virginia+dc	Local news. (Moderated)
clari.local.virginia+dc.briefs	Local news Briefs. (Moderated)
clari.local.washington	Local news. (Moderated)
clari.local.washington.briefs	Local news Briefs. (Moderated)
clari.local.wisconsin	Local news. (Moderated)
clari.local.wisconsin.briefs	Local news Briefs. (Moderated)
clari.matrix_news	Monthly journal on the internet. (Moderated)
clari.nb.apple	Newsbytes Apple/Macintosh news. (Moderated)
clari.nb.business	Newsbytes business & industry news. (Moderated)
clari.nb.general	Newsbytes general computer news. (Moderated)

clari.* (continued):

clari.nb.govt	Newsbytes legal and government computer news. (Moderated)
clari.nb.ibm	Newsbytes IBM PC World coverage. (Moderated)
clari.nb.review	Newsbytes new product reviews. (Moderated)
clari.nb.telecom	Newsbytes telecom & online industry news. (Moderated)
clari.nb.top	Newsbytes top stories (crossposted). (Moderated)
clari.nb.trends	Newsbytes new developments & trends. (Moderated)
clari.nb.unix	Newsbytes Unix news. (Moderated)
clari.net.admin	Announcements for news admins at ClariNet sites. (Moderated)
clari.net.announce	Announcements for all ClariNet readers. (Moderated)
clari.net.newusers	Online info about ClariNet. (Moderated)
clari.net.products	New ClariNet products. (Moderated)
clari.net.talk	Discussion of ClariNet—only unmoderated group.
clari.news.almanac	Daily almanac - quotes, "this date in history" etc. (Moderated)
clari.news.arts	Stage, drama & other fine arts. (Moderated)
clari.news.aviation	Aviation industry and mishaps. (Moderated)
clari.news.books	Books & publishing. (Moderated)
clari.news.briefs	Regular news summaries. (Moderated)
clari.news.bulletin	Major breaking stories of the week. (Moderated)
clari.news.canada	News related to Canada. (Moderated)
clari.news.cast	Regular U.S. news summary. (Moderated)
clari.news.children	Stories related to children and parenting. (Moderated)
clari.news.consumer	Consumer news, car reviews etc. (Moderated)

clari.news.demonstration	Demonstrations around the world. (Moderated)
clari.news.disaster	Major problems, accidents & natural disasters. (Moderated)
clari.news.economy	General economic news. (Moderated)
clari.news.election	News regarding both US and international elections. (Moderated)
clari.news.entertain	Entertainment industry news & features. (Moderated)
clari.news.europe	News related to Europe. (Moderated)
clari.news.features	Unclassified feature stories. (Moderated)
clari.news.fighting	Clashes around the world. (Moderated)
clari.news.flash	Ultra-important once-a-year news flashes. (Moderated)
clari.news.goodnews	Stories of success and survival. (Moderated)
clari.news.gov	General Government related stories. (Moderated)
clari.news.gov.agency	Government agencies, FBI etc. (Moderated)
clari.news.gov.budget	Budgets at all levels. (Moderated)
clari.news.gov.corrupt	Government corruption, kickbacks etc. (Moderated)
clari.news.gov.international	International government-related stories. (Moderated)
clari.news.gov.officials	Government officials & their problems. (Moderated)
clari.news.gov.state	State government stories of national importance. (Moderated)
clari.news.gov.taxes	Tax laws, trials etc. (Moderated)
clari.news.gov.usa	US Federal government news. (High volume). (Moderated)
clari.news.group	Special interest groups not covered in their own group. (Moderated)
clari.news.group.blacks	News of interest to black people. (Moderated)
clari.news.group.gays	Homosexuality & Gay Rights. (Moderated)

clari.* (continued):

clari.news.group.jews	Jews & Jewish interests. (Moderated)
clari.news.group.women	Women's issues and abortion. (Moderated)
clari.news.headlines	Hourly list of the top U.S./World headlines. (Moderated)
clari.news.hot.east_europe	News from Eastern Europe. (Moderated)
clari.news.hot.somalia	News from Somalia. (Moderated)
clari.news.hot.ussr	News from the Soviet Union. (Moderated)
clari.news.interest	Human interest stories. (Moderated)
clari.news.interest.animals	Animals in the news. (Moderated)
clari.news.interest.history	Human interest stories & history in the making. (Moderated)
clari.news.interest.people	Famous people in the news. (Moderated)
clari.news.interest.people.column	Daily "People" column—tidbits on celebs. (Moderated)
clari.news.interest.quirks	Unusual or funny news stories. (Moderated)
clari.news.issues	Stories on major issues not covered in their own group. (Moderated)
clari.news.issues.civil_rights	Freedom, Racism, Civil Rights Issues. (Moderated)
clari.news.issues.conflict	Conflict between groups around the world. (Moderated)
clari.news.issues.family	Family, Child abuse, etc. (Moderated)
clari.news.labor	Unions, strikes. (Moderated)
clari.news.labor.strike	Strikes. (Moderated)
clari.news.law	General group for law related issues. (Moderated)
clari.news.law.civil	Civil trials & litigation. (Moderated)
clari.news.law.crime	Major crimes. (Moderated)
clari.news.law.crime.sex	Sex crimes and trials. (Moderated)
clari.news.law.crime.trial	Trials for criminal actions. (Moderated)
clari.news.law.crime.violent	Violent crime & criminals. (Moderated)

clari.news.law.drugs	Drug related crimes & drug stories. (Moderated)
clari.news.law.investigation	Investigation of crimes. (Moderated)
clari.news.law.police	Police & law enforcement. (Moderated)
clari.news.law.prison	Prisons, prisoners & escapes. (Moderated)
clari.news.law.profession	Lawyers, Judges etc. (Moderated)
clari.news.law.supreme	U.S. Supreme court rulings & news. (Moderated)
clari.news.lifestyle	Fashion, leisure etc. (Moderated)
clari.news.military	Military equipment, people & issues. (Moderated)
clari.news.movies	Reviews, news and stories on movie stars. (Moderated)
clari.news.music	Reviews and issues concerning music & musicians. (Moderated)
clari.news.politics	Politicians & politics. (Moderated)
clari.news.politics.people	Politicians & Political Personalities. (Moderated)
clari.news.religion	Religion, religious leaders, televangelists. (Moderated)
clari.news.sex	Sexual issues, sex-related political stories. (Moderated)
clari.news.terrorism	Terrorist actions & related news around the world. (Moderated)
clari.news.top	Top US news stories. (Moderated)
clari.news.top.world	Top international news stories. (Moderated)
clari.news.trends	Surveys and trends. (Moderated)
clari.news.trouble	Less major accidents, problems & mishaps. (Moderated)
clari.news.tv	TV news, reviews & stars. (Moderated)
clari.news.urgent	Major breaking stories of the day. (Moderated)
clari.news.weather	Weather and temperature reports. (Moderated)

Other Hierarchies

clari.* (continued):

clari.sfbay.briefs	Twice daily news roundups for SF Bay Area. (Moderated)
clari.sfbay.entertain	Reviews and entertainment news for SF Bay Area. (Moderated)
clari.sfbay.fire	Stories from Fire Depts. of the SF Bay. (Moderated)
clari.sfbay.general	Main stories for SF Bay Area. (Moderated)
clari.sfbay.misc	Shorter general items for SF Bay Area. (Moderated)
clari.sfbay.police	Stories from the Police Depts. of the SF Bay. (Moderated)
clari.sfbay.roads	Reports from Caltrans and the CHP. (Moderated)
clari.sfbay.short	Very short items for SF Bay Area. (Moderated)
clari.sfbay.weather	SF Bay and California Weather reports. (Moderated)
clari.sports.baseball	Baseball scores, stories, stats. (Moderated)
clari.sports.baseball.games	Baseball games & box scores. (Moderated)
clari.sports.basketball	Basketball coverage. (Moderated)
clari.sports.basketball.college	College basketball coverage. (Moderated)
clari.sports.features	Sports feature stories. (Moderated)
clari.sports.football	Pro football coverage. (Moderated)
clari.sports.football.college	College football coverage. (Moderated)
clari.sports.hockey	NHL coverage. (Moderated)
clari.sports.misc	Other sports, plus general sports news. (Moderated)
clari.sports.motor	Racing, Motor Sports. (Moderated)
clari.sports.olympic	The Olympic Games. (Moderated)
clari.sports.tennis	Tennis news & scores. (Moderated)
clari.sports.top	Top sports news. (Moderated)
clari.tw.aerospace	Aerospace industry and companies. (Moderated)

clari.tw.computers	Computer industry, applications and developments. (Moderated)
clari.tw.defense	Defense industry issues. (Moderated)
clari.tw.education	Stories involving Universities & colleges. (Moderated)
clari.tw.electronics	Electronics makers and sellers. (Moderated)
clari.tw.environment	Environmental news, hazardous waste, forests. (Moderated)
clari.tw.health	Disease, medicine, health care, sick celebs. (Moderated)
clari.tw.health.aids	AIDS stories, research, political issues. (Moderated)
clari.tw.misc	General technical industry stories. (Moderated)
clari.tw.nuclear	Nuclear power & waste. (Moderated)
clari.tw.science	General science stories. (Moderated)
clari.tw.space	NASA, Astronomy & spaceflight. (Moderated)
clari.tw.stocks	Regular reports on computer & technology stock prices. (Moderated)
clari.tw.telecom	Phones, Satellites, Media & general Telecom. (Moderated)

clari:

ClariNet: How it works (Jul 92)

ClariNet Electronic Newspaper Introduction (Oct 92)

ClariNet frequently asked questions (Jul 92)

ClariNet news reading basics (Jul 92)

Decoding ClariNet special article headers (Oct 92)

Description of ClariNet newsgroup Standing stories (Jul 92)

Picking which ClariNet newsgroups you wish to read (Jul 92)

Other Hierarchies

gnu.*:

This set of newsgroups contains discussion about the GNU Project of the Free Software Foundation.

gnu.announce	Status and announcements from the Project. (Moderated)
gnu.bash.bug	Bourne Again SHell bug reports and suggested fixes. (Moderated)
gnu.chess	Announcements about the GNU Chess program.
gnu.emacs.announce	Announcements about GNU Emacs. (Moderated)
gnu.emacs.bug	GNU Emacs bug reports and suggested fixes. (Moderated)
gnu.emacs.gnews	News reading under GNU Emacs using Weemba's
gnu.emacs.gnus	News reading under GNU Emacs using GNUS (in English).
gnu.emacs.help	User queries and answers.
gnu.emacs.sources	ONLY (please!) C and Lisp source code for GNU Emacs.
gnu.emacs.vm.bug	Bug reports on the Emacs VM mail package.
gnu.emacs.vm.info	Information about the Emacs VM mail package.
gnu.emacs.vms	VMS port of GNU Emacs.
gnu.epoch.misc	The Epoch X11 extensions to Emacs.
gnu.g++.announce	Announcements about the GNU C++ Compiler. (Moderated)
gnu.g++.bug	g++ bug reports and suggested fixes. (Moderated)
gnu.g++.help	GNU C++ compiler (G++) user queries and answers.
gnu.g++.lib.bug	g++ library bug reports/suggested fixes. (Moderated)
gnu.gcc.announce	Announcements about the GNU C Compiler. (Moderated)

gnu.gcc.bug	GNU C Compiler bug reports/suggested fixes. (Moderated)
gnu.gcc.help	GNU C Compiler (gcc) user queries and answers.
gnu.gdb.bug	gcc/g++ DeBugger bugs and suggested fixes. (Moderated)
gnu.ghostscript.bug	GNU Ghostscript interpreter bugs. (Moderated)
gnu.gnusenet.config	GNU's Not Usenet administration and configuration.
gnu.gnusenet.test	GNU's Not Usenet alternative hierarchy testing.
gnu.groff.bug	Bugs in the GNU roff programs. (Moderated)
gnu.misc.discuss	Serious discussion about GNU and freed software.
gnu.smalltalk.bug	Bugs in GNU Smalltalk. (Moderated)
gnu.utils.bug	GNU utilities bugs (e.g., make, gawk. ls). (Moderated)

gnu.epoch.misc:

GNU Epoch FAQ (Info version)
GNU Epoch FAQ (LaTeXinfo version)

gnu.g++.help:

FAQ for g++ and libg++, plain text version [Revised 15 Aug 1993]
FAQ for g++ and libg++, texinfo version [Revised 15 Aug 1993]

HEPnet.*:

The topic of discussion in this set of newsgroups is high-energy nuclear physics. It has no listed FAQs.

hepnet.admin	Discussions among hepnet.* netnews administrators.
hepnet.announce	Announcement of general interest.
hepnet.conferences	Discussions of conference and workshops.
hepnet.freehep	Discussions about the freehep archives.

HEPnet. (continued):*

hepnet.general	Discussions of general interest.
hepnet.hepix	Discussions on the use of Unix.
hepnet.heplib	Discussions about HEPLIB.
hepnet.jobs	Job announcements and discussions.
hepnet.lang.c++	Discussions of the use of C++.
hepnet.test	Test postings.
hepnet.videoconf	Discussions on the use of videoconferencing.

ieee.:*

Discussion concerning the Institute of Electrical and Electronic Engineers are contained in this set of newsgroups. It has no listed FAQs.

ieee.announce	General Announcements for IEEE community.
ieee.config	Postings about managing the ieee.* groups.
ieee.general	IEEE - General discussion.
ieee.pcnfs	Discussion & tips on PC-NFS.
ieee.rab.announce	Regional Activities Board - Announcements.
ieee.rab.general	Regional Activities Board - General discussion.
ieee.region1	Region 1 Announcements.
ieee.tab.announce	Technical Activities Board - Announcements.
ieee.tab.general	Technical Activities Board - General discussion.
ieee.tcos	The Technical Committee on Operating Systems. (Moderated)
ieee.usab.announce	USAB - Announcements.
ieee.usab.general	USAB - General discussion.

inet/DDN:

This set of newsgroups is very similar to those contained in the traditional USENET hierarchy but they are circulated via a different mechanism. There are no listed FAQs.

comp.ai.edu	Applications of Artificial Intelligence to Education.
comp.ai.vision	Artificial Intelligence Vision Research. (Moderated)
comp.dcom.lans.hyperchannel	Hyperchannel networks within an IP network.
comp.editors	Topics related to computerized text editing.
comp.edu.composition	Writing instruction in computer-based classrooms.
comp.lang.asm370	Programming in IBM System/370 Assembly Language.
comp.lang.clu	The CLU language & related topics.
comp.lang.forth.mac	The CSI MacForth programming environment.
comp.lang.icon	Topics related to the ICON programming language.
comp.lang.idl	IDL (Interface Description Language) related topics.
comp.lang.lisp.franz	The Franz Lisp programming language.
comp.lang.lisp.x	The XLISP language system.
comp.lang.rexx	The REXX command language.
comp.lang.scheme.c	The Scheme language environment.
comp.lang.visual	Visual programming languages.
comp.lsi.cad	Electrical Computer Aided Design.
comp.mail.multi-media	Multimedia Mail.
comp.music	Applications of computers in music research.
comp.networks.noctools. - announce	Info and announcements about NOC tools. (Moderated)
comp.networks.noctools.bugs	Bug reports and fixes for NOC tools.
comp.networks.noctools.d	Discussion about NOC tools.

inet/DDN (continued):

comp.networks.noctools.-submissions	New NOC tools submissions.
comp.networks.noctools.tools	Descriptions of available NOC tools. (Moderated)
comp.networks.noctools.wanted	Requests for NOC software.
comp.org.isoc.interest	Discussion about the Internet Society.
comp.os.aos	Topics related to Data General's AOS/VS.
comp.os.cpm.amethyst	Discussion of Amethyst, CP/M-80 software package.
comp.os.msdos.4dos	The 4DOS command processor for MS-DOS.
comp.os.rsts	Topics related to the PDP-11 RSTS/E operating system.
comp.os.v	The V distributed operating system from Stanford.
comp.periphs.printers	Information on printers.
comp.protocols.iso.dev-environ	The ISO Development Environment.
comp.protocols.iso.x400	X400 mail protocol discussions.
comp.protocols.iso.x400.gateway	X400 mail gateway discussions. (Moderated)
comp.protocols.pcnet	Topics related to PCNET (a personal computer network).
comp.protocols.snmp	The Simple Network Management Protocol.
comp.protocols.tcp-ip.domains	Topics related to Domain Style names.
comp.protocols.time.ntp	The network time protocol.
comp.security.announce	Announcements from the CERT about security. (Moderated)
comp.soft-sys.andrew	The Andrew system from CMU.
comp.soft-sys.nextstep	The NeXTstep computing environment.
comp.std.announce	Announcements about standards activities. (Moderated)
comp.sys.cdc	Control Data Corporation Computers (e.g., Cybers).

comp.sys.handhelds	Handheld computers and programmable calculators.
comp.sys.intel.ipsc310	Anything related to the Intel 310.
comp.sys.northstar	Northstar microcomputer users.
comp.sys.super	Supercomputers.
comp.sys.ti.explorer	The Texas Instruments Explorer.
comp.sys.zenith	Heath terminals and related Zenith products.
comp.terminals.bitgraph	The BB&N BitGraph Terminal.
comp.terminals.tty5620	AT&T Dot Mapped Display Terminals (5620 and BLIT).
comp.theory	Theoretical Computer Science.
comp.theory.cell-automata	Discussion of all aspects of cellular automata.
comp.theory.dynamic-sys	Ergodic Theory and Dynamical Systems.
comp.theory.self-org-sys	Topics related to self-organization.
comp.unix.cray	Cray computers and their operating systems.
comp.unix.solaris	Discussions about the Solaris operating system.
comp.windows.x.announce	X Consortium announcements. (Moderated)
comp.windows.x.motif	The Motif GUI for the X Window System.
ddn.mgt-bulletin	The DDN Management Bulletin from NIC.DDN.MIL (Moderated)
ddn.newsletter	The DDN Newsletter from NIC.DDN.MIL (Moderated)
news.software.nntp	The Network News Transfer Protocol.
rec.games.vectrex	The Vectrex game system.
rec.mag.fsfnet	A Science Fiction "fanzine." (Moderated)
sci.bio.technology	Any topic relating to biotechnology.
sci.math.num-analysis	Numerical Analysis.
sci.philosophy.meta	Discussions within the scope of "MetaPhilosophy."
soc.culture.esperanto	The neutral international language Esperanto.

info.*:

This set of newsgroups contains topics of local interest to the University of Illinois. It has no listed FAQs.

info.admin	Administrative messages regarding info.* groups (usenet@ux1.cso.uiuc.edu). (Moderated)
info.big-internet	*Issues facing a huge Internet (big-internet@munnari.oz.au). (Moderated)
info.bind	*The Berkeley BIND server (bind@arpa.berkeley.edu). (Moderated)
info.brl-cad	BRL's Solid Modeling CAD system (cad@brl.mil). (Moderated)
info.bytecounters	*NSstat network analysis program. (bytecounters@venera.isi.edu). (Moderated)
info.convex	Convex Corp machines (info-convex@pemrac.space.swri.edu). (Moderated)
info.firearms	Non-political firearms discussions (firearms@cs.cmu.edu). (Moderated)
info.firearms.politics	Political firearms discussions (firearms-politics@cs.cmu.edu). (Moderated)
info.gated	*Cornell's GATED program (gated-people@devvax.tn.cornell.edu). (Moderated)
info.grass.programmer	GRASS geographic information system programmer issues (grassp-list @moon.cecer.army.mil). (Moderated)
info.grass.user	GRASS geographic information system user issues (grassu-list@moon.cecer.army.mil). (Moderated)
info.ietf	*Internet Engineering Task Force (IETF) discussions (ietf@venera.isi.edu). (Moderated)
info.ietf.hosts	*IETF host requirements discussions (ietf-hosts@nnsc.nsf.net). (Moderated)
info.ietf.isoc	*Internet Society discussions (isoc-interest@relay.sgi.com). (Moderated)

info.ietf.njm	*Jo-MAAN - the Joint Monitoring Access between Adjacent Networks IETF working group (njm@merit.edu). (Moderated)
info.ietf.smtp	*IETF SMTP extension discussions (ietf-smtp@dimacs.rutgers.edu). (Moderated)
info.isode	*The ISO Development Environment package (isode@nic.ddn.mil). (Moderated)
info.jethro-tull	Discussions about Jethro Tull's music (jtull@remus.rutgers.edu). (Moderated)
info.labmgr	Computer lab managers list (labmgr@ukcc.uky.edu). (Moderated)
info.mach	The Mach operating system (info-mach@cs.cmu.edu). (Moderated)
info.mh.workers	*MH development discussions (mh-workers@ics.uci.edu). (Moderated)
info.nets	Inter-network connectivity (info-nets@think.com).
info.nsf.grants	*NSF grant notes (grants@note.nsf.gov). (Moderated)
info.nsfnet.cert	*Computer Emergency Response Team announcements (nsfnet-cert@merit.edu). (Moderated)
info.nsfnet.status	NSFnet status reports. (Moderated)
info.nupop	Northwestern University's POP for PCs (nupop@casbah.acns.nwu.edu). (Moderated)
info.nysersnmp	*The SNMP software distributed by PSI (nysersnmp@nisc.nyser.net). (Moderated)
info.osf	*OSF Electronic Bulletin mailings (roma@uiuc.edu). (Moderated)
info.pem-dev	*IETF privacy enhanced mail discussions (pem-dev@tis.com). (Moderated)
info.ph	Qi, ph, sendmail/phquery discussions (info-ph@uxc.cso.uiuc.edu). (Moderated)
info.rfc	*Announcements of newly released RFCs (rfc-request@nic.ddn.mil). (Moderated)

Other Hierarchies

info.* (continued):

info.slug	Care and feeding of Symbolics Lisp machines (slug@iu.ai.sri.com). (Moderated)
info.snmp	*SNMP (Simple Gateway/Network Monitoring Protocol) (snmp@nisc.nyser.net). (Moderated)
info.solbourne	Discussions & info about Solbourne computers (info-solbourne@acsu.buffalo.edu). (Moderated)
info.sun-managers	*Sun-managers digest (sun-managers@rice.edu). (Moderated)
info.sun-nets	*Sun-nets (nee Sun Spots) digest (sun-nets@umiacs.umd.edu). (Moderated)
info.theorynt	Theory list (theorynt@vm1.nodak.edu). (Moderated)
info.unix-sw	Software available for anonymous FTP (unix-sw-request@wsmr-simtel20.army.mil). (Moderated)
info.wisenet	Women In Science and Engineering NETwork (wisenet@uicvm.uic.edu). (Moderated)

k12.*:

This set of newsgroups contains topics of interest to K-12 educators. It has no listed FAQs.

k12.ed.art	Arts & crafts curricula in K-12 education.
k12.ed.business	Business education curricula in grades K-12.
k12.ed.comp.literacy	Teaching computer literacy in grades K-12.
k12.ed.health-pe	Health and Physical Education curricula in grades K-12.
k12.ed.life-skills	Home Economics, career education, and school counseling.
k12.ed.math	Mathematics curriculum in K-12 education.
k12.ed.music	Music and Performing Arts curriculum in K-12 education.

k12.ed.science	Science curriculum in K-12 education.
k12.ed.soc-studies	Social Studies and History curriculum in K-12 education.
k12.ed.special	Educating students with handicaps and/or special needs.
k12.ed.tag	K-12 education for gifted and talented students.
k12.ed.tech	Industrial arts & vocational education in grades K-12.
k12.library	Implementing info technologies in school libraries.
k12.lang.art	The art of teaching language skills in grades K-12.
k12.lang.deutsch-eng	Bilingual German/English practice with native speakers.
k12.lang.esp-eng	Bilingual Spanish/English practice with native speakers.
k12.lang.francais	French practice with native speakers.
k12.lang.russian	Bilingual Russian/English practice with native speakers.
k12.sys.projects	Discussion of potential projects.
k12.sys.ch0	Current projects.
k12.sys.ch1	Current projects.
k12.sys.ch2	Current projects.
k12.sys.ch3	Current projects.
k12.sys.ch4	Current projects.
k12.sys.ch5	Current projects.
k12.sys.ch6	Current projects.
k12.sys.ch7	Current projects.
k12.sys.ch8	Current projects.
k12.sys.ch9	Current projects.
k12.sys.ch10	Current projects.
k12.sys.ch11	Current projects.
k12.sys.ch12	Current projects.

k12.* (continued):

k12.chat.elementary	Casual conversation for elementary students, grades K-5.
k12.chat.junior	Casual conversation for students in grades 6-8.
k12.chat.senior	Casual conversation for high school students.
k12.chat.teacher	Casual conversation for teachers of grades K-12.

relcom.*:

This is a hierarchy of Russian language newsgroups. It has no listed FAQs.

relcom.ads	Non-commercial ads. (Moderated)
relcom.archives	Messages about new items on archive sites.
relcom.archives.d	Discussions on file servers, archives.
relcom.bbs	BBS news.
relcom.commerce.audio-video	Audio & video equipment.
relcom.commerce.chemical	Chemical production.
relcom.commerce.computers	Computer hardware.
relcom.commerce.construction	Construction materials and equipment.
relcom.commerce.consume	Cosmetics, parfumes, dresses, shoes.
relcom.commerce.energy	Gas, coal, oil, fuel, generators, etc.
relcom.commerce.estate	Real estate.
relcom.commerce.food	Food & drinks (including alcoholic).
relcom.commerce.food.drinks	Spirits and soft drinks.
relcom.commerce.food.sweet	Sweets and sugar.
relcom.commerce.household	All for house - furniture, freezers, ovens, etc.
relcom.commerce.infoserv	Information services.
relcom.commerce.jobs	Jobs offered/wanted.
relcom.commerce.machinery	Machinery, plant equipment.
relcom.commerce.medicine	Medical services, equipment, drugs.
relcom.commerce.metals	Metals and metal products.
relcom.commerce.money	Credits, deposits, currency.

relcom.commerce.orgtech	Office equipment.
relcom.commerce.other	Miscelannia.
relcom.commerce.software	Software.
relcom.commerce.stocks	Stocks and bonds.
relcom.commerce.talk	Discussions about commercial groups.
relcom.commerce.tobacco	Cigarettes and tobacco.
relcom.commerce.tour	Tourism, leisure and entertainment opportunities.
relcom.commerce.transport	Vehicles and spare parts.
relcom.comp.binaries	Binary codes of computer programs. (Moderated)
relcom.comp.dbms.foxpro	FoxPro database development system.
relcom.comp.demo	Demo versions of various software. (Moderated)
relcom.comp.demo.d	Discussions on demonstration programs.
relcom.comp.lang.pascal	Using of Pascal programming language.
relcom.comp.os.os2	FIDOnet area, OS/2 operational system.
relcom.comp.os.vms	VMS operational system.
relcom.comp.os.windows	FIDOnet area, MS-Windows operational system.
relcom.comp.os.windows.prog	FIDOnet area, programming under MS-Windows.
relcom.comp.sources.d	Discussions on sources.
relcom.comp.sources.misc	Software sources. (Moderated)
relcom.currency	Discussion of Russian currency
relcom.exnet	Discussions on ExNet electronic exchange.
relcom.exnet.quote	ExNet quotes.
relcom.expo	Exhibitions and fairs announcements and reviews. (Moderated)
relcom.fido.flirt	FIDOnet, just talking of love.
relcom.fido.ru.hacker	FIDOnet, hackers and crackers (legal!).
relcom.fido.ru.modem	Inter-network discussion on modems.
relcom.fido.ru.networks	Inter-network discussion of global nets.

Other Hierarchies

relcom.* (continued):

relcom.fido.ru.strack	FIDOnet, digitized sound.
relcom.fido.ru.unix	Inter-network challenge to OS Unix.
relcom.fido.su.books	FIDOnet, for book readers and lovers.
relcom.fido.su.c-c++	FIDOnet, C & C++ language.
relcom.fido.su.dbms	FIDOnet, database management systems.
relcom.fido.su.general	FIDOnet, about everything and nothing.
relcom.fido.su.hardw	FIDOnet, computer hardware.
relcom.fido.su.magic	FIDOnet, magic and occult sciences.
relcom.fido.su.softw	FIDOnet, software in general.
relcom.fido.su.tolkien	FIDOnet, creations of J.R.R Tolkien.
relcom.fido.su.virus	FIDOnet, viruses and vaccines.
relcom.humor	Ha-ha-ha. Jokes, you know them, funny.
relcom.infomarket.quote	Ex-USSR exchanges's quotes /ASMP/. (Moderated)
relcom.infomarket.talk	Discussion on market development /ASMP/. (Moderated)
relcom.jusinf	Information on laws by "Justicinform". (Moderated)
relcom.kids	About kids.
relcom.lan	Inter-network discussion on local area networks.
relcom.maps	Relcom maps.
relcom.msdos	MS-DOS software.
relcom.music	Music lovers.
relcom.netnews	Announcements and articles important for all netters.
relcom.netnews.big	General BIG articles.
relcom.newusers	Q&A of new Relcom users.
relcom.penpals	To find friends, colleagues, etc.
relcom.politics	Political discussions.
relcom.postmasters	For RELCOM postmasters, official. (Moderated)

relcom.postmasters.d	Discussion of postmaster's troubles and bright ideas.
relcom.relarn.general	Scientific academical subnet RELARN: general issues. (Moderated)
relcom.renews	Net magazine RENEWS. (Moderated)
relcom.sources	Superseded by relcom.comp.sources.misc. (Moderated)
relcom.spbnews	Political & economic news digest by SPB-News Agency. (Moderated)
relcom.talk	Unfettered talk.
relcom.tcpip	TCP/IP protocols and their implementation.
relcom.terms	Discussion of various terms and terminology.
relcom.test	"Wow, does it really work?".
relcom.wtc	Commercial proposals of World Trade Centers.
relcom.x	X Windows discussion.

VMSnet.*:

This set of newsgroups contains discussion of topics of interest to VAX/VMS users. It has no listed FAQs.

vmsnet.admin	Administration of the VMSnet newsgroups.
vmsnet.alpha	Discussion about Alpha AXP architecture, systems, porting, etc.
vmsnet.announce	General announcements of interest to all. (Moderated)
vmsnet.announce.newusers	Orientation info for new users. (Moderated)
vmsnet.databases.rdb	DEC's Rdb relational DBMS and related topics.
vmsnet.decus.journal	The DECUServe Journal. (Moderated)
vmsnet.decus.lugs	Discussion of DECUS Local User Groups and related issues.
vmsnet.employment	Jobs sought/offered, workplace and employment related issues.
vmsnet.internals	VMS internals, MACRO-32, Bliss, etc., gatewayed to MACRO32 list.

VMSnet.* (continued):

vmsnet.mail.misc	Other electronic mail software.
vmsnet.mail.pmdf	PMDF email system, gatewayed to ipmdf mailing list.
vmsnet.mail.mx	MX email system, gatewayed to MX mailing list.
vmsnet.misc	General VMS topics not covered elsewhere.
vmsnet.networks.desktop.misc	Other desktop integration software.
vmsnet.networks.-desktop.-pathworks	DEC Pathworks desktop integration software.
vmsnet.networks.-management.decmcc	DECmcc and related software.
vmsnet.networks.management.-misc	Other network management solutions.
vmsnet.networks.misc	General networking topics not covered elsewhere.
vmsnet.networks.tcp-ip.cmu-tek	CMU-TEK TCP/IP package, gatewayed to cmu-tek - tcp+@andrew.cmu.edu.
vmsnet.networks.tcp-ip.misc	Other TCP/IP solutions for VMS.
vmsnet.networks.tcp-ip.multinet	TGV's Multinet TCP/IP, gatewayed to info-multinet.
vmsnet.networks.tcp-ip.tcpware	Discussion of Process Software's TCPWARE TCP/IP software.
vmsnet.networks.tcp-ip.ucx	DEC's VMS/Ultrix Connection (or TCP/IP services for VMS) product.
vmsnet.networks.tcp-ip.wintcp	The Wollongong Group's WIN-TCP TCP/IP software.
vmsnet.pdp-11	PDP-11 hardware and software, gatewayed to info-pdp11.
vmsnet.sources	Source code postings ONLY. (Moderated)
vmsnet.sources.d	Discussion about or requests for sources.
vmsnet.sources.games	Recreational software postings.
vmsnet.sysmgt	VMS system management.

vmsnet.test	Test messages.
vmsnet.tpu	TPU language and applications, gatewayed to info-tpu.
vmsnet.uucp	DECUS uucp software, gatewayed to vmsnet mailing list.
vmsnet.vms-posix	Discussion about VMS POSIX.

Accessing USENET

3

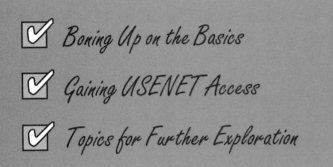

☑ *Boning Up on the Basics*

☑ *Gaining USENET Access*

☑ *Topics for Further Exploration*

If you are a regular computer user skip this chapter. This chapter outlines some basic concepts that all who want to gain USENET access should be familiar with. It will describe some fundamental computer concepts and point the reader in the right direction for further, more detailed reading.

Boning Up on the Basics

USENET Basics

If you have made it this far into the book, you know that USENET is a method of exchanging information with people around the world using computers. You know that there are hundreds of thousands of conversations going on at any one time in the form of USENET newsgroups. You also know that the depth and breadth of the subjects covered in USENET newsgroups is increasing at an exponential rate.

Before trying to gain access to USENET there are a few basic concepts that, if you understand them ahead of time, will make your USENET experience more rewarding.

Computer Basics

You don't necessarily need to understand how your computer works to successfully use it but you do need to have a basic understanding of how to use a computer. The set of things you will need to know about will depend on how you will be accessing USENET. Whether you access USENET from a personal computer at home, or a remote computer at work will determine which items you need to bone up on along the way.

A *personal computer* (PC) is a computer that is self contained. That is to say that all of its parts are within a cable's reach. Those parts usually consist of a *keyboard*, a *video display terminal* (VDT), a *central processing unit* (CPU), one or more *hard disks*, one or more *floppy disk drives*, a *mouse*, a *printer* (optionally), any number of special purpose *boards* installed internally (such as a *modem*, or *FAX board*) and cables and connectors to hook them all together. A PC was designed to be used by one person at a time.

A *remote computer* is usually a larger version of functionally the same equipment. It allows more than one person to access it at the same time so it usually has many keyboards and

VDTs hooked up to it. Remote computers come in all shapes and sizes. The equipment that makes up a remote computer usually has a much a greater capacity than that which makes up a personal computer.

Both types of computers keep track of information in the form of *computer files* stored on their hard or floppy disks. Computer files come in many varieties. Some files contain information that you put in them. Some files contain instructions to perform jobs. Some computer files contain pictures. Others still contain sound. Accessing USENET newsgroups will require that you use files to run programs, read parts of conversations, write bits of conversation and possibly even store information for later use.

If you were to read something interesting that you wanted to share with someone else, in the days before computers, you would probably make a photocopy of the original. You would then either hand it to the person you had in mind directly or put it in an envelope and mail it to them. Doing this required much leg work. Especially if you didn't have direct access to a copier.

Using a computer to save some interesting reading is as easy as typing an "s" in most news reader programs. Sharing it with someone else requires only the typing of their e-mail address. If I happen upon a joke that I like, with a few keystrokes I can send it to a dozen friends all at one time and all with out leaving my chair. Much easier than trying to remember it until I see them.

Computer File Systems

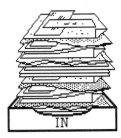

If you will be using your very own personal computer to access USENET's newsgroups, take some time to become familiar with your *directory* and *file system*. Browse the user's guide for your particular *operating system* and learn how to manage your computers files.

Here are some of the basic operations for managing files that will come in handy when managing and exchanging information using USENET's newsgroups:

✔ Viewing a disk's directory structure

✔ Changing to a different disk

✔ Creating a file using an editor or word processor

✔ Editing a file using an editor or word processor

✔ Copying a file to another file

✔ Copying a file to a floppy disk

✔ Printing a file

✔ Deleting a file

✔ Creating a directory

✔ Moving a file between directories

If you will be using a *terminal* connected to a remote computer via a modem to access USENET, you will have less control over your directory and file system than you would with a PC but there are still a few things you will need to understand.

Remote computers assign users login accounts. A login account usually consists of a *username* and *password* to access the remote computer, a bit of *disk space* for creating and managing files and possibly (but not always) access to special commands to make some of the things that you want to do easier to do. The last mentioned here is highly *service provider* dependent. Some service providers provide an elaborate *user interface* to guide its users through the basic functions. Others provide only access to the remote computer's operating system and expect the user to know what to tell it to get the job done.

Should you find yourself selecting a service provider, choose one that provides the appropriate level of user assistance for your needs. If this will be your first time spending any amount of time in front of a computer keyboard, you will prefer an interface that gives you instructions along the way. If you are a Unix *hacker*, chances are you wouldn't be happy confined to the options a menu driven interface would provide. Your service provider will supply you with the necessary reading material to guide you through the services it provides.

Editors

An *editor* is a program that allows you to create a file. There are many varieties of editors and *word processors* available on both personal computers and remote computers. The trick for you will be finding one that is both easy for you to use and one that is readily supported. For interacting with USENET's newsgroups you will want to be able to create *flat text files*—no fancy *fonts*. Once again your service provider will be able to supply you with the necessary reading material to do this.

If you will be paying a service provider for your USENET *connection time*, you may want to learn how to create files on your personal computer and then transfer them to the remote computer you are using to access USENET. This may be a more economical approach for posting long articles.

Terminals, Terminal Emulators and Communication

Remote computers interact with people using terminals. If you happen to be accessing a remote computer from a personal computer, you must first convince it that you are one of its terminals. This you do using a *terminal emulation program* running on your personal computer.

Terminals (and *terminal emulators*) come in all shapes and sizes. Each uses a different communication *protocol* to interact with the computer it is connected to. Making sure that both your terminal and the computer it is connected to are talking the same language is one *configuration* obstacle that you will have to overcome.

If you will be accessing USENET using someone else's equipment (your school's or employer's) the computer system administration department will have this all worked out for you. If you will be accessing USENET from home, your service provider will be able to give you a hand setting up the proper *terminal mode*. This will probably be the most frustrating part of your USENET experience but don't despair. You will not be doing anything that hasn't been done many times before by other people. It just may take a little bit of time to get the answers from the experts about what you need to do to do the same. In the process of doing this you will hear words like *baud rate, handshaking* and *parity.* Trust the experts. These are well defined and understood. They will guide you through the process of setting these parameters in meaningful way for both your computer and the remote computer you will be accessing.

News Readers

Once you have established an effective way of communicating with your remote computer, you will be getting to know your local news reader program. Just as there are many different types of editors and terminals available, there are many types of news reader programs available. Each is different. Each has advantages and disadvantages. All attempt to do the same job which is giving you access in an orderly manner to the files that make up the USENET newsgroups.

You will probably have very little control over which news reader you have access to. Whichever one it is, your service provider will be able to tell you which one you will be using. The service provider will probably also be able to supply you will the necessary reading material to successfully navigate USENET's newsgroups using your news reader.

"Appendix C—A Word About News Readers" is an overview of some available news readers. It contains a command summary for a few of the more common ones. It will also direct you to further reading on the subject.

This chapter will help you evaluate the best avenue for you to get access to USENET's newsgroups. It will direct you to the right people and arm you with the appropriate questions to ask them. There are many different configurations possible for accessing USENET's newsgroups. This will help you find the easiest one available to you.

17

Gaining USENET Access

Typical Configurations

Most people access USENET's newsgroups using equipment owned by their employer or educational facility. The reason for this is the amount of equipment both hardware and software needed to access USENET is not trivial. USENET is a valuable work resource which is why many employers support it. USENET is also great fun. Many people spend a considerable amount of time browsing and interacting with USENET's newsgroups. Because USENET can be a time sink, people who access USENET from their employer's equipment usually do so during non-work time. Many dial up the remote computer at work using a terminal or personal computer available from home.

People who do not have access to USENET from an employer or educational facility can pay for access to USENET from what is called a service provider. "Appendix A—*Getting USENET Access*" contains a list of service providers. Using a service provider assumes that you have the appropriate equipment available from home to access the remote computer at the service provider's site.

Equipment You Will Need

Whether you will be accessing USENET from someone else's equipment or your own there is some basic equipment you will need. The following outlines the basic equipment needed.

- ✔ Video Display Terminal (or PC with Terminal Emulator)
- ✔ Keyboard
- ✔ Connection to Remote Computer with USENET Newsgroup Feed (can be direct via cable or indirect via modem and telephone)
- ✔ Account on Remote Computer (username, password, minimal disk space, possibly e-mail access)

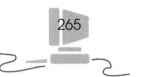

✔ Available News Reader Program

✔ Available Editor Program

If the equipment mentioned above isn't available to you through work or school, you can purchase or rent all of the items listed and any associated peripheral items. Your local computer store will gladly help you define any items you may need if you tell them what it is you are trying to do. Your needs and preferences will determine the cost of the items. It can be as little as a few hundred dollars or as much as a couple thousand. (Are the advantages of using someone else's equipment becoming more apparent to you now?)

Pursuing Existing Avenues

What if you don't know whether or not your employer has access to USENET's newsgroups? Here are a couple of items you can use to gauge the possibility. Do you (or others around you) have a PC sitting on your desk? Does your company use electronic mail to communicate among its employees? Does your company use electronic mail to communicate with other institutions? Is there a computer systems administration group on site where you work? Do you have an account on any of the larger computers at work?

If the answer to any of these questions is yes, there is a good possibility that your company already has access to USENET's newsgroups. Especially if you know there is a team of computer system administrators on site.

Determining whether or not the proper equipment exists is the first step. The next step is to determine whether or not your company subscribes to USENET's newsgroups. If you have a computer system administration group, go ask them. They are the ones who would know. Find your local hacker and ask "Are you familiar with USENET?" If the answer is no, well, go talk to someone else in the department. If the answer is yes, then ask "Do we subscribe to USENET's newsgroups?" If the answer again is yes, you are in business. Your next task is to find out what you need to do to gain access.

Do not be afraid if you do not have a PC or terminal already sitting on your desk. Old ones have become quite common. The old ones have been replaced with newer faster ones

so it is not uncommon for companies to have a closet full of old ones around for people to use. Some companies will even let you take one home to use to work from home.

If the person you are talking to seems unwilling to spend the necessary time with you to learn how to properly access your site's USENET newsgroups, ask for a referral. Find out the name of someone in the company who is currently using USENET and might be willing to help a new user get started. There is usually someone around who is willing to serve as a USENET champion.

Encouraging Avenues to Exist

If you determine that your company has the necessary equipment in place but doesn't currently subscribe to the USENET newsgroups, you may be able to encourage them to do so. The first thing you must do is find someone who is technically capable of the computer tasks, who finds the idea appealing and who has the time to devote to establishing a USENET newsgroup feed. Doing so is not a trivial task but it is one that is well defined. The right person will not have trouble finding the necessary support for accomplishing the task.

Hand the person of choice a copy of "Appendix A— *Getting USENET Access*" and let them read it. It contains much of the information needed to get started establishing a USENET newsgroup feed including references to further reading material.

Creating Your Own Avenue

If you have determined that you have the appropriate equipment to access USENET from home, you must now select a service provider. Determine what your goals are. Do you just want to browse? Do you really want to interact with other people? Do you need access to material that may be archived somewhere? Do you want to collect information? Will you be able to store information on your personal computer or do you need to rent space on someone else's? Do you want to be able to send and receive electronic mail?

You should have a clear understanding of what it is you want to do before shopping for a service provider. There are many service providers who will happily charge you for services that you don't need. Being clear in your own mind about

what you want to use USENET for will make it easier to evaluate the different service providers.

Start with the list of service providers in "Appendix A, *Getting USENET Access*." Call and request information from the service providers that are local to your area. The "local" part may or may not be important depending on the provider. If you live in New York, you may not want to pay the cost of a two hour phone call to California. The service provider should be able to tell you what type of equipment you will need to best access the service provider's remote computer.

In summary, to establish your own connection to USENET's newsgroups, find a service provider that is compatible with the equipment that you own, purchase what you are missing and subscribe to the service. The service provider should be able to guide you through the process of configuring your system.

This chapter concludes our journey to the electronic community that is USENET. In here you will find some strange animals that will empower you to make the most of your USENET adventures. Covered here are tools developed to facilitate information gathering and information sharing. This chapter will give you an overview of the tool, how it is used and where to go for more information about it.

18

Topics for Further Exploration

Archie

There is such a thing called an "archie anonymous ftp database." A *database* is a collection of information. *Anonymous ftp* is a method of accessing a remote computer for information. Anonymous ftp databases are collections of information about computers that have information to make available to other people. Archie is a program that searches these databases.

If you know that information exists somewhere about a certain topic but don't know where, use archie. Let's look at an example of how it works. There is a valuable document available called "The Internet Resource Guide." It contains a list of various Internet resources available to the Internet using public such as online library catalogs, data archives, online white pages directory, networks, network information centers and computer resources. The guide used to be available from nnsc.nsf.net using anonymous ftp. It has since moved to a different site.

Archie can be used to help locate this document. From a computer that has the archie program available type "archie resource-guide." Here is a sample of what archie returns:

```
Host aramis.rutgers.edu

  Location: /
    DIRECTORY drwxr-xr-x          512 Dec 15 02:07 resource-guide

Host athene.uni-paderborn.de

  Location: /doc/FAQ/comp.answers/prolog
    DIRECTORY drwxr-xr-x          512 Dec 15 12:33 resource-guide
  Location: /doc/FAQ/news.answers/prolog
    DIRECTORY drwxr-xr-x          512 Dec 15 12:01 resource-guide

Host athos.rutgers.edu

  Location: /
    DIRECTORY drwxr-xr-x          512 Dec 15 02:07 resource-guide

Host bloom-picayune.mit.edu

  Location: /pub/usenet-by-group/comp.answers/prolog
    DIRECTORY drwxrwxr-x          512 Dec 13 20:07 resource-guide
  Location: /pub/usenet-by-group/news.answers/prolog
    DIRECTORY drwxrwxr-x          512 Dec 13 20:07 resource-guide
  Location: /pub/usenet-by-hierarchy/comp/answers/prolog
    DIRECTORY drwxrwxr-x          512 Dec 13 20:07 resource-guide
  Location: /pub/usenet-by-hierarchy/news/answers/prolog
    DIRECTORY drwxrwxr-x          512 Dec 13 20:07 resource-guide
```

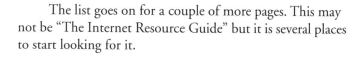

The list goes on for a couple of more pages. This may not be "The Internet Resource Guide" but it is several places to start looking for it.

Electronic Mail

Instant gratification is just one of the positive features of *electronic mail* (e-mail). Sending someone a brief message is as simple as typing a few keystrokes. Sending someone (or a group of people for that matter) an entire document is just as easy. Especially if the document already exists in a computer file. Within minutes you can receive a reply to your message (from the other side of the world even) as well.

Sharing information is what USENET's newsgroups are all about. E-mail allows you to restrict your conversation to just the people you want to talk to. If you have USENET access, getting an e-mail address is usually just a form away. Ask the same people who provided your USENET connection about an e-mail account. They will be able to supply you with the appropriate information.

File Transfers and "anonymous ftp"

File transfers are very important. A file transfer is the fundamental way of going about exchanging information between computers. In the process of searching for information, you may be referred to a remote machine that contains just what you are looking for. to get the information you will need to know how to transfer a file. One very popular way of doing this is using what is called "anonymous ftp." ftp is a user interface to the File Transfer Protocol. It is a program that will allow you to transfer files between computers. Anonymous ftp is a way of making files available to people.

In my search for "The Internet Resource Guide" I eventually was directed to the appropriate ftp site to retrieve the document. Using anonymous ftp I was able to remotely log on to the site's computer, find the file I had been referred to and transfer it back to my computer. Here is what the session

looked like. The bold text is the only text that I personally typed.

```
fristrup@hplabs 1021$ ftp ds.internic.net
Connected to ds.internic.net.
220- InterNIC Directory and Database Services
220-
220-Welcome to InterNIC Directory and Database Services pro-
vided by AT&T.
220-These services are partially supported through a cooperative
agreement
220-with the National Science Foundation.
220-
220-Your comments and suggestions for improvement are wel-
come, and can be
220-mailed to admin@ds.internic.net.
220-
220-AT&T MAKES NO WARRANTY OR GUARANTEE, OR PROMISE,
EXPRESS OR IMPLIED,
220-CONCERNING THE CONTENT OR ACCURACY OF THE INTER-
NIC DIRECTORY ENTRIES
220-AND DATABASE FILES STORED AND MAINTAINED BY AT&T. AT&T
EXPRESSLY
220-DISCLAIMS AND EXCLUDES ALL EXPRESS WARRANTIES AND
IMPLIED WARRANTIES
220-OF MERCHANTABLILITY AND FITNESS FOR A PARTICULAR PUR-
POSE.
220-
220-            *****************************
220-
220 ds.internic.net FTP server ready.
Name (ds.internic.net:fristrup): anonymous
331 Guest login ok, send ident as password.
Password: fristrup@hpl.hp.com
230 Guest login ok, access restrictions apply.
Remote system type is UNIX.
Using binary mode to transfer files.
ftp> dir
200 PORT command successful.
150 Opening ASCII mode data connection for /bin/ls.
total 447
-rw-r--r-- 1 101        30      413 Jul 15 21:47 .Links
-rw-r--r-- 1 101        1       10 Apr 16 1993 .cshrc
drwxr-xr-x 6 101        30      512 Aug 19 19:06 .ds
d--x--x--x 2 root       1       512 Feb 8 1993 bin
drwxr-xr-x 2 root       1       512 Feb 8 1993 dev
drwxr-xr-x 25 101       30      1024 Jan 6 02:00 dirofdirs
d--x--x--x 2 root       1       512 Feb 8 1993 etc
drwxr-xr-x 3 101        1       1024 Jan 6 04:53 fyi
drwxrwxr-x 4 101        60      2048 Jan 6 04:51 iesg
drwxrwxr-x145 101       60      3584 Jan 6 04:51 ietf
drwxrwxrwx 4 101        60      512 Nov 22 17:56 incoming
drwxrwxr-x 3 101        60      40448 Jan 6 13:46 internet-drafts
```

```
drwxr-xr-x 5 101        30      1024 Nov 9 19:21 internic.info
drwxrwxr-x 12 101       60      2048 Nov 25 04:52 isoc
drwxr-xr-x 2 root       root    8192 Feb 3 1993 lost+found
-rw-r--r-- 1 101        30      349260 Jan 6 10:13 ls-lR
drwxr-xr-x 4 101        30      512 Nov 24 19:50 nsf
drwxr-xr-x 82 101       1       2048 Sep 17 16:33 policies-proce
                                dures
drwxr-xr-x 12 101       1       512 Dec 28 16:15 pub
drwxr-xr-x 11 101       1       1024 Jun 17 1993 resource-guide
lrwxrwxrwx 1 101        30      14 Aug 10 18:48 resources -> /ftp/
                                dirofdirs
drwxr-xr-x 3 101        1       19968 Jan 6 04:56 rfc
drwxr-xr-x 3 101        1       1536 Nov 17 16:23 std
drwxr-xr-x 4 root       1       512 Feb 8 1993 usr
226 Transfer complete.
ftp> cd resource-guide
250 CWD command successful.
ftp> dir
200 PORT command successful.
150 Opening ASCII mode data connection for /bin/ls.
total 2412
drwxr-xr-x 2 101        30      512 Dec 25 1992 announce
drwxr-xr-x 2 101        30      1024 Feb 22 1993 chapter.1
drwxr-xr-x 2 101        30      1536 Mar 15 1993 chapter.2
drwxr-xr-x 2 101        30      2048 Mar 15 1993 chapter.3
drwxr-xr-x 2 101        30      512 Nov 13 1992 chapter.4
drwxr-xr-x 2 101        30      3072 Mar 16 1993 chapter.5
drwxr-xr-x 2 101        30      512 Dec 4 1992 chapter.6
drwxr-xr-x 2 101        30      1024 Nov 13 1992 chapter.M
drwxr-xr-x 2 101        30      512 Jun 17 1993 front-matter
-rw-r--r-- 1 101        30      21062 Mar 17 1993 index-
                                resource-guide
-rw-r--r-- 1 101        30      25953 Mar 14 1993 ls-lsR
-rw-r--r-- 1 101        30      11182 Jun 17 1993 overview
-rw-r--r-- 1 101        30      2779 Jun 17 1993 privacy-
                                accuracy
-rw-r--r-- 1 101        30      17267 Jan 21 1993 resource-
                                guide-help
-rw-r--r-- 1 101        30      5125 Nov 11 1992 toc.ps
-rw-r--r-- 1 101        30      547 Nov 11 1992 toc.txt
-rw-r--r-- 1 101        30      578238 Mar 17 1993
                                wholeguide.txt
226 Transfer complete.
ftp> get wholeguide.txt
200 PORT command successful.
150 Opening BINARY mode data connection for wholeguide.txt
(578238 bytes).
226 Transfer complete.
578238 bytes received in 14.42 seconds (39.16 Kbytes/s)
ftp> quit
221 Goodbye.
fristrup@hplabs 1022$
```

This was a minimal investment to retrieve a hefty 100-page document that is full of valuable information.

Gopher

The Internet Gopher is a distributed document delivery service. It allows a user to access various types of data residing on multiple hosts in a seamless fashion. This is accomplished by presenting the user a hierarchical arrangement of documents. The program accepts simple queries and responds by sending a document. Here is an example of what a gopher screen looks like:

```
Internet Gopher Information Client v1.12S
Root gopher server: gopher.micro.umn.edu
--> 1. Information About Gopher/
     2. Computer Information/
     3. Discussion Groups/
     4. Fun & Games/
     5. Internet file server (ftp) sites/
     6. Libraries/
     7. News/
     8. Other Gopher and Information Servers/
     9. Phone Books/
    10. Search Gopher Titles at the University of Minnesota <?>
    11. Search lots of places at the University of Minnesota <?>
    12. University of Minnesota Campus Information/
Press ? for Help, q to Quit, u to go up a menu Page: 1/1
```

The gopher interface is menu driven. It presents its user with a list of the available options at any one time. If you have access to gopher, it is the best place to look for documentation on it is in gopher itself. If you have questions about gopher, ask the people in the "comp.infosystems.gopher" newsgroup.

Mailing Lists

You may find yourself without the time to browse all of your favorite USENET newsgroups all of the time. One way that you can keep up on all that is happening in your topics of interest (assuming you have an e-mail address) is to place your name on a mailing list. There are hundreds of mailing lists available. Your favorite newsgroup will be able to refer you to the appropriate one for your topic of interest. Belonging to a mailing list will assure that you receive the latest information on the happenings in your subject area.

There is a wonderful book available that covers the subject of mailing lists and interest groups. It is called *Internet*

Mailing Lists by SRI International. It contains over 300 pages of available mailing lists. If you think that your time might be better spent devoted only to those topics you love, pick up a copy of this book. You may be able to save yourself some time and make some new friends in the process.

Remote Access via Telnet

The "telnet" program is a user interface to the TELNET protocol. Telnet is used to communicate with another computer using the TELNET protocol. Telnet allows a person sitting at one *workstation* to communicate with a computer halfway around the world as if that computer were in the same room.

In your USENET browsings you may find yourself referred to a remote host's resources (programs and data). An example of using a remote computer's resources would be accessing New York City's public library, from Hawaii. To get to that remote computer you may have to learn a little bit about using telnet. *The Whole Internet* by Ed Krol (O'Reilly and Associates, Inc.) devotes an entire chapter to using telnet. Also try the *man pages* or help files that may be available of the computer you are using.

WAIS

WAIS is a distributed text searching system. It is for working with collections of data. It searches through indexed material and finds articles based on what they contain. *The Whole Internet* by Ed Krol (O'Reilly & Associates, Inc.) devotes a chapter to its use. Or, you can take it for a spin yourself by telneting to quake.think.com and logging on as "wais." If you have any questions about it, try asking the people in the "comp.infosystems.wais" newsgroup.

World Wide Web

The World Wide Web (WWW) is an attempt to organize all the information available on the Internet using *hypertext*. Hypertext is a method of presenting information where selected words in the body of the text can be expanded into further reading at any time. Different types of user interfaces are available for it. You can access WWW by telneting to info.cern.ch. No log on is necessary. For further reading, *The Whole Internet* by Ed Krol (O'Reilly & Associates, Inc.) devotes a chapter to it. There is also a newsgroup devoted to it called "comp.infosystems.www."

The articles contained in this appendix were retrieved from rtfm.mit.edu using anonymous ftp. With the exception of typesetting, no modifications have been made to the article content.

A

Articles from the Source

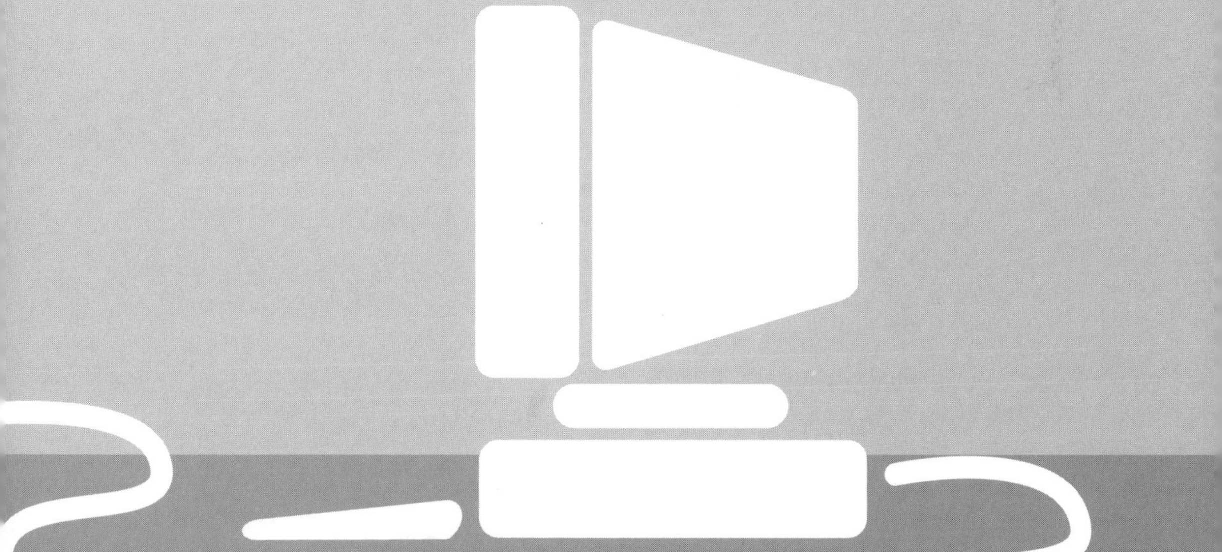

What is USENET?

The following article describes what USENET is. It is the closest thing there is to a USENET definition. It is an article that is posted periodically to the newsgroup "news.announce.newusers". It is entitled "What is USENET/Part 1". Chip Salzenberg is the original author. Gene Spafford maintained it until May of 1993. It is considered required reading for those new to USENET.

What is USENET/Part 1

Archive-name: what-is-usenet/part1
Original from: chip@tct.com (Chip Salzenberg)
Comment: edited until 5/93 by spaf@cs.purdue.edu (Gene Spafford)
Last-change: 19 July 1992 by spaf@cs.purdue.edu (Gene Spafford)

The first thing to understand about Usenet is that it is widely misunderstood. Every day on Usenet, the "blind men and the elephant" phenomenon is evident, in spades. In my opinion, more flame wars arise because of a lack of understanding of the nature of Usenet than from any other source. And consider that such flame wars arise, of necessity, among people who are on Usenet. Imagine, then, how poorly understood Usenet must be by those outside!

Any essay on the nature of Usenet cannot ignore the erroneous impressions held by many Usenet users. Therefore, this article will treat falsehoods first. Keep reading for truth. (Beauty, alas, is not relevant to Usenet.)

What Usenet Is Not

1. Usenet is not an organization.

    No person or group has authority over Usenet as a whole. No one controls who gets a news feed, which articles are propagated where, who can post articles, or anything else. There is no "Usenet Incorporated," nor is there a "Usenet User's Group." You're on your own.

    Granted, there are various activities organized by means of Usenet newsgroups. The newsgroup creation process is one such

activity. But it would be a mistake to equate Usenet with the organized activities it makes possible. If they were to stop tomorrow, Usenet would go on without them.

2. Usenet is not a democracy.

    Since there is no person or group in charge of Usenet as a whole -- i.e. there is no Usenet "government" -- it follows that Usenet cannot be a democracy, autocracy, or any other kind of "-acy." (But see "The Camel's Nose?" below.)

3. Usenet is not fair.

    After all, who shall decide what's fair? For that matter, if someone is behaving unfairly, who's going to stop him? Neither you nor I, that's certain.

4. Usenet is not a right.

    Some people misunderstand their local right of "freedom of speech" to mean that they have a legal right to use others' computers to say what they wish in whatever way they wish, and the owners of said computers have no right to stop them.

    Those people are wrong. Freedom of speech also means freedom not to speak. If I choose not to use my computer to aid your speech, that is my right. Freedom of the press belongs to those who own one.

5. Usenet is not a public utility.

    Some Usenet sites are publicly funded or subsidized. Most of them, by plain count, are not. There is no government monopoly on Usenet, and little or no government control.

6. Usenet is not an academic network.

    It is no surprise that many Usenet sites are universities, research labs or other academic institutions. Usenet originated with a link between two universities, and the exchange of idea and information is what such institutions are all about. But the passage of years has changed Usenet's character. Today, by plain count, most Usenet sites are commercial entities.

7.   Usenet is not an advertising medium.

Because of Usenet's roots in academia, and because Usenet depends so heavily on cooperation (sometimes among competitors), custom dictates that advertising be kept to a minimum. It is tolerated if it is infrequent, informative, and low-hype.

The "comp.newprod" newsgroup is NOT an exception to this rule: product announcements are screened by a moderator in an attempt to keep the hype-to-information ratio in check.

If you must engage in flackery for your company, use the "biz" hierarchy, which is explicitly "advertising-allowed", and which (like all of Usenet) is carried only by those sites that want it.

8.   Usenet is not the Internet.

The Internet is a wide-ranging network, parts of which are subsidized by various governments. It carries many kinds of traffic, of which Usenet is only one. And the Internet is only one of the various networks carrying Usenet traffic.

9.   Usenet is not a UUCP network.

UUCP is a protocol (actually a "protocol suite," but that's a technical quibble) for sending data over point-to-point connections, typically using dialup modems. Sites use UUCP to carry many kinds of traffic, of which Usenet is only one. And UUCP is only one of the various transports carrying Usenet traffic.

10. Usenet is not a United States network.

It is true that Usenet originated in the United States, and the fastest growth in Usenet sites has been there. Nowadays, however, Usenet extends worldwide.

The heaviest concentrations of Usenet sites outside the U.S. seem to be in Canada, Europe, Australia and Japan.

Keep Usenet's worldwide nature in mind when you post articles. Even those who can read your language may have a culture wildly different from yours. When your words are read, they might not mean what you think they mean.

11. Usenet is not a UNIX network.

     Don't assume that everyone is using "rn" on a UNIX machine. Among the systems used to read and post to Usenet are Vaxen running VMS, IBM mainframes, Amigas, and MS-DOS PCs.

12. Usenet is not an ASCII network.

     The A in ASCII stands for "American". Sites in other countries often use character sets better suited to their language(s) of choice; such are typically, though not always, supersets of ASCII. Even in the United States, ASCII is not universally used: IBM mainframes use (shudder) EBCDIC. Ignore non-ASCII sites if you like, but they exist.

13. Usenet is not software.

     There are dozens of software packages used at various sites to transport and read Usenet articles. So no one program or package can be called "the Usenet software."

     Software designed to support Usenet traffic can be (and is) used for other kinds of communication, usually without risk of mixing the two. Such private communication networks are typically kept distinct from Usenet by the invention of newsgroup names different from the universally-recognized ones.

Well, enough negativity.

What Usenet Is

Usenet is the set of people who exchange articles tagged with one or more universally-recognized labels, called "newsgroups" (or "groups" for short).

(Note that the term "newsgroup" is correct, while "area," "base," "board," "bboard," "conference," "round table," "SIG," etc. are incorrect. If you want to be understood, be accurate.)

Diversity

If the above definition of Usenet sounds vague, that's because it is.

It is almost impossible to generalize over all Usenet sites in any non-trivial way. Usenet encompasses government agencies, large

universities, high schools, businesses of all sizes, home computers of all descriptions, etc., etc.

(In response to the above paragraphs, it has been written that there is nothing vague about a network that carries megabytes of traffic per day. I agree. But at the fringes of Usenet, traffic is not so heavy. In the shadowy world of news-mail gateways and mailing lists, the line between Usenet and not-Usenet becomes very hard to draw.)

Control

Every administrator controls his own site. No one has any real control over any site but his own.

The administrator gets her power from the owner of the system she administers. As long as her job performance pleases the owner, she can do whatever she pleases, up to and including cutting off Usenet entirely. Them's the breaks.

Sites are not entirely without influence on their neighbors, however. There is a vague notion of "upstream" and "downstream" related to the direction of high-volume news flow. To the extent that "upstream" sites decide what traffic they will carry for their "downstream" neighbors, those "upstream" sites have some influence on their neighbors' participation in Usenet. But such influence is usually easy to circumvent; and heavy-handed manipulation typically results in a backlash of resentment.

Periodic Postings

To help hold Usenet together, various articles (including this one) are periodically posted in newsgroups in the "news" hierarchy. These articles are provided as a public service by various volunteers. They are few but valuable. Learn them well.

Among the periodic postings are lists of active newsgroups, both "standard" (for lack of a better term) and "alternative." These lists, maintained by Gene Spafford, reflect his personal view of Usenet, and as such are not "official" in any sense of the word. However, if you're looking for a description of subjects discussed on Usenet, or if you're starting up a new Usenet site, Gene's lists are an eminently reasonable place to start.

Propagation

In the old days, when UUCP over long-distance dialup lines was the dominant means of article transmission, a few well-connected sites had real influence in determining which newsgroups would be carried where. Those sites called themselves "the backbone."

But things have changed. Nowadays, even the smallest Internet site has connectivity the likes of which the backbone admin of yesteryear could only dream. In addition, in the U.S., the advent of cheaper long-distance calls and high-speed modems has made long-distance Usenet feeds thinkable for smaller companies.

There is only one pre-eminent site for UUCP transport of Usenet in the U.S., namely UUNET. But UUNET isn't a player in the propagation wars, because it never refuses any traffic. UUNET charges by the minute, after all; and besides, to refuse based on content might jeopardize its legal status as an enhanced service provider.

All of the above applies to the U.S. In Europe, different cost structures favored the creation of strictly controlled hierarchical organizations with central registries. This is all very unlike the traditional mode of U.S. sites (pick a name, get the software, get a feed, you're on). Europe's "benign monopolies," long uncontested, now face competition from looser organizations patterned after the U.S. model.

Newsgroup Creation

The document that describes the current procedure for creating a new newsgroup is entitled "How To Create A New Newsgroup." Its common name, however, is "the guidelines."

If you follow the guidelines, it is probable that your group will be created and will be widely propagated.

HOWEVER: Because of the nature of Usenet, there is no way for any user to enforce the results of a newsgroup vote (or any other decision, for that matter). Therefore, for your new newsgroup to be propagated widely, you must not only follow the letter of the guidelines; you must also follow its spirit. And you must not allow even a whiff of shady dealings or dirty tricks to mar the vote. In other words, don't tick off system administrators; they will get their revenge.

So, you may ask: How is a new user supposed to know anything about the "spirit" of the guidelines? Obviously, he can't. This fact leads inexorably to the following recommendation:

 >> If you are a new user, don't try to create a new newsgroup. <<
If you have a good newsgroup idea, then read the "news.groups" newsgroup for a while (six months, at least) to find out how things work. If you're too impatient to wait six months, then you really need to learn; read "news.groups" for a year instead. If you just can't wait, find a Usenet old hand to run the vote for you.

Readers may think this advice unnecessarily strict. Ignore it at your peril. It is embarrassing to speak before learning. It is foolish to jump into a society you don't understand with your mouth open. And it is futile to try to force your will on people who can tune you out with the press of a key.

The Camel's Nose?

As was observed above in "What Usenet Is Not," Usenet as a whole is not a democracy. However, there is exactly one feature of Usenet that has a form of democracy: newsgroup creation.

A new newsgroup is unlikely to be widely propagated unless its sponsor follows the newsgroup creation guidelines; and the current guidelines require a new newsgroup to pass an open vote.

There are those who consider the newsgroup creation process to be a remarkably powerful form of democracy, since without any coercion, its decisions are almost always carried out. In their view, the democratic aspect of newsgroup creation is the precursor to an organized and democratic Usenet Of The Future.

On the other hand, some consider the democratic aspect of the newsgroup creation process a sham and a fraud, since there is no power of enforcement behind its decisions, and since there appears little likelihood that any such power of enforcement will ever be given it. For them, the appearance of democracy is only a tool used to keep proponents of flawed newsgroup proposals from complaining about their losses.

So, is Usenet on its way to full democracy? Or will property rights and mistrust of central authority win the day? Beats me.

If You are Unhappy...

Property rights being what they are, there is no higher authority on Usenet than the people who own the machines on which Usenet traffic is carried. If the owner of the machine you use says, "We will not carry alt.sex on this machine," and you are not happy with that order, you have no Usenet recourse. What can we outsiders do, after all?

That doesn't mean you are without options. Depending on the nature of your site, you may have some internal political recourse. Or you might find external pressure helpful. Or, with a minimal investment, you can get a feed of your own from somewhere else. Computers capable of taking Usenet feeds are down in the $500 range now, and UNIX-capable boxes are going for under $2000, and there are at least two UNIX lookalikes in the $100 price range.

No matter what, though, appealing to "Usenet" won't help. Even if those who read such an appeal are sympathetic to your cause, they will almost certainly have even less influence at your site than you do.

By the same token, if you don't like what some user at another site is doing, only the administrator and owner of that site have any authority to do anything about it. Persuade them that the user in question is a problem for them, and they might do something -- if they feel like it, that is.

If the user in question is the administrator or owner of the site from which she posts, forget it; you can't win. If you can, arrange for your newsreading software to ignore articles from her; and chalk one up to experience.

Words to Live by #1:
Usenet as Society

Those who have never tried electronic communication may not be aware of what a "social skill" really is. One social skill that must be learned, is that other people have points of view that are not only different, but *threatening*, to your own. In turn, your opinions may be threatening to others. There is nothing wrong with this. Your beliefs need not be hidden behind a facade, as happens with face-to-face conversation. Not everybody in the world is a bosom buddy, but you can still have a meaningful conversation with them. The person who cannot do this lacks in social skills.

                                        -- Nick Szabo

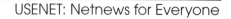
Words to Live by #2:
Usenet as Anarchy

Anarchy means having to put up with things that really piss you off.
-- Unknown

--

Gene Spafford
Software Engineering Research Center & Dept. of Computer Sciences
Purdue University, W. Lafayette IN 47907-1398
Internet: spaf@cs.purdue.eduphone: (317) 494-7825

How to Use USENET (Proper Netiquette)

This article is entitled "A Primer on How to Work with the USENET Community". It is a periodic posting to "news.announce.newusers". It describes proper USENET etiquette (also known as Netiquette). It was written originally by Chuq Von Rospach with modifications by Gene Spafford.

A Primer on How to Work with the USENET Community

Archive-name: usenet-primer/part1
Original-author: chuq@apple.COM (Chuq Von Rospach)
Comment: enhanced & edited until 5/93 by spaf@cs.purdue.edu (Gene Spafford)
Last-change: 25 Apr 1993 by spaf@cs.purdue.edu (Gene Spafford)

A Primer on How to Work With the USENET Community
Chuq Von Rospach

*** You now have access to Usenet, a network of thousands of computers. Other documents or your system administrator will provide detailed technical documentation. This message describes the Usenet culture and customs that have developed over time. All new users should read this message to find out how Usenet works. ***
*** (Old users could read it, too, to refresh their memories.) ***

USENET is a large collection of computers that share data with each other. It is the people on these computers that make USENET worth the effort to read and maintain, and for USENET to function properly those people must be able to interact in productive ways. This document is intended as a guide to using the net in ways that will be pleasant and productive for everyone.

This document is not intended to teach you how to use USENET. Instead, it is a guide to using it politely, effectively and efficiently. Communication by computer is new to almost everybody, and there are certain aspects that can make it a frustrating experience until you get used to them. This document should help you avoid the worst traps.

The easiest way to learn how to use USENET is to watch how others use it. Start reading the news and try to figure out what people are doing and why. After a couple of weeks you will start understanding why certain things are done and what things shouldn't be done. There are documents available describing the technical details of how to use the software. These are different depending on which programs you use to access the news. You can get copies of these from your system administrator. If you do not know who that person is, they can be contacted on most systems by mailing to account "usenet".

Never Forget that the Person on the Other Side is Human

Because your interaction with the network is through a computer it is easy to forget that there are people "out there." Situations arise where emotions erupt into a verbal free-for-all that can lead to hurt feelings.

Please remember that people all over the world are reading your words. Do not attack people if you cannot persuade them with your presentation of the facts. Screaming, cursing, and abusing others only serves to make people think less of you and less willing to help you when you need it.

If you are upset at something or someone, wait until you have had a chance to calm down and think about it. A cup of (decaf!) coffee or a good night's sleep works wonders on your perspective. Hasty words create more problems than they solve. Try not to say anything to others you would not say to them in person in a room full of people.

Don't Blame System Admins for their Users' Behavior

Sometimes, you may find it necessary to write to a system administrator about something concerning his or her site. Maybe it is a case of the

software not working, or a control message escaped, or maybe one of the users at that site has done something you feel requires comment. No matter how steamed you may be, be polite to the sysadmin -- he or she may not have any idea of what you are going to say, and may not have any part in the incidents involved. By being civil and temperate, you are more likely to obtain their courteous attention and assistance.

Be Careful What You Say About Others

Please remember -- you read netnews; so do as many as 3,000,000 other people. This group quite possibly includes your boss, your friend's boss, your girl friend's brother's best friend and one of your father's beer buddies. Information posted on the net can come back to haunt you or the person you are talking about.

Think twice before you post personal information about yourself or others. This applies especially strongly to groups like soc.singles and alt.sex but even postings in groups like talk.politics.misc have included information about the personal life of third parties that could get them into serious trouble if it got into the wrong hands.

Be Brief

Never say in ten words what you can say in fewer. Say it succinctly and it will have a greater impact. Remember that the longer you make your article, the fewer people will bother to read it.

Your Postings Reflect Upon You -- Be Proud of Them

Most people on USENET will know you only by what you say and how well you say it. They may someday be your co-workers or friends. Take some time to make sure each posting is something that will not embarrass you later. Minimize your spelling errors and make sure that the article is easy to read and understand. Writing is an art and to do it well requires practice. Since much of how people judge you on the net is based on your writing, such time is well spent.

Use Descriptive Titles

The subject line of an article is there to enable a person with a limited amount of time to decide whether or not to read your article. Tell people what the article is about before they read it. A title like "Car for Sale" to rec.autos does not help as much as "66 MG Midget for sale:

Beaverton OR." Don't expect people to read your article to find out what it is about because many of them won't bother. Some sites truncate the length of the subject line to 40 characters so keep your subjects short and to the point.

Think About Your Audience

When you post an article, think about the people you are trying to reach. Asking UNIX(*) questions on rec.autos will not reach as many of the people you want to reach as if you asked them on comp.unix.questions or comp.unix.internals. Try to get the most appropriate audience for your message, not the widest.

It is considered bad form to post both to misc.misc, soc.net-people, or misc.wanted and to some other newsgroup. If it belongs in that other newsgroup, it does not belong in misc.misc, soc.net-people, or misc.wanted.

If your message is of interest to a limited geographic area (apartments, car sales, meetings, concerts, etc...), restrict the distribution of the message to your local area. Some areas have special newsgroups with geographical limitations, and the recent versions of the news software allow you to limit the distribution of material sent to world-wide newsgroups. Check with your system administrator to see what newsgroups are available and how to use them.

If you want to try a test of something, do not use a world-wide newsgroup! Messages in misc.misc that say "This is a test" are likely to cause large numbers of caustic messages to flow into your mailbox. There are newsgroups that are local to your computer or area that should be used. Your system administrator can tell you what they are.

Be familiar with the group you are posting to before you post! You shouldn't post to groups you do not read, or post to groups you've only read a few articles from -- you may not be familiar with the on-going conventions and themes of the group. One normally does not join a conversation by just walking up and talking. Instead, you listen first and then join in if you have something pertinent to contribute.

Be Careful with Humor and Sarcasm

Without the voice inflections and body language of personal communications, it is easy for a remark meant to be funny to be misinterpreted. Subtle humor tends to get lost, so take steps to make

sure that people realize you are trying to be funny. The net has developed a symbol called the smiley face. It looks like ":-)" and points out sections of articles with humorous intent. No matter how broad the humor or satire, it is safer to remind people that you are being funny. But also be aware that quite frequently satire is posted without any explicit indications. If an article outrages you strongly, you should ask yourself if it just may have been unmarked satire. Several self-proclaimed connoisseurs refuse to use smiley faces, so take heed or you may make a temporary fool of yourself.

Only Post a Message Once

Avoid posting messages to more than one newsgroup unless you are sure it is appropriate. If you do post to multiple newsgroups, do not post to each group separately. Instead, specify all the groups on a single copy of the message. This reduces network overhead and lets people who subscribe to more than one of those groups see the message once instead of having to wade through each copy.

Please Rotate Messages With Questionable Content

Certain newsgroups (such as rec.humor) have messages in them that may be offensive to some people. To make sure that these messages are not read unless they are explicitly requested, these messages should be encrypted. The standard encryption method is to rotate each letter by thirteen characters so that an "a" becomes an "n". This is known on the network as "rot13" and when you rotate a message the word "rot13" should be in the "Subject:" line. Most of the software used to read usenet articles have some way of encrypting and decrypting messages. Your system administrator can tell you how the software on your system works, or you can use the Unix command "tr (a-z)(A-Z) (n-z)(a-m)(N-Z)(A-M)". (Note that some versions of Unix don't require the () in the "tr" command. In fact, some systems will get upset if you use them in an unquoted manner. The following should work for everyone, but may be shortened on some systems:

tr '(a-m)(n-z)(A-M)(N-Z)' '(n-z)(a-m)(N-Z)(A-M)'

Don't forget the single quotes!)

Summarize What You are Following Up

When you are following up someone's article, please summarize the parts of the article to which you are responding. This allows readers to

appreciate your comments rather than trying to remember what the original article said. It is also possible for your response to get to some sites before the original article.

Summarization is best done by including appropriate quotes from the original article. Do not include the entire article since it will irritate the people who have already seen it. Even if you are responding to the entire article, summarize only the major points you are discussing.

When Summarizing, Summarize!

When you request information from the network, it is common courtesy to report your findings so that others can benefit as well. The best way of doing this is to take all the responses that you received and edit them into a single article that is posted to the places where you originally posted your question. Take the time to strip headers, combine duplicate information, and write a short summary. Try to credit the information to the people that sent it to you, where possible.

Use Mail, Don't Post a Follow-up

One of the biggest problems we have on the network is that when someone asks a question, many people send out identical answers.
When this happens, dozens of identical answers pour through the net.
Mail your answer to the person and suggest that they summarize to the network. This way the net will only see a single copy of the answers, no matter how many people answer the question.

If you post a question, please remind people to send you the answers by mail and at least offer to summarize them to the network.

Read All Follow-ups and Don't Repeat What Has Already Been Said

Before you submit a follow-up to a message, read the rest of the messages in the newsgroup to see whether someone has already said what you want to say. If someone has, don't repeat it.

Check the Headers When Following Up

The news software has provisions to specify that follow-ups to an article should go to a specific set of newsgroups -- possibly different from the newsgroups to which the original article was posted. Sometimes the groups chosen for follow-ups are totally

inappropriate, especially as a thread of discussion changes with repeated postings. You should carefully check the groups and distributions given in the header and edit them as appropriate. If you change the groups named in the header, or if you direct follow-ups to a particular group, say so in the body of the message -- not everyone reads the headers of postings.

Be Careful About Copyrights and Licenses

Once something is posted onto the network, it is *probably* in the public domain unless you own the appropriate rights (most notably, if you wrote the thing yourself) and you post it with a valid copyright notice; a court would have to decide the specifics and there are arguments for both sides of the issue. Now that the US has ratified the Berne convention, the issue is even murkier (if you are a poster in the US). For all practical purposes, though, assume that you effectively give up the copyright if you don't put in a notice. Of course, the *information* becomes public, so you mustn't post trade secrets that way.

When posting material to the network, keep in mind that material that is UNIX-related may be restricted by the license you or your company signed with AT&T and be careful not to violate it. You should also be aware that posting movie reviews, song lyrics, or anything else published under a copyright could cause you, your company, or members of the net community to be held liable for damages, so we highly recommend caution in using this material.

Cite Appropriate References

If you are using facts to support a cause, state where they came from. Don't take someone else's ideas and use them as your own. You don't want someone pretending that your ideas are theirs; show them the same respect.

Mark or Rotate Answers and Spoilers

When you post something (like a movie review that discusses a detail of the plot) which might spoil a surprise for other people, please mark your message with a warning so that they can skip the message. Another alternative would be to use the "rot13" protocol to encrypt the message so it cannot be read accidentally. When you post a message with a spoiler in it make sure the word "spoiler" is part of the "Subject:" line.

Spelling Flames Considered Harmful

Every few months a plague descends on USENET called the spelling flame. It starts out when someone posts an article correcting the spelling or grammar in some article. The immediate result seems to be for everyone on the net to turn into a 6th grade English teacher and pick apart each other's postings for a few weeks. This is not productive and tends to cause people who used to be friends to get angry with each other. It is important to remember that we all make mistakes, and that there are many users on the net who use English as a second language. There are also a number of people who suffer from dyslexia and who have difficulty noticing their spelling mistakes. If you feel that you must make a comment on the quality of a posting, please do so by mail, not on the network.

Don't Overdo Signatures

Signatures are nice, and many people can have a signature added to their postings automatically by placing it in a file called "$HOME/.signature". Don't overdo it. Signatures can tell the world something about you, but keep them short. A signature that is longer than the message itself is considered to be in bad taste. The main purpose of a signature is to help people locate you, not to tell your life story. Every signature should include at least your return address relative to a major, known site on the network and a proper domain-format address. Your system administrator can give this to you. Some news posters attempt to enforce a 4 line limit on signature files -- an amount that should be more than sufficient to provide a return address and attribution.

Limit Line Length and Avoid Control Characters

Try to keep your text in a generic format. Many (if not most) of the people reading Usenet do so from 80 column terminals or from workstations with 80 column terminal windows. Try to keep your lines of text to less than 80 characters for optimal readability. If people quote part of your article in a followup, short lines will probably show up better, too.

Also realize that there are many, many different forms of terminals in use. If you enter special control characters in your message, it may result in your message being unreadable on some terminal types; a character sequence that causes reverse video on your screen may

result in a keyboard lock and graphics mode on someone else's terminal. You should also try to avoid the use of tabs, too, since they may also be interpreted differently on terminals other than your own.

Summary of Things to Remember

Never forget that the person on the other side is human
Don't blame system admins for their users' behavior
Be careful what you say about others
Be brief
Your postings reflect upon you; be proud of them
Use descriptive titles
Think about your audience
Be careful with humor and sarcasm
Only post a message once
Please rotate material with questionable content
Summarize what you are following up
Use mail, don't post a follow-up
Read all follow-ups and don't repeat what has already been said
Double-check follow-up newsgroups and distributions.
Be careful about copyrights and licenses
Cite appropriate references
When summarizing, summarize
Mark or rotate answers or spoilers
Spelling flames considered harmful
Don't overdo signatures
Limit line length and avoid control characters

(*)UNIX is a registered trademark of UNIX Systems Laboratories.

This document is in the public domain and may be reproduced or excerpted by anyone wishing to do so.

--

Gene Spafford
Software Engineering Research Center & Dept. of Computer Sciences
Purdue University, W. Lafayette IN 47907-1398
Internet: spaf@cs.purdue.eduphone: (317) 494-7825

Frequently Asked Questions About USENET

This article is titled "Answers to Frequently Asked Questions about Usenet". It is a periodic posting to "news.announce.newusers" and considered recommended reading for the user that is new to USENET. It was written by Jerry Schwarz and enhanced by Gene Spafford.

Answers to Frequently Asked Questions about Usenet

Archive-name: usenet-faq/part1
Original-author: jerry@eagle.UUCP (Jerry Schwarz)
Comment: enhanced & edited until 5/93 by spaf@cs.purdue.edu (Gene Spafford)
Last-change: 25 Apr 1993 by spaf@cs.purdue.edu (Gene Spafford)

Frequently Submitted/Asked Items

This document discusses some questions and topics that occur repeatedly on USENET. They frequently are submitted by new users, and result in many followups, sometimes swamping groups for weeks. The purpose of this note is to head off these annoying events by answering some questions and warning about the inevitable consequence of asking others. If you don't like these answers, let the poster of this article know.

Note that some newsgroups have their own special "Frequent Questions & Answers" posting. You should read a group for a while before posting any questions, because the answers may already be present. Comp.unix.questions and comp.unix.internals are examples -- Steve Hayman regularly posts an article that answers common questions, including some of the ones asked here.

This list is often referred to as FAQ -- the Frequently Asked Questions. If you are a new user of the Usenet and don't find an answer to your questions here, you can try asking in the news.newusers.questions group. You might also read through other FAQ lists, cross-posted to the news.answers group.

Contents

1.   What does UNIX stand for?

2.   What is the derivation of "foo" as a filler word?

3.   Is a machine at "foo" on the net?

4.   What does "rc" at the end of files like .newsrc mean?

5.   What does :-) mean?

6.   How do I decrypt jokes in rec.humor?

7.   misc.misc or misc.wanted: Is John Doe out there anywhere?

8.   sci.math: Proofs that 1=0.

9.   rec.games.*: Where can I get the source for empire or rogue?

10. comp.unix.questions: How do I remove files with non-ascii characters in their names?

11. comp.unix.internals: There is a bug in the way UNIX handles protection for programs that run suid, or any other report of bugs with standard software.

12. Volatile topics, e.g., soc.women: What do you think about abortion?

13. soc.singles: What do MOTOS, MOTSS, and MOTAS stand for? What does LJBF mean?

14. soc.singles and elsewhere: What does HASA stand for?

15. sci.space.shuttle: Shouldn't this group be merged with sci.space?

16. How do I use the "Distribution" feature?

17. Why do some people put funny lines ("bug killers") at the beginning of their articles?

18. What is the address or phone number of the "foo" company?

19. What is the origin of the name "grep"?

20. How do I get from BITNET to UUCP, Internet to BITNET, JANET etc. etc.?

21. Didn't some state once pass a law setting pi equal to 3?

22. Where can I get the necessary software to get a "smart" mail system running on my machine that will take advantage of the postings in comp.mail.maps? (E.g., pathalias, smail, etc.)

23. What is "food for the NSA line-eater"?

24. Does anyone know the {pinouts, schematics, switch settings, what does jumper J3 do} for widget X?

25. What is "anonymous ftp"?

26. What is UUNET?

27. Isn't the posting mechanism broken? When I post an article to both a moderated group and unmoderated groups, it gets mailed to the moderator and not posted to the unmoderated groups.

28. comp.arch and elsewhere: What do FYI and IMHO mean?

29. Would someone repost {large software distribution}?

30. How do I contact the moderator of an Internet mailing list rather than post to the entire list?

31. I see BTW (or "btw"), wrt and RTFM in postings. What do they mean?

32. Are there any restrictions on posting e-mail someone sends to me?

33. What's an FQDN?

34. How do you pronounce "char" in C, "ioctl" in UNIX, the character "#", etc., etc.?

35. How do you pronounce "TeX"?

36. What is the last year of the 20th century A.D.?

37. I heard these stories about a dying child wanting postcards/get-well cards/business cards to get in the Guinness Book of World Records. Where can I post the address for people to help?

38. I just heard about a scheme the FCC has to implement a tax on modems! Where can I post a message so everyone will hear about this and do something to prevent it?

39. Is there a public access Unix system near me? How can I get access to system for news and mail?

40. In rec.pets: My pet has suddenly developed the following symptoms .... Is it serious? In sci.med: I have these symptoms.... Is it serious?

41. I have this great idea to make money. Alternatively, wouldn't an electronic chain letter be a nifty idea?

42. Where can I get archives of Usenet postings?

43. Is it possible to post messages to the Usenet via electronic mail?

44. Is it possible to read Usenet newsgroups via electronic mail?

45. How do I get the news software to include a signature with my postings?

46. I'm on Bitnet -- can I connect to the net?

Questions and Answers

1. What does UNIX stand for?

   It is not an acronym, but is a pun on "Multics". Multics is a large operating system that was being developed shortly before UNIX was created. Brian Kernighan is credited with the name.

2. What is the derivation of "foo" as a filler word?

   The favorite story is that it comes from "fubar" which is an acronym for "fouled up beyond all recognition", which is supposed to be a military term. (Various forms of this exist, "fouled" usually being replaced by a stronger word.) "Foo" and "Bar" have the same derivation.

3. Is a machine at "foo" on the net?

   These questions belong in news.config (if anywhere), but in fact your best bet is usually to phone somebody at "foo" to find out. If you don't know anybody at "foo" you can always try calling and asking for the "comp center." Also, see the newsgroup comp.mail.maps where maps of USENET and the uucp network are posted regularly. If you have access to telnet, connect to nic.ddn.mil and try the "whois" command. (See also the answer to question #7, below.)

4. What does "rc" at the end of files like .newsrc mean?

    It is related to the phrase "run commands." It is used for any
    file that contains startup information for a command. The use of
    "rc" in startup files derives from the /etc/rc command file used
    to start multi-user UNIX.

5. What does :-) mean?

    This is the net convention for a "smiley face". It means that
    something is being said in jest. If it doesn't look like a smiley
    face to you, flop your head over to the left and look again.
    Variants exist and mean related things; for instance, :-(is sad.

    Collections of smileys are posted to various newsgroups from
    time to time. One was posted to comp.sources.misc in v23i102.

6. How do I decrypt jokes in rec.humor?

    The standard cypher used in rec.humor is called "rot13." Each
    letter is replaced by the letter 13 farther along in the alphabet
    (cycling around at the end). Most systems have a built-in
    command to decrypt such articles; readnews and nn have the "D"
    command, emacs/gnus has the "^C^R" combination, rn has the "X" or
    "^X" commands, notes has "%" or "R", and VMS news has the
    read/rot13 command. If your system doesn't have a program to
    encrypt and decrypt these, you can quickly create a shell script
    using "tr":

    tr A-Za-z N-ZA-Mn-za-m
    On some versions of UNIX, the "tr" command should be written as:
    tr "(a-m)(n-z)(A-M)(N-Z)" "(n-z)(a-m)(N-Z)(A-M)"

7. misc.misc or misc.wanted: Is John Doe out there anywhere?

    I suspect that these items are people looking for Freshman room-
    mates that they haven't seen in ten years. If you have some idea
    where the person is, you are usually better off calling the
    organization. For example, if you call any Bell Labs location and
    request John Doe's number they can give it to you even if he works
    at a different location. If you must try the net, use newsgroup
    soc.net-people *NOT* misc.misc or misc.wanted. Also, you can try
    the "whois" command (see item #3). There is a periodic posting
    in the news.newusers.questions and news.answers newsgroups that
    gives information on other ways to locate people.

8. sci.math: Proofs that 1=0.

   Almost everyone has seen one or more of these in high school. They are almost always based on either division by 0, confusing the positive and negative square roots of a number, or performing some ill-defined operation.

9. rec.games.*: Where can I get the source for empire or rogue?

   You can't get the source of rogue. The authors of the game, as is their right, have chosen not to make the sources available. However, several rogue-like games have been posted to the comp.sources.games group and they are available in the archives.

   You can obtain the source to a version of empire if you provide a tape and SASE *plus* a photocopy of your UNIX source license. To obtain further info, contact mcnc!rti-sel!polyof!john. You can also call John at +1 516 454-5191 (9am-9pm EST only).

   Sites with Internet access can ftp several versions of empire from site g.ms.uky.edu

   Also, please note that the wizards' passwords in games like these are usually system-dependent and it does no good to ask the net-at-large what they are.

10. comp.unix.questions: How do I remove files with non-ascii characters in their names?

    You can try to find a pattern that uniquely identifies the file. This sometimes fails because a peculiarity of some shells is that they strip off the highorder bit of characters in command lines. Next, you can try an rm -i, or rm -r. Finally, you can mess around with i-node numbers and "find".

    Some Emacs editors allow you to directly edit a directory, and this provides yet another way to remove a file with a funny name (assuming you have Emacs and figure out how to use it!).

    To remove a file named "-" from your directory, simply do:
    rm ./-

11. comp.unix.internals: There is a bug in the way UNIX handles protection for programs that run suid, or any other report of bugs with standard software.

There are indeed problems with the treatment of protection in setuid programs. When this is brought up, suggestions for changes range from implementing a full capability list arrangement to new kernel calls for allowing more control over when the effective id is used and when the real id is used to control accesses. Sooner or later you can expect this to be improved. For now you just have to live with it.

Always discuss suspected bugs or problems with your site software experts before you post to the net. It is likely that the bugs have already been reported. They might also be local changes and not something you need to describe to the whole Usenet.

12. Volatile topics, e.g., soc.women: What do you think about abortion?

Although abortion might appear to be an appropriate topic for soc.women, more heat than light is generated when it is brought up. All abortion-related discussion should take place in the newsgroup talk.abortion. If your site administrators have chosen not to receive this group, you should respect this and not post articles about abortion at all.

This principle applies to other topics: religious upbringing of children should be restricted to talk.religion.misc and kept out of misc.kids. Similarly, rape discussions should be kept to talk.rape and not in soc.singles, alt.sex and/or soc.women, Zionism discussions should be kept to talk.politics.mideast and not in soc.culture.jewish; likewise, evangelical and proseletyzing discussions of Jesus or of religions other than Judaism should go to newsgroups for the appropriate religion or to talk.religion.misc or alt.messianic. Any attempts to proselytize any religious view belongs in talk.religion.misc, if they belong on the net at all. Discussions on the merits of Affirmative Action and racial quotas belong in a talk.politics subgroup or alt.discrimination, not in soc.culture.african.american. Discussions about evolution vs. creationism should be confined to the talk.origins group.

USENET newsgroups are named for mostly historical reasons, and are not intended to be fully general discussion groups for everything about the named topic. Please accept this and post articles in their appropriate forums.

13. soc.singles: What do MOTOS, MOTSS, MOTAS, and SO stand for? What does LJBF mean?

Member of the opposite sex, member of the same sex, and member of the appropriate sex, respectively. SO stands for "significant other."

LJBF means "Let's just be friends." This phrase is often heard when you least want it.

14. soc.singles and elsewhere: What does HASA stand for?

The acronym HASA originated with the Heathen and Atheistic SCUM Alliance; the Hedonistic Asti-Spumante Alliance, Heroes Against Spaghetti Altering, the Society for Creative Atheism (SCATHE), SASA, SALSA, PASTA, and many others too numerous to mention all followed. HASA started in (what is now) talk.religion.misc and also turns up in soc.singles, talk.bizarre, et al. because members post there too.

15. sci.space.shuttle: Shouldn't this group be merged with sci.space?

No. sci.space.shuttle is for timely news bulletins. sci.space is for discussions.

16. How do I use the "Distribution" feature?

When your posting software (e.g., Pnews or postnews) prompts you for a distribution, it's asking how widely distributed you want your article. The set of possible replies is different, depending on where you are, but at Bell Labs in Murray Hill, New Jersey, possibilities include (for example):

local	local to this machine
mh	Bell Labs, Murray Hill Branch
nj	all sites in New Jersey
btl	All Bell Labs machines
att	All AT&T machines
usa	Everywhere in the USA
na	Everywhere in North America
world	Everywhere on USENET in the world

Many of the posting programs will provide a list of distributions, if your site admin has kept the files up-to-date.

If you hit return, you'll get the default, which is usually "world.". This default is often not appropriate -- PLEASE take a moment to think about how far away people are likely to be interested in what you have to say. Used car ads, housing wanted ads, and things for sale other than specialized equipment like computers certainly shouldn't be distributed to Europe and Korea, or even to the next state.

It is generally not possible to post an article to a distribution that your own machine does not receive. For instance, if you live in Indiana, you can't post an article for distribution only in New Jersey or Germany unless your site happens to exchange those particular distributions with another site. Try mailing the article to someone in the appropriate area and asking them to post it for you.

If you cannot determine what distributions are valid for your site, ask someone locally rather than posting a query to the whole network!

17. Why do some people put funny lines ("bug killers") at the beginning of their articles?

Some earlier versions (mid-80s) of news had a bug which would drop the first 512 or 1024 bytes of text of certain articles. The bug was triggered whenever the article started with whitespace (a blank or a tab). A fix many people adopted was to begin their articles with a line containing a character other than white space. This gradually evolved into the habit of including amusing first lines.

The original bug has since been fixed in newer version of news, and sites running older versions of news have applied a patch to prevent articles from losing text. The "bug-killer" lines are therefore probably no longer needed, but they linger on.

18. What is the address or phone number of the "foo" company?

Try the white and yellow pages of your phone directory, first; a sales representative will surely know, and if you're a potential customer they will be who you're looking for. Phone books for other cities are usually available in libraries of any size. Whoever buys or recommends things for your company will probably have some buyer's guides or national company directories. Call or visit the reference desk of your library; they have several company and organization directories and many will answer questions like this over the phone. Remember if you only know the city where the company is, you can telephone to find out their full address or a dealer. Calls to 1-800-555-1212 will reveal if the company has an "800" number you can call for information. The network is NOT a free resource, although it may look like that to some people. It is far better to spend a few minutes of your own time researching an answer rather than broadcast your laziness and/or ineptitude to the net.

19. What is the origin of the name "grep"?

The original UNIX text editor "ed" has a construct g/re/p, where "re" stands for a regular expression, to Globally search for matches to the Regular Expression and Print the lines containing them. This was so often used that it was packaged up into its own command, thus named "grep". According to Dennis Ritchie, this is the true origin of the command.

20. How do I get from BITNET to UUCP, Internet to BITNET, JANET etc.?

There are so many networks and mail systems in use now, it would take a book to describe all of them and how to send mail between them. Luckily, there are a couple of excellent books that do exactly that, and in a helpful, easy-to-use manner:

"!%@:: A Directory of Electronic Mail Addressing & Networks" by Donnalyn Frey and Rick Adams, O'Reilly & Associates, Inc., 2nd edition 1990.

"The Matrix: Computer Networks and Conferencing Systems Worldwide" by John Quarterman, Digital Press, 1990.

Another excellent book to have on your bookshelf (to keep those two company) is "The User's Directory of Computer Networks" edited by Tracy LaQuey, Digital Press, 1990.

21. Didn't some state once pass a law setting pi equal to 3?

   Indiana House Bill #246 was introduced on 18 January 1897, and
   referred to the Committee on Canals "midst general cheerfulness."
   The text states, "the ratio of the diameter and circumference is
   as five-fourths to four", which makes pi 3.2 (not 3), but there
   are internal contradictions in the bill as well as contradictions
   with reality. The author was a mathematical crank. The bill was
   passed by the state House on 5 February, but indefinitely tabled
   by the state Senate, in part thanks to the fortuitous presence
   on other business of a Purdue professor of mathematics.
   For details, including an annotated text of the bill, read the
   article by D. Singmaster in "The Mathematical Intelligencer" v7
   #2, pp 69-72.

22. Where can I get the necessary software to get a "smart"
   mail system running on my machine that will take advantage
   of the postings in comp.mail.maps? (E.g., pathalias, smail, etc.)

   There are a couple of packages available through the supporters of
   the comp.sources.unix archives. If sites next to you don't have
   what you want, contact your nearest comp.sources.unix archive, or
   the moderator. Information on archive sites, and indices of
   comp.sources.unix back issues are posted regularly in
   comp.sources.unix and comp.sources.d.

23. What is "food for the NSA line-eater"?

   This refers to the alleged scanning of all USENET traffic by the
   National Security Agency (and possibly other intelligence
   organizations) for interesting keywords. The "food" is believed
   to contain some of those keywords in the fond hope of overloading
   NSA's poor computers. A little thought should convince anyone
   that this is unlikely to occur. Other posters have taken up this
   practice, either as an ambiguous form of political statement, or
   as an attempt at humor. The bottom line is that excessive
   signatures in any form are discouraged, the joke has worn stale
   amongst long-time net readers, and there are specific newsgroups
   for the discussion of politics.

24. Does anyone know the {pinouts, schematics, switch settings, what does jumper J3 do} for widget X?

These postings are almost always inappropriate unless the manufacturer has gone out of business or no longer supports the device. If neither of these is the case, you're likely to get a better and faster response by simply telephoning the manufacturer.

25. What is "anonymous ftp"?

"FTP" stands for File Transfer Protocol; on many systems, it's also the name of a user-level program that implements that protocol. This program allows a user to transfer files to and from a remote network site, provided that network site is reachable via the Internet or a similar facility. (Ftp is also usable on many local-area networks.)

"Anonymous FTP" indicates that a user may log into the remote system as user "anonymous" with an arbitrary password. A common convention is that some sort of identification is supplied as the password, e.g. "mumble@foo". This is sometimes useful to those sites that track ftp usage. Also note that most sites restrict when transfers can be made, or at least suggest that large transfers be made only during non-peak hours.

26. What is UUNET?

UUNET is a for-profit communications service designed to provide access to USENET news, mail, and various source archives at low cost by obtaining volume discounts. Charges are calculated to recover costs.

For more information send your US mail address to info@uunet.uu.net (uunet!info).

27. Isn't the posting mechanism broken? When I post an article to both a moderated group and unmoderated groups, it gets mailed to the moderator and not posted to the unmoderated groups.

This is a question that is debated every few months. The answer is "No, it was designed to work that way." The software is designed so that the moderator can crosspost the article so it appears in the regular groups as well as the moderated group, if

appropriate. If the article were to be posted immediately to the unmoderated groups, the moderated group name would have to be deleted from the header and you would lose the crossposting.

Whether or not this is correct behavior is a matter of opinion. If you want your article to go out immediately to the unmoderated groups, post it twice -- once to the unmoderated groups and once to the moderated groups.

28. comp.arch and elsewhere: What do FYI and IMHO mean?

Those are abbreviations for common phrases. FYI is "For Your Information" and IMHO is "In My Humble Opinion" or "In My Honest Opinion." This is used sarcastically as often as not.

29. Would someone repost {large software distribution}?

This question should never be posted unless you are reporting a widespread problem in article propagation. Lamentably, there ARE occasional glitches in article transport. Large source or binary postings, by their sheer size, are an inviting target.

If the problem is isolated, it is much better to take it upon yourself to obtain the bad portions of the program than to ask thousands of sites to spend thousands of dollars to needlessly move several hundred kilobytes of code. There are archive sites around the net that make most source/binary newsgroups available via anonymous FTP and UUCP. If you get desperate, you can always mail the author a blank disk or magnetic tape with provisions for return postage.

30. How do I contact the moderator of an Internet mailing list rather than post to the entire list?

To do this you should know that there are, by convention, two mailing addresses for every mailing list (except where noted by the List of Lists):

list@host(e.g. xpert@expo.lcs.mit.edu)
list-request@host(e.g. xpert-request@expo.lcs.mit.edu)

When you have something for everyone on the mailing list to read, mail to the list@host address. HOWEVER, if you have an administrative request to make (e.g. "please add me to this list", "please remove me from this list", "where are the archives?", "what is this mailer error I got from sending to this list?"), it

should be directed to the list-request@host address, which goes only to the mailing list administrator.

It is considered to be in bad taste to send administrative requests to the entire mailing list in question, and if (as is often the case) the administrator does not read the mailing list (i.e. he just takes care of the admin tasks for the list), he will not see your request if you don't send it to the right address.

31. I see BTW (or "btw"), wrt and RTFM in postings. What do they mean?

BTW is shorthand for "by the way." WRT is "With respect to". RTFM is generally used as an admonition and means "read the f*ing manual" (choice of f-words varies according to reader). The implication is that the answer to a query or complaint is easy to find if one looks in the appropriate location FIRST. Most FAQ postings (Frequently-Asked Questions) that answer these questions may be found cross-posted in news.answers.

32. Are there any restrictions on posting e-mail someone sends to me?

At a minimum, it is only polite for you to contact the author of the letter and secure her or his permission to post it to the net.

On a more serious note, it can be argued that posting someone's e-mail to the net without their permission is a violation of copyright law. Under that law, even though a letter was addressed to you, it does not grant you the right to publish the contents, as that is the work of the author and the author retains copyright (even if no explicit copyright mark appears).

Basically, your letters are your intellectual property. If someone publishes your letters they are violating your copyright. This principle is well-founded in "paper media," and while untested in electronic forums such as Usenet, the same would probably apply if tested in court.

33. What's an FQDN?

A fully-qualified domain name. That is, a hostname containing full, dotted qualification of its name up to the root of the Internet domain naming system tree. Example: uiucuxc is the

single-word hostname (suitable for, e.g., UUCP transport purposes) of the machine whose FQDN is uxc.cso.uiuc.edu.

34. How do you pronounce "char" in C, "ioctl" in UNIX, the character "#", etc., etc.?

Opinions differ. Pick pronunciations close to what your colleagues use. After all, they're the ones you need to communicate with.

35. How do you pronounce "TeX"?

To quote Donald Knuth, the creator of TeX: "Insiders pronounce the X of TeX as a Greek chi, not as an 'x', so that TeX rhymes with the word blecchhh. It's the 'ch' sound in Scottish words like loch or German words like ach; it's a Spanish 'j' and a Russian 'kh'. When you say it correctly to your computer, the terminal may become slightly moist." (*The TeXbook*, 1986, Addison Wesley, page 1)

36. What is the last year of the 20th century A.D.?

The A.D. (Latin, Anno Domini, In the Year of Our Lord) system was devised before "origin 0 counting" was invented. The year during which Jesus was (incorrectly) assumed to have been born was numbered 1. (The preceding year was 1 B.C.) So the 1st century was 1 to 100, the 2nd was 101 to 200, the 20th is 1901 to 2000. This is standard terminology no matter how much some of you may dislike it. However, "a" century is any span of 100 years; so if you want to celebrate the end of "the century", meaning the 1900's, on December 31, 1999, nobody will stop you. It just isn't the end of the "20th century A.D.".

37. I heard these stories about a dying child wanting postcards/get-well cards/business cards to get in the Guinness Book of World Records. Where can I post the address for people to help?

Post it to "junk," or better yet, don't post it at all. The story of the little boy keeps popping up, even though his mother and the agencies involved have been appealing for people to stop. So many postcards were sent that the agencies involved in the effort don't know what to do with them. The Guinness people have

recorded the boy, Craig Shergold, as the record holder in the category. However, they will not accept claims for a new try at the record. For confirmation, you can see page 24 of the 29 July 1990 NY Times or call the publisher of the Guinness Book (in the US, call "Facts on File" @ 212-683-2244).

According to the 1993 edition of the GBWR, on page 213: Craig Shergold (born 1979) of Carshalton, Surrey when undergoing cancer chemo-therapy was sent a record 33 million get-well cards until May 1991 when his mother pleaded for no more. A successful 5 hour operation on a brain tumour by neurosurgeon Neal Kassel at Virginia University, Charlottesville, USA in March 1991 greatly improved his condition.

If you want to do something noble, donate the cost of a stamp and postcard (or more) to a worthwhile charity like UNICEF or the International Red Cross (Red Crescent, Red Magen David). There are tens of thousands of children dying around the world daily, and they could use more than a postcard.

38. I just heard about a scheme the FCC has to implement a tax on modems! Where can I post a message so everyone will hear about this and do something to prevent it?

Post it the same place as the articles in response to #37, above. This is an old, old story that just won't die. Something like this was proposed many YEARS back and defeated. However, the rumor keeps spreading and people who hear about it for the first time get all upset. Before posting stories like this, check with the organizations involved (like the FCC) to see if the story is true and current.

39. Is there a public access Unix system near me? How can I get access to system for news and mail?

Phil Eschallier posts a list of open access Unix sites (he calls them "Nixpub" sites) on a regular basis to the following newsgroups: comp.misc and alt.bbs. Check his posting for information on sites you can contact.

Furthermore, a list of open access sites that are not necessarily Unix sites is posted regularly in alt.bbs.lists; see the postings entitled "NetPub listing" for more information.

40. In rec.pets: My pet has suddenly developed the following symptoms .... Is it serious? In sci.med: I have these symptoms.... Is it serious?

Could be. The only way to tell for sure is to see an expert. The network reaches a vast audience with considerable talent, but that can never replace the expert observation and diagnosis of a trained professional. Do yourself or your pet a big favor -- if there is a problem, go see an appropriate practitioner. If there is a serious problem, it is important that it is dealt with promptly.

41. I have this great idea to make money. Alternatively, wouldn't an electronic chain letter be a nifty idea?

In a few words: don't even think about it. Trying to use the net to make vast sums of money or send chain letters is a very bad idea. First of all, it is an inappropriate use of resources, and tends to use up vast amounts of net bandwidth. Second, such usage of the net tends to produce extremely negative reactions by people on the net, adding even more to the volume -- most of it directed to you. Users, particularly system admins, do not like that kind of activity, and they will flood your mailbox with notices to that effect.

And last, and perhaps most important, some of this activity is against the law in many places. In the US, you can (and will) be reported by hacked-off system administrators for suspicion of wire fraud or mail fraud. In one incident, at *least* a half dozen people reported the poster to Postal Service inspectors; I'm not sure what the outcome was, but it probably was not a nice experience.

Bottom line: don't try clever schemes to sell things, solicit donations, or run any kind of pyramid or Ponzi scheme. Also, don't start or support electronic chain letters.

42. Where can I get archives of Usenet postings?

Most Usenet newsgroups are not archived in any organized fashion, though it's likely that if you look hard enough someone will have kept much or most of the traffic (either on disk or on some tape

gathering dust somewhere). The volume on Usenet is simply too high to keep everything on rotating magnetic media forever, however. The signal-to-noise ratio is too low in many groups to make them good candidates for archiving.

One person's signal is another person's noise; if you're lucky, you'll find someone who has been keeping the good parts of a particular newsgroup in their own personal stash to save up for later. How to get access to a group that *is* archived depends on what kind of group it is:

* The "sources" and "binaries" groups are generally archived at multiple sites; for more information about getting access to them, see the posting entitled "How to find sources" in comp.sources.wanted.

* Some non-source newsgroups can be found by asking "archie" about the group name. See the comp.sources.wanted posting mentioned above for information about how to use "archie."

* In other groups, if the group has a Frequently Asked Questions posting or another periodic posting about the group, check that posting to see if it mentions where the group is archived. If not, then you'll have to post a message in the newsgroup and ask if it is archived anywhere.

43. Is it possible to post messages to the Usenet via electronic mail?

There are a few sites on the Usenet that offer a full-scale mail to news gateway, so that you can post via E-mail to any newsgroup support.

One of them is decwrl.dec.com. To use its gateway, you mail the message you wish to post to newsgroup.name.usenet@decwrl.dec.com. For example, to post to news.newusers.questions, you would send your message to news.newusers.questions.usenet@decwrl.dec.com.

Mail-to-news gateways of this sort tend to be overloaded. Therefore, please do not use this gateway or any other similar gateway if you have other posting access to the Usenet.

44. Is it possible to read Usenet newsgroups via electronic mail?

Most Usenet newsgroups do not correspond to any mailing list, so the conventional answer to this question is "no" for most groups. However, there are some newsgroups that are gatewayed to mailing lists. For a list of them, see the "List of Active Newsgroups" posting in news.announce.newusers.

If you know a Usenet site admin who is willing to act as a personal gateway for you, you might be able to get him/her to set up his/her system to forward messages from individual newsgroups to you via E-mail. However, most admins don't like to do this because it adds to the outgoing traffic from their site, so don't post messages to the net saying, "Hey, is there someone willing to gateway newsgroups to me?"

45. How do I get the news software to include a signature with my postings?

This is a question that is best answered by examining the documentation for the software you're using, as the answer varies depending on the software.

However, if you're reading news on a Unix machine, then you can probably get a signature to appear on your outgoing messages by creating a file called ".signature" in your home directory. Two important things to remember are:

1. Many article-posting programs will restrict the length of the signature. For example, the "inews" program will often only include the first four lines. This is not something you should be trying to find a way to defeat; it is there for a reason. If your signature is too long, according to the software, then shorten it. Even if the software does not complain, keep your .signature under four lines as a courtesy to others.

2. Under some news configurations, your .signature file must be world-readable, and your home directory world-executable, for your signature to be included correctly in your articles. If your .signature does not get included, try running these commands:

   chmod a+x $HOME
   chmod a+r $HOME/.signature

46. I'm on BitNet -- can I connect to the Usenet?

Many BitNet sites also have connections to other networks. Some
of these sites may be receiving Usenet with NNTP or by other
methods. IBM VM/CMS sites which only have a connection to BitNet
may still gain access to Usenet if they get a software package
called NetNews, which is available from Penn State University at
no charge. The PSU NetNews software allows sites to receive
Usenet news over BITNET. Talk to your local site administrators
to find out if your site has this software installed and how to
access it from your account. Also, contact your favorite BITNET
LISTSERV and get the list NETNWS-L. That list carries info on
the necessary procedures and software.

--

Gene Spafford
Software Engineering Research Center & Dept. of Computer Sciences
Purdue University, W. Lafayette IN 47907-1398
Internet: spaf@cs.purdue.eduphone: (317) 494-7825

Getting USENET Access

This article is titled "How to become a USENET site".
It is a periodic posting to "news.announce.newusers". It was
written by Jonathan I. Kamens. He credits (at the end of the
article) many other kind people with providing information
for it.

How to Become a USENET Site

Archive-name: site-setup
Version: $Id: site-setup,v 1.115 1993/07/18 19:59:28 jik Exp $

This article attempts to summarize, in a general way, the steps
involved in setting up a machine to be on the USENET.

It assumes that you already have some sort of USENET access
(otherwise, how did you get this article?), or at the very least, that
you have ftp or mail server access to get to some of the files
mentioned in it, and that you are trying to configure your own site to
be on the USENET after using some other site for some period of time.
If this assumption is incorrect, then ask whoever made this article

available to you to help you get access to the resources mentioned below.

Before reading this posting, you should be familiar with the contents of the introductory postings in the news.announce.newusers newsgroup, most importantly the posting entitled "USENET Software: History and Sources". Many of the terms used below are defined in those postings. The news.announce.newusers postings are accessible in the periodic posting archive on rtfm.mit.edu (18.70.0.224), in /pub/usenet via anonymous ftp, or via E-mail by sending a message to mail-server@rtfm.mit.edu (send a message with "help" in the body to get more information).

There are five basic steps involved in configuring a machine to be a USENET site.

1. Make the decision -- do you *really* want to do this?

    If you just want to read USENET yourself, then putting your machine onto the USENET is probably not what you want to do. The process of doing so can be time-consuming, and regular maintenance is also required. Furthermore, the resources consumed by a full USENET setup on a machine are significant:
    - disk space for the programs (a few Mb for the binaries, another couple of Mb for any sources you keep online);
    - disk space for the articles - currently (as of December, 1992) as much as 1200Mb a month, although it is possible to minimize the amount of disk space consumed by articles by carefully selecting which newsgroups and/or hierarchies you wish to receive;
    - modem time (possibly long-distance) transferring the articles to your machine (assuming that you are using a modem rather than an Internet NNTP connection); and
    - fees if you're paying someone to provide you with a news feed.

    You might choose, instead, to get an account on a public-access USENET site on which you can read news by dialing up. See, for example, the "Nixpub posting" articles in comp.misc and the "NetPub listing" articles in alt.bbs.lists for lists of such sites.

    Even if there are no public-access USENET sites that are a local phone call away from you, you might still choose this approach, especially if you only read a few (low traffic) groups. Using a

public-access site that is accessible via PC Pursuit or some other packet network might still be cheaper and/or easier than setting up the feed, transferring the news and configuring your machine to store news locally.

You should be sure that the benefits you are going to get by storing news locally are going to outweigh the costs before deciding to proceed. In summary, however, let me say that this decision is not always a clear one. To explain why, let me include an alternative perspective, from joe@jshark.rn.com, on why getting a feed may be appropriate even for a single-user machine:

>When you get to long distance calls, reading the news on-line gets the
>cost rising fast. A few seconds to skip an article you've no interest
>in, maybe a minute to take in a good one plus more time to save it and
>download it later. But when the whole lot is batched together (as
>news), a) it only takes a few minutes and b) it's all conveniently
>automated. Sure, configuring the hardware and software may take a
>(small) time - but it's something you only do once.
>
>And unless you want to get comp.*, the disk space needed is not that
>great. (20Mb disks are about 100 dollars over here; the saving in
>phone charges would pay for that in a few months)
>
>I also find that replying takes time, and this is where on-line
>"reading" would start to really burn dollars! The alternative, {
>download - logout - compose reply - dial back in - login - post (or
>mail) reply}, is a) inconvenient and b) still costly.
>
>Perhaps I see "news administration" as a simple task *because* I only
>provide news to one other site and get a very limited feed. (No
>overflowing disks, no "disappearing inodes", neither angry users nor
>management.) The initial stages were a bit fraught (200kb batches
>being bounced back because of permission problems :-( ), but very
>little effort now. I have an impression, based on your address and
>past postings, that you are involved in "system management" at MIT so
>you see things from a "major site" point of view??

2. Find a site to feed you news and/or mail.

In order to make your machine a USENET site, you need to find other sites on the USENET that are willing to feed you news and/or mail. You might want to locate more than one such site if you want higher reliability.

Finding feeds for a UUCP site.

If you are going to be using a modem (and, presumably, UUCP) to transfer your news and mail, then there are several resources you can use when trying to locate a feed site:

a. *Comp.mail.maps*

Find the postings in the comp.mail.maps newsgroup for your state, country, or whatever. Look in it for sites that sound like they are local to you. Contact their administrators and ask if they would be wi lling to give you a feed.

Comp.mail.maps is archived at several anonymous ftp and mail server sites, including ftp.uu.net, so you can examine map entries even if the maps have expired at your news-reading site (or if you do not currently have USENET access). See the article entitled "UUCP map for README" in the comp.mail.maps newsgroup or archives for more information about the maps.

The comp.mail.maps postings are also archived in rtfm.mit.edu's periodic posting archive, which was mentioned in detail above.

b. *News.admin.misc*

Post a message to news.admin.misc. If at all possible, post it with a restricted distribution, so that only people who are likely to be able to give you a feed will have to get it (e.g. if you have posting access on a machine in Massachusetts, and the site you're setting up is going to be in Massachusetts, then post with a distribution of "ne").

Note that you can post to news.admin.misc even if you do not have direct USENET access right now, as long as you have E-mail access -- send your message to news.admin.misc.usenet@decwrl.dec.com. However, if you use this gateway, you probably can't use a restricted distribution as described above, since the gateway probably isn't in the distribution you want to post to, and besides,

it's not clear that it listens to the "Distribution:" header in postings that are mailed to it. (Other gateways: news.admin.misc@pws.bull.com, news-admin-misc@cs.utexas.edu, news.admin.misc@news.cs.indiana.edu)

When posting your message, try to be as specific as possible. Mention where you are, how you intend to transfer news from your feed site to you (e.g. what kind of modem, how fast), approximately how many newsgroups you are going to want to get and from which hierarchies, and perhaps what kind of machine it's all for. A descriptive Subject line such as "news feed wanted -- Boston, MA" is also useful.

If there is a regional hierarchy for the distribution in which you want a feed, then you might want to post a message in one of the regional newsgroups as well, or cross-post your message to one of the regional newsgroups. Look first for an "admin" group (e.g. "ne.admin"), then (if there is no admin group) a "config" group, then for a "wanted" group.

c. *Commercial services*

If all else fails, you may have to resort to paying someone to provide you with a feed. I know about the following service providers:

a2i communications
1211 Park Avenue #202
San Jose, CA 95126
Data: (408) 293-9010 (v.32bis, v.32), (408) 293-9020 (PEP)
(log in as "guest")
Telnet: a2i.rahul.net (192.160.13.1) (log in as "guest")
Ftp: ftp.rahul.net (192.160.13.1), get /pub/BLURB
info@rahul.net (a daemon will auto-reply)
(UUCP, news feeds, mail feeds, MX forwarding, name service)

Anterior Technology
P.O. Box 1206
Menlo Park, CA 94026-1206
Voice: (415) 328-5615
Fax: (415) 322-1753
info@fernwood.mpk.ca.us
(UUCP, connectivity, name service, MX forwarding, news feeds)

CERFnet
P.O. Box 85608
San Diego, CA 92186-9784
Voice: (800) 876-CERF
help@cerf.net
(connectivity, name service, MX forwarding, news feeds)

Colorado SuperNet, Inc.
Attn: David C. Menges
Colorado School of Mines
1500 Illinois
Golden, CO 80401
Voice: 303-273-3471
dcm@csn.org
(UUCP, news feeds)

Demon Internet Systems
internet@demon.co.uk
(Internet access, SLIP, PPP, name service)

DMConnection
267 Cox St.
Hudson, Ma. 01749
Voice: (508) 568-1618
Fax: (508) 562-1133
info@dmc.com (a daemon will respond, followed by a human being,
if necessary)
(UUCP, news feeds, mail feeds, MX forwarding, file servers, mailing lists,
anonymous FTP and UUCP address to archives, domain registration,
FTP, SLIP, etc.)

ExNet Systems Ltd
60 Sunningdale Avenue
Hanworth
Middlesex, TW13 5JT, UK
Voice/Fax: +44 81 755 0077
exnet@exnet.co.uk
(UUCP, mail and news feeds)

Gordian
20361 Irvine Ave
Santa Ana Heights, CA 92707 (Orange County)
Voice: (714) 850 0205

Fax: (714) 850 0533
E-mail: uucp-request@gordian.com
(UUCP, name service, MX forwarding, news feeds (for SoCal sites only))

Hatch Communications
8635 Falmouth Ave., Suite 105
Playa del Rey, CA 90293
Voice: (310) 305-8758
E-mail: info@hatch.socal.com
(UUCP Usenet news and e-mail, SLIP connections for ftp and telnet)

HoloNet
Information Access Technologies, Inc.
46 Shattuck Square, Suite 11
Berkeley, CA 94704-1152
Voice: 510-704-0160, Fax: 510-704-8019, Modem: 704-1058
Telnet: holonet.net
E-mail: info@holonet.net (automated reply)
Support: support@holonet.net
(UUCP/USENET feeds, local to 850+ cities nationwide)

infocom Public Access Unix,
White Bridge House,
Old Bath Road,
CHARVIL, Berkshire,
United Kingdom,
RG10 9QJ.
Voice: +44 (0) 734 344000
Fax: +44 (0) 734 320988
Data: +44 (0) 734 340055 (you can register online interactively)
E-mail: info@infocom.co.uk (send a message with ALL in the subject)
(UUCP, Usenet Feeds and Internet Email to UNIX, DOS, ATARI,
AMIGA, MAC)

JvNCnet
B6 von Neumann Hall
Princeton University
Princeton, NJ 08543
Voice: (800) 35-TIGER
market@jvnc.net
(connectivity, name service, MX forwarding, news feeds)

MSEN, Inc.
628 Brooks Street
Ann Arbor, MI 48103
Voice: (313) 998-4562
Ftp: ftp.msen.com (148.59.1.2), see /pub/vendor/msen/*
info@msen.com
(UUCP, connectivity, name service, MX forwarding, news feeds)

MV Communications, Inc.
P.O. Box 4963
Manchester, NH 03108-4963
Voice: (603) 429-2223
Data: (603) 429-1735 (log in as "info" or "rates")
info@mv.mv.com
(UUCP, name service, MX forwarding, news feeds)

NEARnet (New England Academic and Research Network)
10 Moulton Street
Cambridge, MA 02138
Voice: (617) 873-8730
Fax: (617) 873-5620
nearnet-join@nic.near.net
(connectivity, name service, MX forwarding, news feeds (for
NEARnet sites))

Netcom - Online Communication Services
4000 Moorpark Avenue - Suite 209
San Jose, CA 95117
Voice: (408) 554-UNIX
Data: (408) 241-9760 (login guest, no password)
Telnet: netcom.netcom.com (192.100.81.100) (login guest)
E-mail: info@netcom.com
(UUCP, connectivity, name service, MX forwarding, news feeds,
other services)

Northwest Nexus Inc.
P.O. Box 40597
Bellevue, WA 98015-4597
Voice: (206) 455-3505
Data: (206) 382-6245 (log in as "new")
Fax: (206) 455-4672
info@nwnexus.wa.com

(Internet access, SLIP/PPP (dial-up, dedicated, 56k, FT-1), UUCP, news feeds, mail feeds, MX forwarding, name service, NIC registration, Nutshell books)

Performance Systems International, Inc.
11800 Sunrise Valley Drive, Suite 1100
Reston, VA 22091
Voice: (703) 620-6651 or (800) 827-7482
Computerized info: all-info@psi.com
Human-based info: info@psi.com
(UUCP, connectivity, name service, MX forwarding, news feeds)

SURAnet
8400 Baltimore Blvd.
College Park, MD 20742
Voice: (301) 982-3214
Fax: (301) 982-4605
E-mail: news-admin@sura.net
(connectivity, name service (for SURAnet sites), news feeds (for SURAnet sites))

TDK Consulting Services
119 University Ave. East
Waterloo, Ontario
Canada N2J 2W9
Voice: (519) 888-0766
Fax: (519) 747-0881
E-mail: info@tdkcs.waterloo.on.ca
(UUCP News/Mail feeds)

UUNET Canada, Inc.
1 Yonge St., Suite 1400
Toronto, Ontario
Canada M5E 1J9
Voice: (416) 368-6621
Fax: (416) 369-0515
info@uunet.ca or uunet-ca@uunet.uu.net
(UUCP, connectivity, name service, MX forwarding, news feeds)

UUNET Technologies Inc.
3110 Fairview Park Drive, Suite 570
Falls Church, VA 22042
Voice: (703) 204-8000

Fax: (703) 204-8001
info@uunet.uu.net
AlterNet (network connectivity) info: alternet-info@uunet.uu.net
(UUCP, connectivity, name service, MX forwarding, news feeds)

UUNORTH, Inc.
Box 445, Station E
Toronto, Ontario
Canada M6H 4E3
Voice: (416) 537-4930 or (416) 225-UNIX
Fax: (416) 537-4890

WIMSEY
Attn: Stuart Lynne
225B Evergreen Dr.
Port Moody, BC, V3H 1S1
Voice: 604-93-7532
sl@vanbc.wimsey.bc.ca
(UUCP, name service, MX forwarding, news feeds)

Xenon Systems
Attn: Julian Macassey
742 1/2 North Hayworth Ave.
Hollywood, CA 90046-7142
Voice: (213) 654-4495
postmaster@bongo.tele.com
(UUCP, news feeds, mail feeds)

Note that some of these are actually network service providers which provide Internet connectivity, but some will also provide news feeds to their customers. For more information about many network service providers, see the anonymous ftp file /nsfnet/referral-list on nnsc.nsf.net.

Some regional network service providers, especially in large urban areas, offer both UUCP and TCP/IP service via modem or leased line. If you can find such a company, the cost of a dedicated (leased line) Internet connection will often be cheaper and more desirable than a UUCP connection, if you plan on using it for a full newsfeed or for frequent downloading. Some companies can offer combined voice and data connections using T1 links, for large-scale users seeking both Internet access and low-cost toll telephone service. For more information about the possibility of hooking up to the

network, see the "How to Get Information about Networks" posting in news.announce.newusers.

NOTE: I am not endorsing any of these companies in any way. I don't know anything about the level or quality of service either of them provides. They are simply the ones I know about. If you know of a site that provides feeds and think it should be mentioned here, please let me know.

d. *Special information for European users*

(This section discusses the various big European networks. There are also smaller service providers, such as ExNet Systems (see above), in Europe.)

In Europe, you can get a feed from one of EUNet's national networks. They charge for feeds but are "non-commercial," which means (I assume) that the fees go to the maintenance of the networks. Most provide help on getting started, can provide source for the mail and news software and lists of sites who have indicated they will provide feeds. They also act as Internet forwarders (see below for more information on this). To contact them, try sending mail to postmaster@country.eu.net or newsmaster@country.eu.net. The "country" in this case should be whatever country you're in.

Note that the national networks have a "no redistribution" policy and have the option to cut off sites which break this rule. There are other groups (such as sublink); see (a) and (b) above for suggestions on how to contact them.

Subscribing to EUNet or to one of the NALnets (National Networks) currently requires to be member of EurOpen either directly or indirectly by being member of a NALUUG (National Unix User Group) affiliated to EurOpen.

In the UK, smaller scale users and individuals can also get news access via Demon Internet Systems. They provide very cheap dialup Internet access, SLIP, PPP and name service entries. Contact them (contact information is given above) for more information.

There are also several other network services providers, already operational (or to become soon available for some of them). Contrary to EUnet which generally accepts any organization as customer, those networks may have restrictions and accept only some

kind of customers (generally academic and/or research) as they are sometimes government funded.

Some of these networks are NORDunet (northern Europe), FUNET (Finland), SWITCH (Switzerland), EASInet (European Academic Supercomputing Initiative, mainly if not totally funded by IBM), DFN (Germany), PIPEX(UK) and RENATER (France).

There are several anonymous ftp sites from which information about all of these networks and about networking in Europe in general might be obtained. They are ftp.switch.ch, ftp.easi.net, ftp.ripe.net, ftp.eu.net, corton.inria.fr and nic.nordu.net.

Note that it is to your advantage to try to find a feed site that is directly on the Internet, if you are not going to be. Getting a feed from a site on the Internet will allow that site to act as your MX forwarder (see section 5 below), and the fact that you are only one hop off of the Internet will make both mail and news delivery fast (assuming that the feed you get from the Internet site is for both mail and news; of course, if you can only find someone willing to forward mail to you but not to traffic with you the heavier load of a news feed, then your mail delivery will still be fast).

Finding feeds for an Internet site.

If you are on the Internet and would like your news feed to be over the Internet rather than over a modem link, then you *might* want to look in the UUCP maps in comp.mail.maps, as mentioned above, since many USENET sites that are on the Internet are mentioned there. News.admin.misc and the commercial services listed above are also viable options. Another option which is relevant only to Internet sites is to send mail to the mailing list nntp-managers@ucbvax.berkeley.edu, and ask if anyone on that list is willing to provide you with a news feed. If you do this, be specific, just as if you were posting to news.admin.misc as described above.

3. Get the software.

    The "USENET Software" posting referenced above goes into quite a bit of detail about the software that is available. There are three components in the software at a USENET site: (a) the software that transports the news (usually using either UUCP or NNTP), (b) the

software that stores the news on the local disks, expires old articles, etc., and (c) the news-readers for looking at the news.

For example, if you're a UNIX site on the Internet and you're going to be getting your news feed over the Internet, then you are probably going to want to get one of the news transport packages mentioned in the "USENET Software" posting (e.g., INN or C News + NNTP), as well as one or more of the UNIX news readers mentioned there.

Since you are probably going to be exchanging mail as well as news, and the mail software that is shipped with the OS you are using might not be powerful enough to handle mail exchanging with the rest of the USENET, you might want to obtain new mail software as well. There are several packages you might choose you use. Discussion of them is beyond the scope of this document; the books referenced below will probably provide some useful information in this area. Furthermore, if you are a UNIX site, the posting by Chris Lewis <clewis@ferret.ocunix.on.ca> entitled "UNIX Email Software Survey FAQ" in news.admin.misc, comp.mail.misc and news.answers provides a good introduction to the UNIX mail software that's out there. Finally, Eric S. Johansson <esj@harvee.billerica.ma.us>'s "FAQ - UUCP Mail, News and Gateway Software for PCs and MACs" posting (actually, the Subject line appears to vary somewhat, and the posting doesn't seem to appear very regularly), in comp.mail.uucp, news.software.readers and vmsnet.uucp, will help you to find out more about the UUCP software that is available to you if you wish to run it on a PC or Macintosh computer.

The basic idea is to go read the "USENET Software" posting, and then to work from there.

Europeans can ask their national backbone site, which will usually either be a software archive or be closely associated with one. UKNET, for example, provides an information pack explaining what is needed and where (and how) to get it.

4.   Do what it says.

Most of the software available for news transport or storage comes with installation instructions. Follow them. This part should be self-explanatory (although the instructions might not be :-).

5.   Register your site on the network.

The "traditional" method of advertising your site to the rest of the USENET after setting it up is to get an entry for it added to the UUCP maps. Doing this involves choosing a name for your site and submitting a map entry indicating the name, other vital statistics, and a list of your feed sites, preferentially weighted. Since many USENET sites still rely exclusively on the UUCP maps for routing mail, you will almost certainly want to register in the maps. To find out more about how to do this, read the "UUCP map for README" posting in comp.mail.maps, referenced above.

However, the past several years have witnessed a dramatic increase in the number of sites choosing to register host names in the Internet Domain Name Service (DNS) hierarchy, in addition to getting a host entry added to the UUCP maps. The DNS hierarchy is becomingly increasingly standardized, and DNS name service is more reliable than the UUCP maps. Therefore, if register a DNS name for your site, put that DNS name in your UUCP map entry as an alias for your site, and use the DNS address rather than the UUCP host name in your mail and USENET postings, both UUCP hosts and hosts that do DNS will be able to get mail to you more efficiently and reliably.

There are two types of DNS host records that are relevant here. If you have opted to contract with a company for a direct connection to the Internet, then you are probably going to want to register an address record advertising what your address will be on the Internet. Hosts which understand DNS can then use that record to connect directly to your machine and deliver mail to it.

If, on the other hand, you are going to be getting your mail via UUCP from some other site, then the host record you will be registering is a Mail eXchange (MX) record. This record announces to the world that mail destined to your host can be directed instead to another host that IS directly on the Internet. That host is your "MX forwarder," and it must be one of your feed sites that knows how to deliver mail to you. In fact, you can have multiple MX records if you have multiple feeds on the Internet and want it to be possible for mail to be routed through all of them (for increased reliability), if they are willing. Note that if you use a commercial service provider for your mail feed, it will probably also be your MX forwarder.

Even if none of your feeds are on the Internet, you may be able to get an MX record, by finding an Internet site that is willing to receive your mail and put it on its way through the correct UUCP route. There are currently at least a couple of sites willing to perform this service for no charge, in order to encourage the increased use of DNS records. You can therefore probably locate an MX forwarder by posting to news.admin.misc and asking if anyone is willing to forward for you.

The procedure for registering a DNS record is quite simple. For some Network Information Centers (the people who handle domain registration, a.k.a. NICs), e.g., the InterNIC (see Internet RFC 1400 for more information about the InterNIC) which handles domain registration for the original Arpanet domains (COM, EDU, etc., as opposed to the geographic domains such as US for the United States, FR for France, etc.), it takes a month or less; others, unfortunately, might take a lot longer. Note that many commercial service providers, such as UUNET, will take care of this for you when you ask for a network connection or news/mail feed from them.

Whether you decide to register an address record or an MX record, you need to decide what your DNS host name is going to be. Since the DNS is arranged in a hierarchy, you need to decide what hierarchy your name will appear in. For example, you might choose to be in the ".us" domain if you are in the United States and want to be in the United States geographical hierarchy. Alternatively, you might choose ".edu" for a University, ".org" for a non-profit organization, ".com" for a commercial company, etc. For more information about the various hierarchies and about choosing a host name, see the "How to Get Information about Networks" posting already referenced.

If you are not in the US, you're theoretically supposed to have no choice about the top-level domain -- it should always be the two-letter ISO code for your country (".fr", ".de", etc.). However, depending on how and how well you are connected to the network, you might be able to get away with being in one of the older domains mentioned above (".edu", ".org", etc.). If you want to find out how to get a host name in a particular European domain, you can probably start by sending mail to hostmaster@mcsun.eu.net and asking for more information.

Once you have determined your host name, you need to determine one or more hosts (preferably two or three, so that even if one is having trouble, the others will fill in for it) that will act as your "name servers," advertising your host name to anyone who asks for it. Note that many hierarchies have their own name servers, which means that when you go through the process of figuring out which domain your host name will be in, you may find some name servers available to you already. Furthermore, if you opt to go with a commercial service provider as described above, your service provider will probably be willing to act as a name server. Different domain-administration organizations may require fewer or more name servers (e.g. the NIC (mentioned below) requires at least two).

Once you've got your host name picked out, you need to submit an application to the authorities for the domain you've chosen. Many of the domains, for example, are managed by the InterNIC -- to submit an application to one of those domains, you would get the file DOMAIN-TEMPLATE.TXT via anonymous ftp from rs.internic.net (ftp://rs.internic.net/templates/domain-template.txt) fill it out, and mail it to hostmaster@internic.net. You will probably determine the correct method for applying for a host name in your domain during the course of investigating which domain to put your host name in.

If you submit an application and don't get any acknowlegement or response in a couple of weeks, it's a good idea to send another note to the same address as you sent your original application to, asking if it was received.

Even if you aren't going to be connecting directly to Internet at the start, if your site is using any TCP/IP-based equipment, you should request a block of IP addresses, to save future transition headaches. Request one Class C address per subnet, or a Class B if your site has a large number of systems on multiple subnets (for the precise guidelines, see Internet RFCs 1366 and 1367). If you don't understand any of this and don't intend on getting on the Internet, don't worry about it. If/when you do decide to get onto the Internet, your service provider should be prepared to help you understand what needs to be done.

Once your application has been approved and your name entered into your name servers' databases, update the mail software on your system and on your MX forwarder's system to recognize and use the new domain.

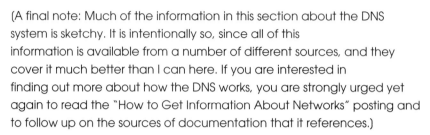

(A final note: Much of the information in this section about the DNS system is sketchy. It is intentionally so, since all of this information is available from a number of different sources, and they cover it much better than I can here. If you are interested in finding out more about how the DNS works, you are strongly urged yet again to read the "How to Get Information About Networks" posting and to follow up on the sources of documentation that it references.)

In addition to the resources already mentioned, there are several books which discuss USENET and/or UUCP maintenance. They include (these entries are culled from the "YABL" posting, by Mitch Wright <mitch@cirrus.com>, in comp.unix.questions):

TITLE: Managing UUCP and USENET
AUTHOR: O'Reilly, Tim
AUTHOR: Todino, Grace
SUBJECT: Introduction
PUBLISHER: O'Reilly & Associates, Inc.
DATE: 1990
PAGES: 289
ISBN: 0-937175-48-X
APPROX_COST: 24.95
KEYWORDS: Nutshell Handbook
SUGGESTED_BY: Mitch Wright <mitch@hq.af.mil>
SUPPLIERS
E-mail: ... uunet!ora!nuts
Phone#: 1-800-338-NUTS

TITLE: Unix Communications
AUTHOR: Anderson, Bart
AUTHOR: Costales, Barry
AUTHOR: Henderson, Harry
SUBJECT: Communication Reference
PUBLISHER: The Waite Group
DATE: 1991
PAGES: 736
ISBN: 0-672-22773-8
APPROX_COST: 29.95
KEYWORDS: UUCP, USENET
COMMENTS Covers everything the end user needs to know about email, USENET and UUCP.

TITLE: Using UUCP and USENET
AUTHOR: Todino, Grace
AUTHOR: Dougherty, Dale
SUBJECT: Introduction
PUBLISHER: O'Reilly & Associates, Inc.
DATE: 1990
PAGES: 210
ISBN: 0-937175-10-2
APPROX_COST: 21.95
KEYWORDS: Nutshell Handbook
SUGGESTED_BY: Mitch Wright <mitch@hq.af.mil>
SUPPLIERS
E-mail: ... uunet!ora!nuts
Phone#: 1-800-338-NUTS

If you are going to be setting up a UUCP/modem USENET site, you will probably find these books quite useful, especially if the UUCP documentation that comes with the OS you're running is sparse.

Comments about, suggestions about or corrections to this posting are welcomed. If you would like to ask me to change this posting in some way, the method I appreciate most is for you to actually make the desired modifications to a copy of the posting, and then to send me the modified posting, or a context diff between my posted version and your modified version (if you do the latter, make sure to include in your mail the "Version:" line from my posted version). Submitting changes in this way makes dealing with them easier for me and helps to avoid misunderstandings about what you are suggesting.

Rich Braun <richb@pioneer.ci.net> provided most of the information above about registering DNS records, and provided other useful comments and suggestions. joe@jshark.rn.com provided some very useful rewriting as well as some different perspectives that helped to make the article more general, as well as providing some specific information about working in Europe, as well as providing other useful comments.

The following people provided useful comments and suggestions about this article:

Vikas Aggarwal <vikas@jvnc.net>
Anton J. Aylward <uunorth@uunorth.UUCP>
Bruno Blissenbach <bubli@purodha.GUN.de>
Oliver Boehmer <oli@odbffm.in.sub.org>
Andy Brager <andyb@wndrsvr.UUCP>
Michael Bryan <michael@resonex.com>
Alan Cox <iiitac@pyr.swan.ac.uk>
John Curran <jcurran@nic.near.net>
Chris Davies <chris@visionware.co.uk>
Christopher Davis <ckd@eff.org>
Paul Eggert <eggert@twinsun.com>
Nathan F. Estey <nestey@copper.Denver.Colorado.EDU>
Stuart Freedman <stuart@orac.HQ.Ileaf.COM>
Margaret D. Gibbs <gibbsm@ll.mit.edu>
David Gilbert <dgilbert@snowhite.cis.uoguelph.ca>
B.J. Herbison <herbison@lassie.ucx.lkg.dec.com>
Dan Horner <liaison@uunet.uu.net>
Brad Isley <bgi@stiatl.salestech.com>
J. Lee Japp <jaapjl@madams.larc.nasa.gov>
Ray.Lampman@Heurikon.Com
Norman Lin <norlin@uokmax.ecn.uoknor.edu>
jmalcom@sura.net
Mark E. Mallett <mem@mv.MV.COM>
Owen Scott Medd <osm@msen.com>
Bertrand Meyer <bertrand@eiffel.com>
Pushpendra Mohta <pushp@cerf.net>
Mark Moraes <moraes@cs.toronto.edu>
Don Nichols <nichols@nvl.army.mil>
Andrew Partan <asp@uunet.uu.net>
Brad Passwaters <bjp@sura.net>
Michel Pollet <michel@trantor.UUCP>
Bob Rieger <bobr@netcom.com>
Rich Salz <rsalz@bbn.com>
Martin Lee Schoffstall <schoff@psi.com>
Russell Schulz <russell@alpha3.ersys.edmonton.ab.ca>
Doug Sewell <doug@ysu.edu>
Barry Shein <bzs@world.std.com>

Vince Skahan <vince@atc.boeing.com>
Shih-ping Spencer Sun <spencer@phoenix.Princeton.edu>
Jerry Sweet <jns@fernwood.mpk.ca.us>
David W. Tamkin <dattier@gagme.chi.il.us>
Christophe Wolfhugel <Christophe.Wolfhugel@grasp1.univ-lyon1.fr>
Steve Yelvington <steve@thelake.mn.org>
--
Jonathan Kamens OpenVision Technologies, Inc. jik@GZA.COM

B

List of the Alternative Hierarchy

List of the Alternative Hierarchy

The following lists appear in the periodic postings to
"news.announce.newusers" and other news newsgroups. The titles of the
articles are "Alternative Newsgroup Hierarchies, Part I" and "Alternative
Newsgroup Hierarchies, Part II."

alt.1d	One-dimensional imaging, & the thinking behind it.
alt.3d	Three-dimensional imaging.
alt.59.79.99	Hut, hut, hike!
alt.abortion.inequity	Paternal obligations of failing to abort unwanted child.
alt.abuse.recovery	Helping victims of abuse to recover.
alt.activism	Activities for activists.
alt.activism.d	A place to discuss issues in alt.activism.
alt.activism.death-penalty	For people opposed to capital punishment.
alt.adjective.noun.verb.verb.verb	The penultimate alt group.
alt.adoption	For those involved with or contemplating adoption.
alt.agriculture.misc	General discussions of agriculture, farming, etc.
alt.aldus.pagemaker	Don't use expensive user support, come here instead.
alt.alien.visitors	Space Aliens on Earth! Abduction! Gov't Cover-up!
alt.amateur-comp	Discussion and input for Amateur Computerist Newsletter.
alt.angst	Anxiety in the modern world.
alt.answers	As if anyone on alt has the answers. (Moderated)
alt.appalachian	Appalachian region awareness, events, and culture.
alt.aquaria	The aquarium & related as a hobby.
alt.archery	Robin Hood had the right idea.
alt.architecture	Building design/construction and related topics.

alt.artcom	Artistic Community, arts & communication.
alt.asian-movies	Movies from Hong Kong, Taiwan and the Chinese mainland.
alt.astrology	Twinkle, twinkle, little planet.
alt.atheism	Godless heathens.
alt.atheism.moderated	Focused Godless heathens. (Moderated)
alt.autos.antique	Discussion of all facets of older automobiles.
alt.autos.rod-n-custom	Vehicles with modified engines and/or appearance.
alt.backrubs	Lower...to the right...aaaah!
alt.basement.graveyard	Another side of the do-it-yourself movement.
alt.bbs	Computer BBS systems & software.
alt.bbs.ads	Ads for various computer BBSs.
alt.bbs.allsysop	SysOp concerns of ALL networks and technologies.
alt.bbs.first-class	The First Class Mac GUI BBS.
alt.bbs.internet	BBSs that are hooked up to the Internet.
alt.bbs.lists	Postings of regional BBS listings.
alt.bbs.pcboard	Technical support for the PCBoard BBS.
alt.bbs.pcbuucp	The commercial PCBoard gateway, PCB-UUCP.
alt.bbs.unixbbs	Discussion of the BBS package UnixBBS.
alt.bbs.uupcb	PCB? I used to do that in the Sixties, man...
alt.beer	Good for what ales ya.
alt.best.of.internet	It was a time of sorrow, it was a time of joy.
alt.bigfoot	Dr. Scholl's gone native.
alt.binaries.multimedia	Sound, text and graphics data rolled in one.
alt.binaries.pictures	Additional volume in the form of huge image files.

alt.binaries.pictures.d	Discussions about picture postings.
alt.binaries.pictures.erotica	Gigabytes of copyright violations.
alt.binaries.pictures.erotica.d	Discussing erotic copyright violations.
alt.binaries.pictures.erotica.female	Copyright violations featuring females.
alt.binaries.pictures.erotica.male	Copyright violations featuring males.
alt.binaries.pictures.erotica.orientals	Copyright violations featuring Asians.
alt.binaries.pictures.fine-art.d	Discussion of the fine-art binaries. (Moderated)
alt.binaries.pictures.fine-art.digitized	Art from conventional media. (Moderated)
alt.binaries.pictures.fine-art.graphics	Art created on computers. (Moderated)
alt.binaries.pictures.fractals	Cheaper just to send the program parameters.
alt.binaries.pictures.misc	Have we saturated the network yet?
alt.binaries.pictures.supermodels	Yet more copyright violations.
alt.binaries.pictures.tasteless	"Eccchh, that last one was *sick*...".
alt.binaries.pictures.utilities	Posting of pictures-related utilities.
alt.binaries.sounds.d	Sounding off.
alt.binaries.sounds.misc	Digitized audio adventures.
alt.binaries.sounds.music	Music samples in MOD/669 format.
alt.bitterness	No matter what it's for, you know how it'll turn out.
alt.books.deryni	Katherine Kurtz's books, especially the Deryni series.
alt.books.isaac-asimov	Fans of the late SF/science author Isaac Asimov.
alt.books.reviews	"If you want to know how it turns out, read it!".
alt.books.technical	Discussion of technical books.
alt.brother-jed	The born-again minister touring US campuses.
alt.buddha.short.fat.guy	Religion. And not religion. Both. Neither.

alt.business.multi-level	Multi-level (network) marketing businesses.
alt.cad	Computer Aided Design.
alt.cad.autocad	CAD as practiced by customers of Autodesk.
alt.california	The state and the state of mind.
alt.callahans	Callahan's bar for puns and fellowship.
alt.cascade	Art or litter you decide.
alt.cd-rom	Discussions of optical storage media.
alt.censorship	Discussion about restricting speech/press.
alt.cereal	Breakfast cereals and their (m)ilk.
alt.cesium	College Educated Students In Universal Mainland.
alt.child-support	Raising children in a split family.
alt.chinchilla	The nature of chinchilla farming in America Today.
alt.chinese.text	Postings in Chinese; Chinese language software.
alt.chinese.text.big5	Posting in Chinese[BIG 5].
alt.clearing.technology	Renegades from the Church of Scientology.
alt.co-ops	Discussion about co-operatives.
alt.cobol	Relationship between programming and stone axes.
alt.collecting.autographs	WOW! You got Pete Rose's? What about Kibo's?
alt.college.college-bowl	Discussions of the College Bowl competition.
alt.college.food	Dining halls, cafeterias, mystery meat, and more.
alt.comedy.british	Discussion of British comedy in a variety of media.
alt.comedy.firesgn-thtre	Firesign Theatre in all its flaming glory.
alt.comics.batman	Marketing mania.

alt.comics.lnh	Interactive net.madness in the superhero genre.
alt.comics.superman	No one knows it is also alt.clark.kent.
alt.comp.acad-freedom.news	Academic freedom issues related to computers. (Moderated)
alt.comp.acad-freedom.talk	Academic freedom issues related to computers.
alt.comp.fsp	A file transport protocol.
alt.computer.consultants	Geeks on Patrol.
alt.config	Alternative subnet discussions and connectivity.
alt.consciousness	Discussions on the study of the human consciousness.
alt.conspiracy	Be paranoid—they're out to get you.
alt.conspiracy.jfk	The Kennedy assassination.
alt.cows.moo.moo.moo	Like cows would cluck or something.
alt.cult-movies	Movies with a cult following.
alt.cult-movies.rocky-horror	Virgin! Virgin! Virgin! Virgin!
alt.culture.alaska	Is this where the ice weasels come from?
alt.culture.argentina	Don't cry for me.
alt.culture.hawaii	Ua Mau Ke Ea O Ka 'Aina I Ka Pono.
alt.culture.indonesia	Indonesian culture, news, etc.
alt.culture.internet	The culture(s) of the Internet.
alt.culture.karnataka	Culture and language of the Indian state of Karnataka.
alt.culture.kerala	People of Keralite origin and the Malayalam language.
alt.culture.ny-upstate	New York State, above Westchester.
alt.culture.oregon	Discussion about the state of Oregon.
alt.culture.us.asian-indian	Asian Indians in the US and Canada.
alt.culture.us.southwest	Basking in the sun of the US's lower left.
alt.culture.usenet	A self-referential oxymoron.
alt.current-events.bosnia	The strife of Bosnia-Herzegovina.

alt.current-events.flood-of-93	How the midwest US was turned into a sea.
alt.cyberpunk	High-tech low-life.
alt.cyberpunk.chatsubo	Literary virtual reality in a cyberpunk hangout.
alt.cyberpunk.tech	Cyberspace and Cyberpunk technology.
alt.cyberspace	Cyberspace and how it should work.
alt.dads-rights	Rights of fathers trying to win custody in court.
alt.data.bad.bad.bad	Evil androids siding with the Borg.
alt.dcom.telecom	Discussion of telecommunications technology.
alt.dear.whitehouse	When Hints from Heloise aren't enough.
alt.decathena	Digital's DECathena product. (Moderated)
alt.dev.null	The ultimate in moderated newsgroups. (Moderated)
alt.devilbunnies	Probably better left undescribed.
alt.discordia	All hail Eris, etc.
alt.discrimination	Quotas, affirmative action, bigotry, persecution.
alt.divination	Divination techniques (e.g., I Ching, Tarot, runes).
alt.dreams	What do they mean?
alt.drugs	Recreational pharmaceuticals and related flames.
alt.drugs.caffeine	All about the world's most-used stimulant drug.
alt.drumcorps	Drum and bugle corps discussion (and related topics).
alt.drwho.creative	Writing about long scarfs and time machines.
alt.emusic	Ethnic, exotic, electronic, elaborate, etc. music.
alt.engr.explosives	Building backyard bombs.

alt.ensign.wesley.die.die.die	We just can't get enough of him.
alt.evil	Tales from the dark side.
alt.exotic-music	Exotic music discussions. *
alt.fan.alok.vijayvargia	Vote early, and vote often.
alt.fan.asprin	The works of Robert Lynn Asprin.
alt.fan.bgcrisis	Priss, the Replicants, the ADP and Bubblegum Crisis.
alt.fan.bill-gates	Fans of the original micro-softie.
alt.fan.dan-quayle	For discussion of the US Vice President.
alt.fan.dave_barry	Electronic fan club for humorist Dave Barry.
alt.fan.debbie.gibson	The world's oldest cheerleader.
alt.fan.devo	Funny hats do not a band make.
alt.fan.dick-depew	Dump on Dick.
alt.fan.disney.afternoon	Disney Afternoon characters & shows.
alt.fan.douglas-adams	Author of "The Meaning of Liff", & other fine works.
alt.fan.eddings	The works of writer David Eddings.
alt.fan.enya	For Enya fandom.
alt.fan.firesign-theatre	The first try for alt.comedy.firesgn-thtre.
alt.fan.frank-zappa	Is that a Sears poncho?
alt.fan.furry	Fans of funny animals, ala Steve Gallacci's book.
alt.fan.g-gordon-liddy	Y'know, I saw him and Rush holding hands in a bar once.
alt.fan.goons	Careful Neddy, it's that dastardly Moriarty again.
alt.fan.greaseman	Fans of Doug Tracht, the DJ.
alt.fan.hofstadter	Douglas Hofstadter and Godel, Escher, Bach.
alt.fan.holmes	Elementary, my dear Watson. Like he ever said that.
alt.fan.howard-stern	Fans of the abrasive radio & TV personality.

alt.fan.james-bond	On his Majesty's Secret Service (& secret linen too).
alt.fan.jen-coolest	Gosh, isn't she just wonderful?
alt.fan.jimmy-buffett	A white sports coat and a pink crustacean.
alt.fan.karla-homolka	Why are there so few hot, exhibitionist, S&M women?
alt.fan.laurie.anderson	Will it be a music concert or a lecture this time?
alt.fan.lemurs	Little critters with BIG eyes.
alt.fan.letterman	One of the top 10 reasons to get the alt groups.
alt.fan.lightbulbs	A hardware problem.
alt.fan.madonna	Nice tits, eh... And how about that puppy?
alt.fan.mike-jittlov	Electronic fan club for animator Mike Jittlov.
alt.fan.monty-python	Electronic fan club for those wacky Brits.
alt.fan.pern	Anne McCaffery's s-f oeuvre.
alt.fan.piers-anthony	For fans of the s-f author Piers Anthony.
alt.fan.pratchett	For fans of Terry Pratchett, s-f humor writer.
alt.fan.robert.mcelwaine	Another favorite net-personality.
alt.fan.ronald-reagan	Jellybeans and all.
alt.fan.rush-limbaugh	Derogation of others for fun and profit.
alt.fan.serdar-argic	All about Armenia, Turkey, genocide, and robot-posting.
alt.fan.spinal-tap	Down on the sex farm.
alt.fan.tank-girl	No, she doesn't make noises like a squirrel. Really.
alt.fan.tolkien	...and in the dark shall find them.
alt.fan.warlord	The War Lord of the West Preservation Fan Club.
alt.fan.wodehouse	Discussion of the works of humour author P.G. Wodehouse.

alt.fandom.cons	Announcements of conventions (SciFi and others).
alt.fandom.misc	Other topics for fans of various kinds.
alt.fashion	All facets of the fashion industry discussed.
alt.feminism	Like soc.feminism, only different.
alt.filesystems.afs	Discussions about AFS, from deployment to development.
alt.fishing	Fishing as a hobby and sport.
alt.flame	Alternative, literate, pithy, succinct screaming.
alt.flame.faggots	Ignore the homophobic twits and they'll go away.
alt.flame.f***ing.faggots	For especially intellectual homophobes.
alt.flame.roommate	Putting the pig on a spit.
alt.folklore.college	Collegiate humor.
alt.folklore.computers	Stories & anecdotes about computers (some true!).
alt.folklore.ghost-stories	Boo!.
alt.folklore.herbs	Discussion of all aspects of herbs and their uses.
alt.folklore.science	The folklore of science, not the science of folklore.
alt.folklore.urban	Urban legends, ala Jan Harold Brunvand.
alt.food.cocacola	& Royal Crown, Pepsi, Dr. Pepper, NEHI, etc...
alt.food.mcdonalds	Carl Sagan's favorite burger place.
alt.funk-you	The altnet, so full of wit!
alt.games.frp.dnd-util	Discussion and creation of utility programs for AD&D.
alt.games.frp.live-action	Discussion of all forms of live-action gaming.
alt.games.gb	The Galactic Bloodshed conquest game.
alt.games.lynx	The Atari Lynx.
alt.games.mk	Struggling in Mortal Kombat!

alt.games.omega	The computer game Omega.
alt.games.sf2	The video game Street Fighter 2.
alt.games.torg	Gateway for TORG mailing list.
alt.games.vga-planets	Discussion of Tim Wisseman's VGA Planets.
alt.games.xpilot	Discussion on all aspects of the X11 game Xpilot.
alt.gathering.rainbow	For discussing the annual Rainbow Gathering.
alt.geek	To fulfill an observed need.
alt.good.morning	Would you like coffee with that?.
alt.good.news	A place for some news that's good news.
alt.gopher	Discussion of the gopher information service.
alt.gothic	The gothic movement: things mournful and dark.
alt.gourmand	Recipes & cooking info. (Moderated)
alt.grad-student.tenured	Most prison terms are finished sooner.
alt.graphics.pixutils	Discussion of pixmap utilities.
alt.great-lakes	Discussions of the Great Lakes and adjacent places.
alt.guitar	You axed for it, you got it.
alt.guitar.bass	Bass guitars.
alt.guitar.tab	Discussions about guitar tablature music.
alt.hackers	Descriptions of projects currently under development.(Moderated)
alt.health.ayurveda	Really old medicine from India.
alt.hemp	It's about knot-tying with rope. Knot!
alt.hi.are.you.cute	Are there a lot of pathetic people on the net or what?
alt.hindu	The Hindu religion. (Moderated)
alt.history.living	A forum for discussing the hobby of living history.

alt.history.what-if	What would the net have been like without this group?
alt.homosexual	Same as alt.sex.homosexual.
alt.horror	The horror genre.
alt.horror.cthulhu	Campus Crusade for Cthulhu, Ctulhu, Ctulu, and the rest.
alt.horror.werewolves	They were wolves, now they're something to be wary of.
alt.hotrod	High speed automobiles. (Moderated)
alt.humor.best-of-usenet	What the moderator thinks is funniest. (Moderated)
alt.humor.best-of-usenet.d	Why everyone else doesn't think it's funny.
alt.hypertext	Discussion of hypertext—uses, transport, etc.
alt.hypnosis	When you awaken, you will forget about this newsgroup.
alt.illuminati	See alt.cabal. Fnord.
alt.image.medical	Medical image exchange discussions.
alt.india.progressive	Progressive politics in the Indian sub-continent. (Moderated)
alt.individualism	Philosophies where individual rights are paramount.
alt.internet.access.wanted	"Oh. OK, how about just an MX record for now?"
alt.internet.services	Not available in the uucp world, even via email.
alt.irc	Internet Relay Chat material.
alt.irc.lamers	See alt.hi.are.you.cute.
alt.is.too	NOT!
alt.japanese.text	Postings in Japanese; Japanese language software.
alt.journalism	General hangout for journalists.
alt.ketchup	Whak* Whak* ...shake... Whak* Damn, all over my tie.

alt.kids-talk	A place for the pre-college set on the net.
alt.kill.the.whales	This newsgroup is evidence for the coming apocalypse.
alt.lang.asm	Assembly languages of various flavors.
alt.lang.basic	The Language That Would Not Die.
alt.lang.intercal	A joke language with a real compiler.
alt.law-enforcement	No, ossifer, there's nothing illegal going on in alt...
alt.life.internet	One big throbbing mass of life, we are.
alt.life.sucks	& then you shrivel up.
alt.locksmithing	You locked your keys in *where*?
alt.lucid-emacs.bug	Bug reports about Lucid Emacs.
alt.lucid-emacs.help	Q&A and general discussion of Lucid Emacs.
alt.magic	For discussion about stage magic.
alt.magick	For discussion about supernatural arts.
alt.magick.sex	Sexuality, spirituality, and magick.
alt.manga	Discussion of non-Western comics.
alt.mcdonalds	Can I get fries with that?
alt.med.cfs	Chronic fatigue syndrome information.
alt.meditation	General discussion of meditation.
alt.meditation.transcendental	Contemplation of states beyond the teeth.
alt.memetics	The evolution of ideas in societies.
alt.messianic	Messianic traditions.
alt.military.cadet	Preparing for the coming apocalypse.
alt.missing-kids	Locating missing children.
alt.msdos.programmer	For the serious MS/DOS programmer (no for sale ads).
alt.mud	Same as rec.games.mud.
alt.mud.cyberworld	"Made for some student," the clueless newsgroup said.
alt.mudders.anonymous	You might as well face it, you're addicted to MUD.

alt.music.a-cappella	Voice only, no /dev/sound.
alt.music.alternative	For groups having 2 or less Platinum-selling albums.
alt.music.canada	Oh, Canada, eh?
alt.music.enya	Gaelic set to spacey music.
alt.music.filk	SF/fantasy related folk music.
alt.music.hardcore	Could be porno set to music.
alt.music.marillion	A progressive band. The Silmarillion is a book.
alt.music.prince	So my Prince came. Make him go away.
alt.music.progressive	Yes, Marillion, Asia, King Crimson, etc.
alt.music.queen	He's dead, Jim.
alt.music.rush	For Rushheads.
alt.music.ska	Discussions of ska (skank) music, bands, and suchlike.
alt.music.tmbg	They Might Be Giants.
alt.music.world	Discussion of music from around the world.
alt.mythology	Zeus rules.
alt.necromicon	Yet another sign of the coming apocalypse.
alt.netgames.bolo	A multiplayer tank game for the Macintosh.
alt.news-media	Don't believe the hype.
alt.news.macedonia	News concerning Macedonia in the Balkan Region.
alt.nick.sucks	Probably.
alt.non.sequitur	Richard Nixon.
alt.online-service	Large commercial online services, and the Internet.
alt.os.multics	30 years old and going strong.
alt.out-of-body	Out of Body Experiences.
alt.overlords	Office of the Omnipotent Overlords of the Omniverse.
alt.pagan	Discussions about paganism & religion.

alt.paranet.abduct	"They replaced Jim-Bob with a look-alike!"
alt.paranet.paranormal	"If it exists, how can supernatural be beyond natural?"
alt.paranet.science	"Maybe if we dissect the psychic..."
alt.paranet.skeptic	"I don't believe they turned you into a newt."
alt.paranet.ufo	"Heck, I guess naming it 'UFO' identifies it."
alt.paranormal	Phenomena which are not scientifically explicable.
alt.parents-teens	Parent-teenager relationships.
alt.party	Parties, celebration and general debauchery.
alt.pave.the.earth	One world, one people, one slab of asphalt.
alt.peeves	Discussion of peeves & related.
alt.personals	Do you really want to meet someone this way?
alt.personals.ads	Geek seeks Dweeb. Object: low-level interfacing.
alt.personals.bondage	Are you tied up this evening?
alt.personals.misc	Dweeb seeks Geek. Object: low-level interfacing.
alt.personals.poly	Hi there, do you multiprocess?
alt.philosophy.objectivism	A product of the Ayn Rand corporation.
alt.politics.british	Politics and a real Queen, too.
alt.politics.clinton	Discussing Slick Willie & Co.
alt.politics.correct	A Neil Bush fan club.
alt.politics.economics	War == Poverty, & other discussions.
alt.politics.elections	Everyone who votes for Quayle gets a free lollipop.
alt.politics.equality	Equality and discrimination.
alt.politics.greens	Green party politics & activities worldwide.

alt.politics.homosexuality	As the name implies
alt.politics.india.progressive	All about Progressive politics in India.
alt.politics.libertarian	The libertarian ideology.
alt.politics.media	There's lies, damn lies, statistics, and news reports.
alt.politics.org.misc	Political organizations.
alt.politics.perot	Discussion of the non-candidate.
alt.politics.radical-left	Who remains after the radicals left?
alt.politics.reform	Political reform.
alt.politics.sex	Not a good idea to mix them, sez Marilyn & Profumo.
alt.politics.usa.constitution	U.S. Constitutional politics.
alt.politics.usa.misc	Miscellaneous USA politics.
alt.politics.usa.republican	Discussions of the USA Republican Party.
alt.polyamory	For those who maintain multiple love relationships.
alt.postmodern	Postmodernism, semiotics, deconstruction, and the like.
alt.president.clinton	Will the CIA undermine his efforts?
alt.prisons	Can I get an alt.* feed in the slammer?
alt.privacy	Privacy issues in cyberspace.
alt.privacy.anon-server	Technical & policy matters of anonymous contact servers.
alt.privacy.clipper	No, really, we can't read it. *snicker*.
alt.prose	Postings of original writings, fictional & otherwise.
alt.psychoactives	Better living through chemistry.
alt.psychology.personality	Personality taxonomy, such as Myers-Briggs.
alt.pub.cloven-shield	S-F role-playing.
alt.pub.dragons-inn	Fantasy virtual reality pub similar to alt.callahans.
alt.pub.havens-rest	Even more S-F role-playing.
alt.punk	Burning them keeps insects away.

alt.ql.creative	The "Quantum Leap" tv show.
alt.quotations	Quotations, quips, .sig lines, witticisms, et al.
alt.radio.pirate	Hide the gear, here comes the magic station-wagons.
alt.radio.scanner	Discussion of scanning radio receivers.
alt.rap	For fans of rap music.
alt.rave	Techno-culture: music, dancing, drugs, dancing...
alt.recovery	For people in recovery programs (e.g., AA, ACA, GA).
alt.recovery.codependency	Recovering from the disease of codependency.
alt.religion.emacs	Emacs. Umacs. We all macs.
alt.religion.kibology	He's Fred, Jim.
alt.religion.monica	Discussion about net-venus Monica and her works.
alt.religion.scientology	He's dead, Jim.
alt.revisionism	"It CAN'T be that way 'cause here's the FACTS."
alt.revolution.counter	Discussions of counter-revolutionary issues.
alt.rhode_island	Discussion of the great little state.
alt.rock-n-roll	Counterpart to alt.sex and alt.drugs.
alt.rock-n-roll.acdc	Dirty deeds done dirt cheap.
alt.rock-n-roll.classic	Classic rock, both the music and its marketing.
alt.rock-n-roll.hard	Music where stance is everything.
alt.rock-n-roll.metal	For the headbangers on the net.
alt.rock-n-roll.metal.gnr	"Axl Rose" is an anagram for "Oral Sex."
alt.rock-n-roll.metal.heavy	Non-sissyboy metal bands.
alt.rock-n-roll.metal.ironmaiden	Sonic torture methods.
alt.rock-n-roll.metal.metallica	Sort of like Formica with more hair.
alt.rock-n-roll.metal.progressive	Slayer teams up with Tom Cora.

alt.rock-n-roll.stones	Gathering plenty of moss by now.
alt.romance	Discussion about the romantic side of love.
alt.romance.chat	Talk about no sex.
alt.rush-limbaugh	Fans of the conservative activist radio announcer.
alt.satanism	Not such a bad dude once you get to know him.
alt.satellite.tv.europe	All about European satellite tv.
alt.save.the.earth	Environmentalist causes.
alt.sci.physics.acoustics	Sound advice.
alt.sci.physics.new-theories	Scientific theories you won't find in journals.
alt.sci.planetary	Studies in planetary science.
alt.sci.sociology	People are really interesting when you watch them.
alt.security	Security issues on computer systems.
alt.security.index	Pointers to good stuff in alt.security. (Moderated)
alt.security.pgp	The Pretty Good Privacy package.
alt.sega.genesis	Another addiction.
alt.self-improve	Self-improvement in less than 14 characters.
alt.sewing	A group that is not as it seams.
alt.sex	Postings of a prurient nature.
alt.sex.bestiality	Happiness is a warm puppy.
alt.sex.bestiality.barney	For people with big, purple newt fetishes.
alt.sex.bondage	Tie me, whip me, make me read the net!
alt.sex.fetish.amputee	They're as sexual as anyone else.
alt.sex.fetish.fa	The group creator couldn't spell "fat" right.
alt.sex.fetish.feet	Kiss them. Now.
alt.sex.fetish.hair	It worked for Rapunsel.
alt.sex.fetish.orientals	The mysteries of Asia are a potent lure.
alt.sex.masturbation	Where one's SO is oneself.

alt.sex.motss	Jesse Helms would not subscribe to this group.
alt.sex.movies	Discussing the ins and outs of certain movies.
alt.sex.pictures	Gigabytes of copyright violations.
alt.sex.pictures.female	Copyright violations featuring mostly females.
alt.sex.pictures.male	Copyright violations featuring mostly males.
alt.sex.stories	For those who need it *NOW*.
alt.sex.stories.d	For those who talk about needing it *NOW*.
alt.sex.wanted	Requests for erotica, either literary or in the flesh.
alt.sex.wizards	Questions for only true sex wizards.
alt.sexual.abuse.recovery	Helping others deal with traumatic experiences.
alt.sexy.bald.captains	More StarTrek.
alt.shenanigans	Practical jokes, pranks, randomness, etc.
alt.shut.the.hell.up.geek	Group for Usenet motto.
alt.skate-board	Discussion of all aspects of skate-boarding.
alt.skinheads	The skinhead culture/anti-culture.
alt.slack	Posting relating to the Church of the Subgenius.
alt.slick.willy.tax.tax.tax	Not just for rich people anymore.
alt.society.anarchy	Societies without rulers.
alt.society.ati	The Activist Times Digest. (Moderated)
alt.society.civil-liberties	Individual rights.
alt.society.civil-liberty	Same as alt.society.civil-liberties.
alt.society.conservatism	Social, cultural, and political conservatism.
alt.society.resistance	Resistance against governments.
alt.society.revolution	Discussions on revolutions
alt.soft-sys.tooltalk	Forum for ToolTalk related issues.
alt.soulmates	But what if Richard Bach's true love lived in Mongolia?

alt.sources	Alternative source code, unmoderated. Caveat Emptor.
alt.sources.d	Discussion of posted sources.
alt.sources.index	Pointers to source code in alt.sources.*. (Moderated)
alt.sources.wanted	Requests for source code.
alt.spam	What is that stuff that doth jiggle in the breeze?
alt.sport.bowling	In the gutter again.
alt.sport.darts	Look what you've done to the wall!
alt.sport.foosball	Table soccer and dizzy little men.
alt.sport.lasertag	Indoor splatball with infrared lasers.
alt.sport.pool	Knock your balls into your pockets for fun.
alt.sports.baseball.atlanta-braves	Atlanta Braves major league baseball.
alt.sports.baseball.balt-orioles	Baltimore Orioles major league baseball.
alt.sports.baseball.chicago-cubs	Chicago Cubs major league baseball.
alt.sports.baseball.cinci-reds	Cincinnati Reds major league baseball.
alt.sports.baseball.col-rockies	Colorado Rockies major league baseball.
alt.sports.baseball.fla-marlins	Florida Marlins major league baseball.
alt.sports.baseball.houston-astros	Houston Astros major league baseball.
alt.sports.baseball.la-dodgers	Los Angels Dodgers baseball talk.
alt.sports.baseball.mke-brewers	For discussion of the Milwaukee Brewers.
alt.sports.baseball.mke-brewers.suck.suck.suck	... and why they suck.
alt.sports.baseball.mn-twins	Minnesota Twins major league baseball.
alt.sports.baseball.montreal-expos	Montreal Expos major league baseball.
alt.sports.baseball.ny-mets	New York Mets baseball talk.
alt.sports.baseball.oakland-as	Oakland A's major league baseball talk.
alt.sports.baseball.phila-phillies	Philadelphia Phillies baseball talk.
alt.sports.baseball.pitt-pirates	Pittsburgh Pirates baseball talk.
alt.sports.baseball.sf-giants	San Francisco Giants baseball talk.
alt.sports.baseball.stl-cardinals	St. Louis Cardinals baseball talk.
alt.sports.football.mn-vikings	Minnesota Vikings football talk.

alt.sports.football.pro.wash-redskins	Washington Redskins football talk.
alt.stagecraft	Technical theatre issues.
alt.startrek.creative	Stories and parodies related to Star Trek.
alt.stupid.religious.discussion	talk.religion.misc's no-nonsense name.
alt.stupidity	Discussion about stupid newsgroups.
alt.suicide.holiday	Talk of why suicides increase at holidays.
alt.super.nes	Discussion of the Super Nintendo video game.
alt.supermodels	Discussing famous & beautiful models.
alt.support	Dealing with emotional situations & experiences.
alt.support.big-folks	Sizeism can be as awful as sexism or racism.
alt.support.diet	Seeking enlightenment through weight loss.
alt.support.mult-sclerosis	Discussion about living with multiple sclerosis.
alt.support.step-parents	Difficulties of being a step-parent.
alt.surfing	Riding the ocean waves.
alt.sustainable.agriculture	Such as the Mekong delta before Agent Orange.
alt.swedish.chef.bork.bork.bork	The beginning of the end.
alt.sys.amiga.demos	Code and talk to show off the Amiga.
alt.sys.amiga.uucp	AmigaUUCP.
alt.sys.intergraph	Support for Intergraph machines.
alt.sys.perq	Keeping the antiques working.
alt.sys.sun	Technical discussion of Sun Microsystems products.
alt.tasteless	Truly disgusting.
alt.tasteless.johan.wevers	The OETLUL of the year.
alt.tasteless.jokes	Sometimes insulting rather than disgusting or humorous.
alt.techno-shamanism	But can they make the name work on SYSV systems?
alt.technology.misc	Another well-focused alt group.

alt.technology.mkt-failure	Promising technologies that failed to sell.
alt.test	Alternative subnetwork testing.
alt.test.my.new.group	Created by a fool on his day.
alt.test.test	More from the people who brought you "BBS systems."
alt.thinking.hurts	Barbie was right.
alt.thrash	Thrashlife.
alt.timewasters	A Dutch computer club; perhaps a microcosm of Usenet...
alt.toolkits.xview	The X windows XView toolkit.
alt.toys.hi-tech	Optimus Prime is my hero.
alt.toys.lego	Snap 'em together.
alt.transgendered	Boys will be girls, and vice-versa.
alt.tv.babylon-5	Casablanca in space.
alt.tv.bh90210	Fans of "Beverly Hills 90210" TV show.
alt.tv.dinosaurs.barney.die.die.die	Squish the saccharine newt.
alt.tv.la-law	For the folks out in la-law land.
alt.tv.mash	Nothing like a good comedy about war and dying.
alt.tv.mst3k	Hey, you robots! Down in front!.
alt.tv.muppets	Miss Piggy on the tube.
alt.tv.mwc	"Married... With Children."
alt.tv.northern-exp	For the TV show with moss growing on it.
alt.tv.prisoner	The Prisoner television series from years ago.
alt.tv.red-dwarf	The British sci-fi/comedy show.
alt.tv.ren-n-stimpy	Some change from Lassie, eh?
alt.tv.rockford-files	But he won't do windows.
alt.tv.seinfeld	A funny guy.
alt.tv.simpsons	Don't have a cow, man!
alt.tv.time-traxx	If you run into Nyssa, let us know.
alt.tv.tiny-toon	Discussion about the "Tiny Toon Adventures" show.
alt.tv.tiny-toon.fandom	Apparently one fan group could not bind them all.

alt.tv.twin-peaks	Discussion about the popular (and unusual) TV show.
alt.unsubscribe-me	Just strap right in to this electric chair here.
alt.usage.english	English grammar, word usages, and related topics.
alt.usenet.offline-reader	Getting your fix offline.
alt.uu.lang.esperanto.misc	Study of Esperanto in Usenet University.
alt.vampyres	Discussion of vampires and related writings, films, etc.
alt.video.games.reviews	What's hot and what's not in video games.
alt.video.laserdisc	LD players and selections available for them.
alt.visa.us	Discussion/information on visas pertaining to US.
alt.war	Not just collateral damage.
alt.war.civil.usa	Discussion of the U.S. Civil War (1861-1865).
alt.war.vietnam	Discussion of all aspects of the Vietnam War.
alt.wedding	Til death or our lawyers do us part.
alt.wesley.crusher.die.die.die	Ensigns just get no respect.
alt.whine	Why me?
alt.whistleblowing	Whistleblowing on fraud, abuse and other corruption.
alt.winsock	Windows Sockets.
alt.wolves	Discussing wolves & wolf-mix dogs.
alt.wonderment.bgjw	By Gosh, Judge Wapner!
alt.zima	Not to be confused with zuma.
alt.zines	Small magazines, mostly noncommercial.
alt.znet.aeo	Atari Explorer Online magazine. (Moderated)
alt.znet.pc	Z*NET International ASCII Magazines (Weekly). (Moderated)

A Word About News Readers

News Reader Basic Functions

A news reader is a software package or program that allows you to interact with the articles in USENET's newsgroups. In general a news reader will allow you to:

✔ Select newsgroups

✔ Page back and forth in a set of newsgroups to determine which to read

✔ Page back and forth in a set of articles to determine which to read

✔ Post a reply to an article

✔ Write an e-mail response to an article's author

✔ Post an original article

✔ Save an article

The way in which a news reader provides these basic functions will vary tremendously depending on the capabilities of the platform (hardware and its operating system software) it is running on. Some news readers are better suited toward one platform or another. Most news readers allow you to set options to personalize your news reading environment. Most allow you to decide in advance which newsgroups you care to subscribe to using the .newsrc file. Ask your system administrator or service provider for more information about how to do either of these.

Types of News Readers Available

There are two fundamental types of news readers available: unthreaded and threaded. An unthreaded news reader presents articles in the order that they are received. An unthreaded news reader leaves it to the person using it to recognize replies to previously posted articles. A threaded news reader, on the other hand, presents the articles and their replies together in a threaded discussion. When reading an article, a threaded news reader will present the articles and all direct replies together.

Some Available News Readers

The following is an overview of some of the available news readers and the platforms they run on. It is by no means a comprehensive list. It also includes news readers that are obsolete but of historical significance.

"A" News

Original news reading software written in Unix shell scripts intended to manage only a few articles per group per day. (Obsolete)

"B" News

Rewritten version of "A" News to handle an increasing volume of news. (Obsolete)

"C" News

One rewritten version of "B" News that uses Network News Transfer Protocol as opposed to UUCP. "C" News can be obtained from cs.toronto.edu. For more information see "News Need Not Be Slow" in the Winter 1987 Usenix Technical Conference Proceedings.

"C" News

A ported version of "C" News for the Commodore Amiga. Can be obtained from ftp.uu.net in the /systems/amiga/dillon directory.

ANU-NEWS

A complete news package for VMS systems. Can be obtained from kuhub.cc.ukans.edu.

Gnews

A macro package that can be used with the GNU Emacs text editor. Can be obtained from most sites carrying GNU archives.

GNUS

A macro package that can be used with the GNU Emacs text editor. Can be obtained from most sites carrying GNU archives.

HyperNews

An NNTP news reader for the Macintosh based on Hy-perCard stack. Can be obtained from many Mac archives.

InterNetNews
(INN)

A rewritten version of "B" News that supports both NNTP and UUCP. Designed to run on Unix hosts that have a socket interface. Can be obtained from ftp.uu.net in the /networking/news/nntp/inn directory. For more information see "InterNetNews: Usenet Transport for Internet Sites" published in the June 1992 Usenix Technical Conference Proceedings.

NewsWatcher

A Macintosh news reader preferred by many Mac users. Can be obtained from ftp.acns.nwu.edu in the /pub/news-watcher directory.

nn

A screen-oriented news reader that presents its user with a menu of subject and sender name lines and allows the pre-selection of articles to read. Can be obtained from dkuug.dk or other widely available sites.

NNMVS

An NNTP based news reader for TSO/ISPF. Can be obtained from info2.rus.uni-stattgart.de in the /pub/comm/news/beginner/software/nnmvs directory and other sites.

NNR

An NNTP based news reader that uses XEDIT for a screen manager. Can be obtained from rusmv1.rus.uni-stuttgart.de in the soft/comm/news/beginner/software/vm-cms/* directory.

notes

Notes was another distributed "news" system that was merged with USENET via gateways doing a protocol translation. (No longer maintained)

PSU NetNews

An IBM VM/SP (CMS) version of USENET software that supports only 3270 terminals and uses XEDIT as a screen driver. Can be obtained from LISTSERV@PSUVM.

readnews
    The oldest USENET news reading interface. Contains a nice balance of simplicity and power. Found on most USENET systems.

rn
    A screen-oriented news reader powerful and popular with Unix users. Can be obtained from lib.tmc.edu using ftp or from archive-server@bcm.tmc.edu using e-mail.

tin
    A threaded screen-oriented news reader based on the older "notes" news reader. Can be obtained from alt.sources.

trn
    A threaded version of rn. Can be obtained from ftp.coe.montana.edu in the /pub/trn directory and other widely available sites.

trumpet
    An intuitive, NNTP based news reader for DOS. Available at most ftp sites.

VM NNTP
    An NNTP server available for VM systems, compatible with Unix NNTP. Assumes PSU NetNews is already installed on the VM system. Can be obtained from the NNTP Package on listserv@blekul11.

VMS/vnews
    A better news reader than ANU-NEWS for VMS systems. Can be obtained from arizona.edu or any site which archives vmsnet.source.

vnews
    A screen-oriented news reader based on "readnews". It is currently distributed with the standard 2.11 source.

xrn
    An X-11 based interface to NNTP. Can be obtained from ftp.uu.net and other widely available sites.

xvnews
    An X-11 based interface to NNTP for use on Sun workstations running OpenWindows. Can be obtained from export.lcs.mit.edu in the contrib directory.

Command Summary for rn

Here is a list of the available commands for the rn news reader. It can be obtained online by typing a "?" from within rn.

Article Selection commands:

n,SP	Find next unread article (follows discussion-tree in threaded groups).
N	Go to next article.
^N	Scan forward for next unread article with same subject.
p,P,^P	Same as n,N,^N, only going backwards.
-	Go to previously displayed article.
<,>	Browse the previous/next selected thread. If no threads are selected, all threads that had unread news upon entry to the group are considered selected for browsing. Entering an empty group browses all threads.
(,)	Go to article's parent/child.
{,}	Go to tree's root/leaf.
t	Display the entire article tree and all its subjects.
number	Go to specified article.
range{,range}:command{:command}	
	Apply one or more commands to one or more ranges of articles. Ranges are of the form: number | number-number. You may use . for the current article, and $ for the last article. Valid commands are: e, j, m, M, s, S, t, T, |, +, and -.
:cmd	Perform a command on all the selected articles.
/pattern/modifiers	
	Scan forward for article containing pattern in the subject line. (Use ?pat? to scan backwards; append h to scan headers, a to scan entire articles, r to scan read articles, c to make case sensitive.)
/pattern/modifiers:command{:command}	
	Apply one or more commands to the set of articles matching pattern. Use a K modifier to save entire command to the KILL file for this newsgroup. Commands m and M, if first, imply an r modifier. Valid commands are the same as for the range command.
f,F	Submit a followup article (F = include this article).
r,R	Reply through net mail (R = include this article).
e dir{| command}	
	Extract to directory using /bin/sh, uudecode, unship, or command.
s ...	Save to file or pipe via sh.
S ...	Save via preferred shell.
w,W	Like s and S but save without the header.
| ...	Same as s | ...
C	Cancel this article, if yours.
^R,v	Restart article (v=verbose).
^X	Restart article, rot13 mode.
c	Catch up (mark all articles as read).
b	Back up one page.

^L	Refresh the screen. You can get back to the pager with this.
X	Refresh screen in rot13 mode.
^	Go to first unread article. Disables subject search mode.
$	Go to end of newsgroup. Disables subject search mode.
#	Print last article number.
&	Print current values of command-line switches.
&switch {switch}	Set or unset more switches.
&&	Print current macro definitions.
&&def	Define a new macro.
j	Junk this article (mark it read). Stays at end of article.
m	Mark article as still unread.
M	Mark article as still unread upon exiting newsgroup or Y command.
Y	Yank back articles marked temporarily read via M.
k	Kill current subject (mark articles as read).
,	Mark current article and its replies as read.
J	Junk entire thread (mark all subjects as read in this thread).
T	Trash current thread (like 'J'), and save command in KILL file.
K	Mark current subject as read, and save command in KILL file.
^K	Edit local KILL file (the one for this newsgroup).
=	List subjects of unread articles.
+	Enter thread selection mode.
U	Unread some news -- prompts for thread, subthread, all, or select.
u	Unsubscribe from this newsgroup.
q	Quit this newsgroup for now.
Q	Quit newsgroup, staying at current newsgroup.

Command Summary for trn

Here is a list of the available commands for the trn news reader. It can be obtained online by typing a "?" from within trn.

*** NEWS NEWS ***

Welcome to trn. There are more options to trn than you want to think about, so we won't list them here. If you want to find out about them, read the manual page(s). There are some important things to remember, though:

* Trn is an extension of rn. Where possible, the command syntax is the same.
* To access all the new features, specify the options -x and -X. These options MAY be on by default, but it won't hurt to be redundant.
* Trn runs in cbreak mode. This means you don't have to type carriage return on single character commands. (There are some multi-character commands.)
* At ANY prompt, you may type 'h' for help. There are many different help menus, depending on the context. Also, typing <esc>h in the middle of a multi-character command will list escape substitutions.
* Typing a space to any prompt means to do the normal thing. You could spend all day reading news and never hit anything but the space bar.

This particular message comes from /usr/local/lib/news/trn/news-news, and will only appear once. If your news administrator puts a new message in here, it will be displayed for you the first time you run trn after the change.

Wayne Davison davison@borland.com

Paging commands:

SP	Display the next page.
x	Display the next page decrypted (rot13).
d	Display half a page more.
CR	Display one more line.
^R,v,^X	Restart the current article (v=verbose header, ^X=rot13).
b	Back up one page.
^L,X	Refresh the screen (X=rot13).
t	Display the entire article tree and all its subjects.
g pat	Go to (search forward within article for) pattern.
G	Search again for current pattern within article.
^G	Search for next line beginning with "Subject:".
TAB	Search for next line beginning with a different character.
q	Quit the pager, go to end of article. Leave article read or unread.
j	Junk this article (mark it read). Goes to end of article.

The following commands skip the rest of the current article, then behave just as if typed to the 'What next?' prompt at the end of the article:

n	Scan forward for next unread article.
N	Go to next article.
^N	Scan forward for next unread article with same title.
p,P,^P	Same as n,N,^N, only going backwards.
-	Go to previously displayed article.
<,>	Browse the previous/next selected thread. If no threads are selected, all threads that had unread news upon

entry to the group are considered
selected for browsing. Entering an empty group
browses all threads.
(.),{.}   Go to parent/child/root/leaf in thread.

The following commands also take you to the end of the article.
Type h at end of article for a description of these commands:

$ & / = ? c C f F k K ^K J , m M number e r R ^R s S u U v w W Y ^ |

(To return to the middle of the article after one of these commands, type ^L.)

Andrew

Andrew N. Schlein
schlein@pipeline.com

Command Summary for tin

Here is a list of the available commands for the tin news reader. It can be obtained online by typing a "h" from within tin.

4$	Goto article 4 ($=goto last article)
^D^U	Down (^U=up) a page
^F^B	Down (^B=up) a page
^K	Kill / Auto select (hot) current article
^L	Redraw page
<CR>	Read current article
<TAB>	Goto next unread article or group
aA	Author forward (A=backward) search
b<SPACE>	Back (<SPACE>=forward) a page
B	Mail bug/comment to Iain.Lea%anl433.uucp@Germany.EU.net
c	Mark all articles as read and goto group selection menu
C	Mark all articles as read and goto next unread group
d	Toggle display of subject only & subject/author
g	Choose a new group by name
h	Command help
I	Toggle inverse video
jk	Down (k=up) a line
K	Mark article/thread as read & goto next unread
l	List articles within current thread
m	Mail article/thread/hot/pattern/tagged articles to someone
M	Menu of configurable options
o	Output article/thread/hot/pattern/tagged articles to printer
np	Goto next (p=previous) group
NP	Goto next (P=previous) unread article
q	Return to previous level
Q	Quit

r	Toggle display to show all / only unread articles
s	Save article/thread/hot/pattern/tagged articles to file
T	Tag current article for crossposting/mailing/piping/printing/saving
u	Toggle display of unthreaded & threaded articles
U	Untag all tagged articles
v	Show version information
w	Post an article to current group
W	List articles posted by user
x	Crosspost current article to another group
zZ	Mark article (Z=thread) as unread
/?	Subject forward (?=backward) search
!	Shell escape
-	Show last message
|	Pipe article/thread/hot/pattern/tagged articles into command
*	Select thread
.	Toggle selection of thread
@	Reverse all selections (all articles)
~	Undo all selections (all articles)
X	Mark all unread articles that have not been selected as read
+	Perform auto-selection on group
=	Mark threads selected if at least one unread art is selected
;	Mark threads selected if at least one unread art is selected

Where to Go for More Information

For an excellent description of how some of the more popular news readers work, pick up a copy of *The Waite Group's Unix Communications* by Bart Anderson, Barry Costales, & Harry Henderson. It is published by SAMS, A Division of Macmillan Computer Publishing.

For more detailed information about a particular news reader, get a printed copy of the manual pages. Your system administrator or service provider will be able to assist you with this.

Recommended Reading

If reading this book has made you curious about other computer communication related topics, you may find the following books useful in satisfying your newly arisen curiosity.

Computer Networks

The following is a pleasant, easy to read book focusing on the Internet network. It discusses in detail many of the topics mentioned in the final chapter of this book:

> Kehoe, Brendon, *Zen and the Art of the Internet: A Beginner's Guide.* 2nd edition. Englewood Cliffs, NJ: PTR Prentice Hall, 1993.

For a more substantial book discussing the Internet and related topics get a copy of:

> Krol, Ed, *The Whole Internet: User's Guide & Catalog.* Sebastopol, CA: O'Reilly & Associates, 1992.

Another good book on the subject of the Internet is:

> LaQuey, Tracy, *The Internet Companion: A Beginner's Guide to Global Networking.* Reading, MA: Addison-Wesley, 1993.

Computer Communications

The following book is particularly good at presenting Unix and computer communications topics in a manner that is both comprehensive and understandable. It has great illustrations and avoids the use of jargon. I highly recommend it.

> Anderson, Bart, Bryan Costales, Harry Henderson (The Waite Group), *UNIX Communications.* Indianapolis, IN: Howard W. Sams & Company, 1987.

Unlike the book mentioned above, the following book on computer communications was written from the perspec-

tive of someone trying to do it from home. It is full of useful, necessarily technical, information.

> Glossbrenner, Alfred, *The Complete Handbook of Personal Computer Communications: Everything You Need to Go Online with the World.* New York, NY: St. Martin's Press, 1983.

Mailing Lists

Here is an incredible resource for mailing lists and special interest groups:

> Hardie, Edward T. L., Vivian Neou, (Editors), *Internet: Mailing Lists.* Menlo Park, CA: SRI International, 1992.

USENET in Particular

The following two books are recommended reading for those who want to get seriously involved in bringing USENET to their site.

> O'Reilly, Tim, Grace Todino, *Managing UUCP and Usenet.* Sebastopol, CA: O'Reilly & Associates, 1989.

> Todino, Grace, Dale Dougherty, *Using UUCP and USENET.* Sebastol, CA: O'Reilly & Associates, 1990.

Glossary

The following definitions are given in the context of USENET usage.

*   An asterisk is a symbol for a wildcard.

*.answers   A newsgroup hierarchy's answer subgroup containing FAQs and other periodic postings that the newsgroup's regular participants recommend that new users review before participating in the newsgroup.

.sig File   A file containing custom information about a person that gets attached to newsgroup postings and/or electronic mail messages in Unix operating systems.

:-(Short hand for an unhappy face. A way to indicate that a previously described event didn't make you happy. Turn head sideways to view.

:-)   Short hand for a happy face. A way to indicate that a previously described event made you happy. Turn head sideways to view.

;-)   Short hand for just kidding. A way to indicate that what you said shouldn't be taken seriously by the reader. Turn head sideways to view.

Access   Having in place properly configured hardware and software to be able to use a remote computer's resources; pertains to communicating with a data processing facility through a data communications link.

Account   A set of parameters on a remote computer to allow a person access to the remote computers resources.

Acronym   A way of saving bandwidth by using the first letter of each word in a frequently used expression.

alt.*   A way to refer to all newsgroups belonging to the Alternative Newsgroup Hierarchy tree.

Alternative Newsgroups   Newsgroups that do not belong to one of the seven core USENET newsgroup hierarchies.

Anonymous ftp   A way to access a remote computer to get information from it without having a user account.

Archie   A program that searches anonymous ftp databases.

Archive A place on a remote computer to save important information about a newsgroup or set of newsgroups; usually a secondary storage medium such as magnetic tape or a mass storage device that operates on semi-direct access and sequential access principles.

Article Text written by a person regarding a newsgroup topic in the form of a computer file distributed via USENET newsgroup management and distribution software from one remote computer to another.

Article Number A number assigned to an article to uniquely identify it.

ASCII Acronym for American Standard Code for Information Interchange; pronounced "as-key."

Band The frequency spectrum between two defined limits.

Bandwidth A quantity of electronic bits of information transmitted over a network.

Baud Rate A unit for measuring the speed of data transmission.

Binary A term used to express a situation in which there is a choice between two states. In arithmetic, binary is expressed as 1 or 0. In electronics, binary is expressed as "on" or "off."

Binaries Computer files in the form of 1's and 0's; a form usable by a computer.

bionet.* A non-USENET newsgroup hierarchy devoted to the discussion of things of a biological nature.

Bit An acronym for Binary Digit; the smallest unit of information in the computer world.

bit.* A non-USENET newsgroup hierarchy devoted to the discussion of things related to technical issues.

Bitmap A picture stored in a computer file.

biz.* A non-USENET newsgroup hierarchy devoted to the discussion of things related to business and business products.

Board Short for "printed circuit board." A piece of equipment installed within a computer designed to do a specific task.

Branch A set of USENET newsgroups.

BTW Acronym for "by the way."

Cable A wire used to connect computer equipment.

Central Processing Unit (CPU)   The component of a computer that executes the arithmetic, logic and data movement instructions of a computer's instruction set.

Champion   A person who will readily promote a product or service.

Charter   A mutually agreed upon purpose for a newsgroup.

clari.*   A non-USENET newsgroup hierarchy devoted to commercial news related services.

Communications Board   The circuit board that enables your computer to communicate with other computers also called a "serial interface."

Communications Settings   The settings that establish an agreement between two computers about how they will communicate.

comp.*   The set of USENET newsgroups devoted to the discussion of things related to computers.

Computer   A multipurpose tool for the management and manipulation of information.

Computer File   A discrete piece of information recognizable by a computer; usually a collection of related records that contain information about a specific group of persons, places or things.

Computer System Administrator   A person whose job it is to manage and maintain a computer and its associated hardware, software and users.

Configuration   A particular arrangement of hardware and software; a collection of equipment including a computer and peripheral devices that make up a computer system.

Connection   A two way communication link between your computer and a remote computer.

Connection Time   Time spent communicating with a remote computer.

Core Newsgroups   Seven officially recognized newsgroups hierarchies that make up USNET newsgroups: comp.*, misc.*, news.*, rec.*, sci.*, soc.* and talk.*.

Cross Posting   Posting an article to more than one newsgroup at a time.

Cursor   A movable, visible mark used to indicate the position on which the next operation will occur on a display surface.

Data   A representation of facts, concepts, or instructions in a formalized manner suitable for communication, interpretation or processing by humans or computers.

Database   A collection of data.

Dial-up   A combination of hardware and software facilities that make it possible for computers to use conventional telephone dialing to make connections with and exchange information with other computers.

Digitize Audio Output   Sound stored in a computer file in binary form.

Directory   An organization of computer files; a table of identifiers and references to the corresponding items of data.

Disk   Short for magnetic disk; a round magnetic media for storing and retrieving information in computer files (can be hard and/or floppy).

Disk Drive   The hardware component that houses and controls the reading and writing of files to a magnetic disk.

Diskette   Also known as a "floppy;" a relatively small flexible magnetic storage medium.

Disk Space   A usable portion of space on a disk for storing computer files.

DOS   An acronym for disk operating system.

E-mail   Short for electronic mail.

Editor   A program designed to allow a person to create computer text files by typing into a keyboard.

Electronic Mail (E-mail)   Messages in the form of electronic signals recognizable by a computer transmitted over a computer network; the use of either communications network facilities or local area network facilities to provide communcation between workstations (a workstation is either a computer or terminal).

Electronic Messages   Electronic signals recognizable by a computer.

Emulation   The ability of one computer to behave like another by means of either a software or hardware feature.

Emulator   A program that allows one computer to behave like another; designed to allow a remote computer to acknowledge a personal computer as one of its own terminals.

FAQ   Acronym for "frequently asked questions." Usually refers to a file that contains a list of a newsgroup's most frequently asked questions and the answers to them.

FAX Board   A printed circuit board installed in a personal computer that does the same job as a FAX machine which is to send and receive printed material over the telephone line.

Feed   Short for newsgroup feed. Refers to one remote computer receiving newsgroup articles from another remote computer.

Fiber Optics   Cable made of clear fiberglass for the transmission of signals via light pulses.

File   A discrete unit of storage on a computer disk, usually a collection of related records that contain information about a specific group of persons, places or things.

File System   A way of organizing computer files that is meaningful to both a computer and its user.

Flame   A vehement disagreement in response to a newsgroup article.

Flat Text File   A computer file containing ASCII characters.

Floppy Disk   A magnetic storage medium that is made out of flexible material.

Follow Up   An article that refers to a previously posted article.

Fonts   A family or assortment of characters of a given size and style.

ftp   A program that uses the File Transfer Protocol to transfer computer files between remote computers. Short for "file transfer protocol."

FYI   An acronym for "for your information."

Gateway   A device that is used to interface two otherwise incompatible network facilities.

gnu.*   A non-USENET newsgroup hierarchy devoted to the discussion of things related to the GNU Project of the Free Software Foundation.

Gopher   A program used to search and retrieve information from different remote computers that are networked together.

Hacker   A person especially good at things related to computers.

Handshaking   A ritual of exchanging signals between two computers before communicating.

Hard Disk   A magnetic medium for storing computer files installed within a computer.

Hardware   Physical equipment associated with computers and their use.

HEPnet.*   A non-USENET set of newsgroups devoted to discussing the topic of high-energy nuclear physics.

Hierarchy   An ordered arrangement of newsgroups.

Host   The primary or controlling computer in a computer network.

Hypertext   A method of presenting information where selected words in the text can be expanded into further reading at any time.

ieee.*   A non-USENET set of newsgroups devoted to the discussion of items concerning the Institute of Electrical and Electronic Engineers.

IMHO   An acronym for "in my humble opinion."

IMNSHO   An acronym for "in my not so humble opinion."

Index   A numbered list of newsgroups and/or articles.

Inet/DDN   A non-USENET set of newsgroups similar in structure to USENET but distributed via a different mechanism.

info.*   A non-USENET set of newsgroups devoted to the discussion of topics of interest to the University of Illinois.

Information Highway   A term coined by the Clinton Administration for the development and implementation of a fiber optic network for information exchange country wide.

Interface   A device (either hardware or software) that makes possible communication between two devices or programs that would otherwise be unable to communicate.

Internet   One of many computer networks.

Internet Address   A registered address for a remote computer on the Internet network.

k12.*   A non-USENET set of newsgroups devoted to the discussion of topics of interest to kindergarten through twelfth grade educators.

Keyboard   A piece of equipment that looks like a typewriter that allows a person to talk to a computer.

LAN   Acronym for local area network; a network of computers that are interconnected without the use of communication facilities.

Log In   The process of accessing a remote computer using predefined parameters.

Login   The predefined parameters used to access a remote computer.

Log Off   The process of closing a dialog with a computer.

Log On   The process of accessing a remote computer using predefined parameters.

Log Out   The process of closing a dialog with a computer.

Lurker   A person who reads the articles of a newsgroup but doesn't frequently participate in the discussion.

Machine   Usually refers to a piece of computer hardware.

Mailing Lists   A list of e-mail addresses of a group of people who are all interested in the same subject.

Man Pages   Short for manual pages, refers to Unix online help files.

misc.*   The set of USENET newsgroups devoted to the discussion of topics that don't fit easily into the other core USENET hierarchies. Short for miscellaneous.

Mode   Short for terminal mode; a particular configuration of terminal (or terminal emulator) parameters for communicating with a remote computer. Allows your computer to appear as one of the remote computers own terminals.

Modem   A device that translates the signals coming from and going to your computer into a form that can be transmitted over standard telephone lines.

Modem Board   A printed circuit board installed within your computer that does the same job as a modem.

Moderator   A person in charge of seeing that only articles sticking to the agreed upon newsgroup charter are posted within a newsgroup.

Monitor   Another name for Video Display Terminal. A device used to display information and programs that are stored on a computer.

Mouse   A device used by graphical user interfaces for communicating with a computer.

Netiquette   A term for USENET Etiquette, a set of preferred USENET operating conventions.

Network   A system of computer communication; an arrangement in which computers and terminal devices are interconnected by means of cables or communication facilities.

Network Protocol   A recognized language for computers to communicate.

Networked Computer   A computer that is recognized by a computer network and is able to communicate with other computers on the network.

News Feed   See Newsgroup Feed.

News Reader   A program that allows a person to interact with a newsgroup and its articles.

news.*   The set of USENET newsgroups devoted to the discussion of things related to USENET, its newsgroups and its users. Contains information that is considered required reading for all USENET participants.

Newsgroup   A collection of articles devoted to the discussion of a particular topic.

Newsgroup Distribution Software   A set of computer programs used to manage the distribution of USENET newsgroups and articles.

Newsgroup Feed   One remote computer receiving USENET newsgroups from another remote computer.

Newsgroup Management Software   A set of computer programs used to manage USENET newsgroups and articles.

Operating System   The set of instructions you can use to tell your computer what it is you would like it do; a set of computer programs that enable a computer configuration to perform basic functions.

Parity   A form of error checking used to increase the chances that each character has been received correctly by your computer.

Password   A secret code word that prevents others from easily accessing one of your computer accounts.

Periodic Postings   Articles that are posted periodically to a newsgroup for the benefit of people who are new to the newsgroup.

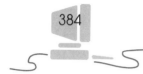

Personal Computer (PC)   A self-contained set of computer equipment consisting of a VDT, a keyboard, a CPU, one or more hard or floppy disk drives, and possibly a mouse.

Post   The process of making a computer file containing an article available to a news-group.

Printer   A device for producing paper copies of computer files.

Program   A computer file that contains a set of instructions for a computer to per-form a particular job.

Protocol   An agreed upon set of communication settings; a convention for informa-tion interchange among devices.

Quota   A limit on the amount of computer resources available to any one account.

rec.*   The set of USENET newsgroups devoted to the discussion of things related to recreation.

Regular   A person who participates regularly in a newsgroup's discussions.

relcom.*   A non-USENET set of newsgroups devoted to the discussion of topics in Russian.

Remote Computer   A computer designed to be used by more than one person at a time accessed via a data communications link.

Reply   An article written and posted that refers to a previously posted article.

Rot 13   A method of encrypting articles to avoid offending the easily offendable.

RTFM   An acronym for "read the f***ing manual."

sci.*   The set of USENET newsgroups devoted to the discussion of things related to scientific issues.

Service Provider   An organization that will provide access to USENET and other electronic resources for a fee.

Signature   A file containing personalized information that gets appended to articles and other electronic messages.

Site   A place where a remote computer resides.

Sneaker Net   Transferring files between computer by physically walking the mag-netic media the file resides on from one computer to another.

Glossary

soc.* The set of USENET newsgroups devoted to the discussion of things related to society and things social.

Software A set of computer files (programs and data) that will allow a computer to do a job.

Spoiler An article containing facts that may spoil an event for someone else.

Subgroup A newsgroup can hierarchically be broken down into further and further detail. Low level newsgroups are sometimes referred to as subgroups or sub-topics.

Subject Line The line of text used by a news reader to describe the contents of a particular article.

Subscribe Putting in place a newsgroup feed to regularly receive newsgroup articles from a remote computer.

Subtopic A newsgroup can hierarchically be broken down into further and further detail. Low level newsgroups are sometimes referred to as subgroups or sub-topics.

Summary A concise write up of all information received regarding a particular request for information.

Supported Items related to computers and their use are said to be supported if there is a defined person or place to go to for help when you have questions.

talk.* The set of USENET newsgroups devoted to the discussion of things people traditionally like to talk about.

Telecommunications A term that refers to the transmission of all kinds of information by different disciplines.

Telnet A method of accessing a remote computer.

Terminal A VDT and keyboard recognized by a remote computer; a device connected to a computer that is used to put information into and retrieve information from a computer.

Terminal Emulator A program used to get a remote computer to recognize a personal computer as one of its own terminals.

Terminal Mode A particular configuration of parameters to allow communication between computers.

Text Words, numbers or special characters that appear on a screen or printer.

Threaded   A method of presenting articles within a newsgroup in a way that shows which articles refer to which other ones.

Tree   A set of newsgroups. Another name for hierarchy.

Unmoderated   A newsgroup that doesn't have a moderator.

Unthreaded   A method of presenting articles within a newsgroup in a way that doesn't automatically show which articles relate to which.

User   A person who uses a computer resource.

User Interface   A program that facilitates communication between a computer and its users.

Username   A parameter used by a remote computer to identify a user.

UUCP   A network protocol.

Video Display Terminal (VDT)   A screen used by a computer to communicate with its user; a terminal device connected to a computer.

VMSnet.*   A non-USENET set of newsgroups devoted to the discussion of topics related to Digital Equipments products.

Voice Recognition   A set of hardware and software devices that will allow a computer to accept vocal command from its user.

WAIS   A distributed text searching system.

World Wide Web (WWW)   A program that organizes information available on the Internet network using hypertext.

Wildcard   A character that can represent any character or letter.

Word Processor   A program designed to make typed text look pleasing.

Workstation   A term used to refer to either a computer or computer terminal.

YMMV   An acronym for "your mileage may vary."

Index

A

Abortion, talk newsgroup, 196, 301
Acronyms, 24
Activism, miscellaneous newsgroup, 106
Administrative requests, 307-8
Aeronautics, science newsgroup, 172
Alternative USENET hierarchy, 198-210
  alt.binaries, 200-202
  alt.fan, 203-6
  alt.sex, 206-8, 301
  alt.tv, 208-10
  list of, 335-57
"A" News, 361
Animation, 129, 131
Announcements, network news newsgroup, 115-16
Anonymous ftp, 270
  defined, 306
  and file transfers, 271-74
Anthropology, science newsgroup, 172
Antiques, recreation newsgroup, 129
ANU-NEWS, 361
Aquaria:
  recreation newsgroup, 129
  scientifically-oriented posting, 172
Archaeology, science newsgroup, 172
Archie, 270-71
Articles, 18, 20, 25, 277-333

limiting distribution of, 28, 289, 302-3
threaded, 20
Artificial Intelligence, computer newsgroup, 48-49
Arts, recreation newsgroup, 129-38
Astronomy, science newsgroup, 173
Attributions, handling, 28
Audience, evaluating, 289
Audio, recreation newsgroup, 138
Automobiles/automotive products, recreation newsgroup, 138-39
Aviation, recreation newsgroup, 139

B

Babylon-5, 13-14
Bandwidth, 24, 28
Benchmarking techniques, 52
Bicycles, recreation newsgroup, 140-41
Binary postings, 52-53
Biology, science newsgroup, 173
bionet.*, 214-16
Biostasis, 174
Birds, recreation newsgroup, 141
Bisexuality, society newsgroup, 184
bit.*, 216-23
BITNET, 304
  connecting to USENET via, 314
biz.*, 224-25

Bizarre topics, 196
"B" News, 361
Boards, 256
Boats, recreation newsgroup, 141
Body decoration, 129, 131
Bonsai, 129, 131
Books:
  miscellaneous newsgroup, 106
  recreation newsgroup, 129, 132
Brevity of posting, 288
BTW, 24, 308
"Bug killers," defined, 303
Bugs, 53
Bulletin board systems, 51-52

C

Central processing unit (CPU), 256
Chemistry, science newsgroup, 173
Children, miscellaneous newsgroup, 32-37, 109
clari.*, 226-35
Client-server technology, computer newsgroups, 54
Climbing, recreation newsgroup, 141
"C" News, 361
Coats of arms, 148
Cognitive engineering, computer newsgroups, 54
Collecting, recreation newsgroup, 141

Index

College/graduate schools, society newsgroup, 184
Comic books, 129, 132
comp.* (computer newsgroups), 47-103
  comp.admin.*, 48
  comp.ai.*, 48-49
  comp.answers, 49-50
  comp.apps, 50
  comp.arch, 51, 307
  comp.archives.*, 251
  comp.bbs.*, 51-52
  comp.benchmarks, 52
  comp.binaries, 52-53
  comp.bugs.*, 53
  comp.cad.*, 54
  comp.client-server, 54
  comp.cog-eng, 54
  comp.compilers, 54
  comp.compression.*, 54
  comp.databases, 55
  comp.dcom.*, 55-56
  comp.doc.*, 56-57
  comp.dsp, 57
  comp.editors, 57
  comp.edu, 57
  comp.emacs, 57
  comp.fonts.*, 57-58
  comp.graphics.*, 58-59
  comp.groupware, 59
  comp.human-factors, 59
  comp.infosystems.*, 60
  comp.lang.*, 60-65
  comp.lsi.*, 65
  comp.mail.*, 65-71, 305
  comp.misc, 71
  comp.multimedia, 71
  comp.music, 71
  comp.newprod, 71
  comp.object.*, 71-72
  comp.org.*, 72
  comp.os.*, 72-78
  comp.parallel, 78

  comp.patents, 78
  comp.periphs.*, 79
  comp.programming, 79
  comp.protocols.*, 79-80
  comp.realtime.*, 80
  comp.research, 80
  comp.risks, 80
  comp.robotics, 80
  comp.security, 81
  comp.simulation, 81
  comp.society.*, 81
  comp.soft-sys, 81
  comp.software, 82
  comp.software-eng, 82
  comp.sources, 82-84, 305
  comp.specification.*, 84
  comp.speech, 84
  comp.std.*, 85
  comp.sw, 85
  comp.sys.*, 85-96
  comp.terminals.*, 97
  comp.text.*, 97
  comp.unix.*, 98-101, 300, 301
  comp.virus, 101-2
  comp.windows.*, 102-3
Compilers, computer newsgroup, 54
Compression, data, computer newsgroup, 54
Computer-aided design (CAD), 54
Computer applications, computer newsgroup, 50
Computer architecture, computer newsgroup, 51
Computer archives, computer newsgroup, 51
Computer basics, 256-57
Computer files, 257
Computer file systems, 257-58

Computer organizations, computer newsgroup, 72
Computer research, computer newsgroup, 80
Computer security, computer newsgroup, 81
Computer software, computer newsgroup, 82
Computer system administration, computer newsgroup, 48
Computer system administrators, 21, 287-88
Computer terminals, 5, 20
Configurations, network news newsgroup, 264
Connection time, 259
Consumer interests, 106-7
Consumers, miscellaneous newsgroup, 106-7
Control characters, avoiding, 293-94
Copyrights/licenses, 292
Couples, society newsgroup, 184
Crafts, recreation newsgroup, 141-42
Cross-postings, avoiding, 28
Cryonics, science newsgroup, 174
Culture, society newsgroup, 185-90, 301-2

D

Dance, 129
  folk-dancing, 142
Databases, 55, 270
Data compression, 54
Data encryption/decryption, science newsgroup, 174-75

Data formats, science newsgroup, 175

Digital communications, 55-56

Digital signal processing, 57

Disney-related items, recreation newsgroup, 129, 132

Distribution, 28, 289, 302-3

Documentation, computer newsgroup, 56-57

Domain Name Service (SDNS), 327-28

E

Economics, science newsgroup, 175

Editors, 258-59
    computer newsgroup, 57

Education:
    computer newsgroup, 57
    miscellaneous newsgroup, 107
    science newsgroup, 175

Electronic chain letters, 311

Electronics, science newsgroup, 175

EMACS, computer newsgroup, 57

E-mail, 271
    computer newsgroup, 65-71
    responding by, 27
    restrictions on posting, 308

Emergency services, miscellaneous newsgroup, 107

Encryption:
    data, 174-75
    of messages, 290

Energy, science newsgroup, 175

Engineering, science newsgroup, 176

Entrepreneurs, miscellaneous newsgroup, 107

Environment:
    science newsgroup, 176
    talk newsgroup, 196

Equestrians, recreation newsgroup, 142

Equipment:
    basic needs, 264-65
    existing equipment, using, 265-66

Erotica, recreation newsgroup, 129, 133

Etiquette, USENET, 26-27

European users, 324-25

Evolution vs. creationism, 196

F

FAQs, 25, 27, 37-38, 295-314

FAX board, 256

Feminism, society newsgroup, 190

Files, 257

File transfers, and anonymous ftp, 271-74

Fine arts, recreation newsgroup, 129, 133

Fitness, miscellaneous newsgroup, 107

Flames, 25
    spelling, 293

Flat text file, 259

Floppy disk drives, 256

Folk-dancing, recreation newsgroup, 142

Follow-ups:
    checking headers for, 291-92

reading before posting, 27

Fonts, computer newsgroup, 57-58

Foo, as filler word, 398

"Foo" company, address/phone number of, 303-5

Food, recreation newsgroup, 142-43

"Food for the NSA line-eater," defined, 305

FQDN (fully-qualified domain name), 308-9

Fractals, science newsgroup, 176

FYI, 24, 307

G

Games, recreation newsgroup, 143-48

Gardens, recreation newsgroup, 148

Geophysical fluid dynamics, science newsgroup, 176

Gnews, 361

gnu.*, 236-37

GNUS, 361

Gopher, 274

Graduate schools, 184

Grammatical errors, 29

Graphics, computer newsgroup, 58-59

"grep," 304

Groupware, computer newsgroup, 59

Guns, recreation newsgroup, 148

H

Handicapped, miscellaneous newsgroup, 108
Hard disk, 256
HASA, defined, 302
Headers, checking for follow-ups, 291-92
Headlines, 108
Health, miscellaneous newsgroup, 108
HEPnet.*, 237-38
Heraldry, recreation newsgroup, 148
Hierarchy, 25
History, society newsgroup, 191
Human-computer interaction, 59
Humor/sarcasm, 148-49, 289-90
Hunting, recreation newsgroup, 149
HyperNews, 362
Hypertext, 275
Hysterics, refraining from, 29

I

Ice skating, recreation newsgroup, 165
ieee.*, 238
Image processing/analysis, science newsgroup, 177
IMHO/IMNSHO, 24, 307
Index, 25
inet/DDN, 239-41
info.*, 242-44
Infosystems, computer newsgroup, 60

Intellectual property rights, miscellaneous newsgroup, 108
Interactive fiction, 130, 133
Internet Gopher, 274
Internet Mailing Lists (SRI International), 274-75
InterNetNews (INN), 362
"Internet Resource Guide," 270-71
Investments, miscellaneous newsgroup, 108

J

Jobs, miscellaneous newsgroup, 109
Juggling, recreation newsgroup, 149

K

k12.*, 244-46
Keyboard, 256
Kites, recreation newsgroup, 149

L

Languages:
    computer, 60-65
    natural, 177
Large-scale integrated circuits, 65
Legal, miscellaneous newsgroup, 110
Libraries, society newsgroup, 191
Line length, 293-94
LJBF, defined, 302
Local-interest articles, 28
Logic, science newsgroup, 177

Lurker, 25

M

Magazines, recreation newsgroup, 149
Mail eXchange (MX) record, 327-28
Mailing lists, 274-75
Man pages, 276
Marching, 130, 133
Martial arts, recreation newsgroup, 149
Materials engineering, science newsgroup, 177
Mathematics, science newsgroup, 177
Medicine, science newsgroup, 178
Memory, science newsgroup, 174
Men, society newsgroup, 191
Mensa, 156
Meteorology, science newsgroup, 176
Military, science newsgroup, 178
misc.* (miscellaneous newsgroups), 104-11
misc.activism, 106
misc. answers, 106
misc.books.*, 106
misc.consumers.*, 106-7
misc.education.*, 107
misc.emergency-services, 107
misc.entrepreneurs, 107
misc.fitness, 107
misc.forsale.*, 107-8
misc.handicap, 108
misc.health.*, 108
misc.int-property, 108
misc.invest.*, 108

misc.* (miscellaneous news-
groups), *continued*
misc.jobs.*, 109
misc.kids, 32-37, 109
    articles, 34-37
    charter, 32
    events, 38
    FAQs, 37-38
    index, 32-34
misc.legal.*, 110
misc.misc, 110, 299
misc.news.*, 110
misc.rural, 110
misc.taxes, 110
misc.test, 110
misc.wanted, 110, 299
misc.writers, 110
misc.writing, 111
Miscellaneous computer top-
    ics, 71
Models, recreation news-
    group, 149-50
Modem, 256
Moderator, 25, 306-7
MOTAS, defined, 302
Motorcycles, recreation
    newsgroup, 150-51
MOTOS, defined, 302
MOTSS:
    defined, 302
    society newsgroup, 101
Movies, 130, 133
Multics, 208
Multimedia technologies,
    computer newsgroup,
    71
Multiple newsgroups, post-
    ing to, 290
Music:
    computer newsgroup, 71
    recreation newsgroup,
    151-55

N

Name-calling, refraining
    from, 29
Naturist/nudist activities,
    recreation newsgroup,
    155-56
Netiquette, See USENET et-
    iquette
Networked computers, 5, 19
Network protocol, 18
New products, computer
    newsgroup, 71
news.* (network news news-
    groups), 112-25
    news.admin.*, 114
    news.announce.*, 115-16
    news.announce.newusers,
    24, 27, 115-16
    news.answers, 116-20
    news.config, 120
    news.groups, 120-21
    news.lists.*, 121-23
    news.misc, 123-24
    news.newsites, 124
    news.newusers.*, 124,
    299
    news.software.*, 124-25
News, miscellaneous news-
    group, 110
News administration, 114
newsfuture, 120
Newsgroup distribution soft-
    ware, 19
Newsgroup management
    software, 19
Newsgroups, 4, 26, 31-38
    articles, 18, 20
    changes in, 21
    moderator, 25
News readers, 5, 20, 26, 260,
    359-68
    "A" News, 361

ANU-NEWS, 361
basic functions of, 360
"B" News, 361
"C" News, 361
Gnews, 361
GNUS, 361
HyperNews, 362
information sources, 368
InterNetNews (INN),
    362
NewsWatcher, 362
nn, 362
NNMVS, 362
NNR, 362
notes, 362
PSU NetNews, 362
readnews, 363
rn, 363
    command summary for,
    364-65
tin, 363
    command summary for,
    367-68
trn, 363
    command summary for,
    365-67
trumpet, 363
types available, 360
VM NNTP, 363
VMSvnews, 363
vnews, 363
xrn, 363
xvnews, 364
News reading software, 19-
    20
NewsWatcher, 362
New user conduct, 27-29
"Nixpub" sites, 310
nn, 362
NNMVS, 362
NNR, 362
Notes, 362

O

Object-oriented programming (OOP), computer newsgroup, 71-72
Operating systems, 85-96
Optics, science newsgroup, 179
Origins, talk newsgroup, 196
O/S2, computer newsgroup, 72-78
Outdoors, 139-40, 156

P

Parallel programming, computer newsgroup, 78
Parents, 109
Password, 258
Patents, computer newsgroup, 78
Penpals, society newsgroup, 192
Perception, 174
Peripherals, 79
Personal computer, definition of, 256
Personal information, posting, 288
Pets, recreation newsgroups, 157-58
Philosophy:
  science newsgroup, 179
  talk newsgroup, 196
Photography, recreation newsgroup, 158
Physical connections, 19
Physics, science newsgroup, 179
Pi, 305
Poems/poetry, 130
Politics:
  society newsgroup, 192

talk newsgroup, 196-97
Posting, 26
  brevity of, 288
  cross-postings, 28
  editing, 288
  of personal information, 288
  previous material included in, 28
  reading follow-ups before, 27
  subject line, 288-89
  summary, 27
Programming, computer newsgroup, 79
Prose, 130, 133
Protocols, computer newsgroup, 79-80, 259
PSU NetNews, 362
Public domain, 292
Puzzles, recreation newsgroup, 158-59

R

Radio, recreation newsgroup, 159-64
Railroad, recreation newsgroups, 164
Rape, talk newsgroup, 197, 301
"rc," 299
readnews, 363
Real-time computing, computer newsgroup, 80
Reasoning, 174
rec.* (recreation newsgroups), 126-69
  rec.answers, 128-29
  rec.antiques, 129
  rec.aquaria, 129
  rec.arts.*, 129-38
  rec.audio, 138

rec.autos, 138-39
rec.aviation, 139
rec.backcountry, 139-40
rec.bicycles.*, 140-41
rec.birds, 141
rec.boats.*, 141
rec.climbing, 141
rec.collecting.*, 141
rec.crafts.*, 141-42
rec.equestrian, 142
rec.folk-dancing, 142
rec.food.*, 142-43
rec.games, 143-48, 300
rec.gardens, 148
rec.guns, 148
rec.heraldry, 148
rec.humor, 148-49, 299
rec.hunting, 149
rec.juggling, 149
rec.kites, 149
rec.mag, 149
rec.martial-arts, 149
rec.misc, 149
rec.models, 149-50
rec.motorcycles, 150-51
rec.music.*, 151-55
rec.nude, 155-56
rec.org, 156
rec.outdoors, 156
rec.pets, 157-58, 311
rec.photo, 158
rec.puzzles.*, 158-59
rec.radio.*, 159-64
rec.railroad, 164
rec.roller-coaster, 164
rec.running, 164
rec.scouting, 164-65
rec.scuba, 165
rec.skate, 165
rec.skiing, 165
rec.skydiving, 165

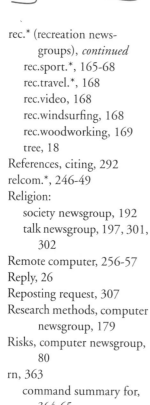

rec.* (recreation news-
    groups), *continued*
    rec.sport.*, 165-68
    rec.travel.*, 168
    rec.video, 168
    rec.windsurfing, 168
    rec.woodworking, 169
    tree, 18
References, citing, 292
relcom.*, 246-49
Religion:
    society newsgroup, 192
    talk newsgroup, 197, 301,
        302
Remote computer, 256-57
Reply, 26
Reposting request, 307
Research methods, computer
    newsgroup, 179
Risks, computer newsgroup,
    80
rn, 363
    command summary for,
        364-65
Robotics, computer news-
    group, 80
Roller coasters/amusement
    park rides, recreation
    newsgroup, 164
"rot13," 290, 292, 299
RTFM, 24, 308
Rumors, talk newsgroup, 197
Running, recreation news-
    group, 164
Rural living, miscellaneous
    newsgroup, 110

S

Sale items, miscellaneous
    newsgroup, 107-8
sci.* (science newsgroup),
    170-80

sci.aeronautics.*, 172
sci.answers, 172
sci.anthropology, 172
sci.aquaria, 172
sci.archaeology, 172
sci.astro.*, 173
sci.bio, 173
sci.chem.*, 173
sci.cognitive, 174
sci.cryonics, 174
sci.crypt, 174-75
sci.data.*, 175
sci.econ.*, 175
sci.education, 175
sci.electronics, 175
sci.energy, 175
sci.engr.*, 176
sci.environment, 176
sci.fractals, 176
sci.geo.*, 176
sci.image, 177
sci.lang.*, 177
sci.logic, 177
sci.materials, 177
sci.math.*, 177, 300
sci.med.*, 178
sci.military, 178
sci.misc., 178
sci.nanotech, 178
sci.optics, 179
sci.philosophy.*, 179
sci.physics, 179
sci.research, 179
sci.skeptic, 179
sci.space.*, 179-80, 302
sci.systems, 180
sci.virtual, 180
Science fiction, 130, 134
Scouting, recreation news-
    group, 164-65
SCUBA diving, recreation
    newsgroup, 165

Service providers, 258, 318-
    23
    selecting, 266-67
Shergold, Craig, 310
Signatures, 293
    including with postings,
        313
Simulation, computer news-
    group, 81
Singles, society newsgroup,
    301, 302
Skiing, recreation news-
    group, 165
Skydiving, recreation news-
    group, 165
Smileys, 24, 299
SO, defined, 302
soc.* (society newsgroup),
    182-92
    soc.answers, 184
    soc.bi, 184
    soc.college, 184
    soc.couples, 184
    soc.culture, 185-90, 301-
        2
    soc.feminism, 190
    soc.history, 191
    soc.libraries.*, 191
    soc.men, 191
    soc.misc., 191
    soc.motss, 101
    soc.net-people, 191, 299
    soc.penpals, 192
    soc.politics, 192
    soc.religion.*, 192
    soc.singles, 301, 302
Society, technology and, 81
Software, computer news-
    group, 82
Software engineering, com-
    puter newsgroup, 82
Software systems, computer
    newsgroup, 81

Solid earth sciences, 176
Sources/source postings, computer newsgroup, 82-84
Space-related topics, science newsgroup, 179-80, 302
Specification, computer newsgroup, 84
Speech, computer newsgroup, 84
Spelling errors, 29
Spelling flames, 293
Spoiler, 26, 292
Sports, recreation newsgroup, 165-68
Standards, computer newsgroup, 85
Startrek, 130, 134-37
Straczynski, J. Michael, 13-14
Subject line, 288-89
    checking, 28
    using "rot13" in, 290
Summary, posting, 27, 290-91
Systems science, 180

T

talk.* (talk newsgroup), 194-97
    talk.abortion, 196
    talk.answers, 196
    talk.bizarre.*, 196, 302
    talk.environment, 196
    talk.origins, 196
    talk.philosophy.*, 196
    talk.politics.*, 196-97
    talk.rape, 197, 301
    talk.religion.*, 197, 301, 302
    talk.rumors, 197
Tantrums, avoiding, 29, 287

Tattoos, 129
Tax laws/advice, miscellaneous newsgroup, 110
Television, 130-31, 137-38, 208-10
TELNET, remote access via, 275
Terminal emulators, 5, 20, 259
Terminal mode, 259
Terminals, 258
    newsgroups, 97
Testing network software, miscellaneous newsgroup, 110
TeX, 309
Text processing issues, computer newsgroup, 97
Theatre, 130, 137
Threaded articles, 20
tin, 363
    command summary for, 367-68
Tolkien, 129, 132
Travel, recreation newsgroup, 168
"tr" command, 290, 299
trn, 363
    command summary for, 365-67
trumpet, 363

U

UNIX:
    computer newsgroup, 98-101
    FAQ, 298, 300, 301
    open access sites, 310
USENET:
    as anarchy, 286
    basics, 256
    Clinton administration's use of, 12

control, 282
control characters, avoiding, 293-94
copyrights/licenses, 292
defined, 278-86
frequently asked questions about, 295-314
future of, 15
gaining access to, 263-67, 314-33
growth/maintenance, 21
history of, 10
how to use, 5-6
line length, 293-94
newsgroups:
    articles, 18
    creation of, 283-84
    hierarchical nature of, 18
    reading via e-mail, 313
new user conduct, 27-29
periodic postings, 282
posting via e-mail, 312
postings, obtaining archives of, 311-12
propagation, 283
references, citing, 292
as a society, 285
structure of, 19-20
terminology, 24-26
users, samples of, 10-14
uses of, 4-5, 15
USENET community, 3-6, 21
    working with, 286-94
USENET etiquette, 280-94
    arguments/tantrums, avoiding, 287
    audience, 289
    brevity, 288
    editing your posting, 288
    evolution of, 26-27
    headers, checking, 291-92
    humor/sarcasm, 148-49, 289-90

USENET etiquette, *continued*
  personal information, posting, 288
  posting to multiple newsgroups, 290
  signatures, 293
  subject line, 288-89
  summarization, 290-91
  system administrators, 287-88
USENET site:
  becoming, 314-33
USENET site:
  registering on the network, 327-33
USENET software, 325-26
User interface, 20, 258
Username, 258
UUCP, 19, 280, 304
UUNET, 283, 306

V

VDT (video display terminal), 256
Video, recreation newsgroup, 168
Virtual worlds, science newsgroup, 180
Viruses, computer newsgroup, 101-2
VM NNTP, 363
VMSnet.*, 249-51
VMSvnews, 363
vnews, 363

W

WAIS, 275
"whois" command, 298, 299
Whole Internet, The (Krol), 275
Windows, computer newsgroup, 102-3

Windsurfing, recreation newsgroup, 168
Woodworking, recreation newsgroup, 169
World Wide Web (WWW), 275
Writers, miscellaneous newsgroup, 110
Writing, miscellaneous newsgroup, 111
WRT (with respect to), 308

X

xrn, 363
xvnews, 364

Y

YMMV, 24